Reintegrating *Severance*

Nora M. Isacoff · Jennifer Dawes
Editors

Reintegrating *Severance*

Interdisciplinary Insights on Apple TV's Dystopian Thriller

palgrave
macmillan

Editors
Nora M. Isacoff
Department of Psychology
Columbia University
New York, NE, USA

Jennifer Dawes
Rhetoric and Writing
University of Arkansas at Little Rock
Little Rock, AR, USA

ISBN 978-3-031-57447-4 ISBN 978-3-031-57448-1 (eBook)
https://doi.org/10.1007/978-3-031-57448-1

Cover Credit: Eoneren/Getty Images

This Palgrave Macmillan imprint is published by the registered company Springer Nature Switzerland AG
The registered company address is: Gewerbestrasse 11, 6330 Cham, Switzerland

Acknowledgments

The editors would like to thank Palgrave Macmillan and particularly Felicity Pleister for commissioning this book. Our contributors also deserve sincere thanks for their enthusiasm for this project. We appreciate their dedication and diverse insights.

Nora M. Isacoff would like to dedicate this book to her fellow scholars and artists at the Diverse Intelligences Summer Institute (DISI), and its directors, Erica Cartmill and Jacob Foster. DISI's steadfast commitment to cultivating and sharing wisdom among the sciences, humanities, and arts is a shining light in this world—and a significant inspiration for this book's perspective.

Jennifer Dawes would like to thank her family for their support during the development of this book from its early stages to the final proof. She would like to dedicate her work on this book to her sister, Amy Dawes Klein, for her enthusiasm and encouragement in all things.

Contents

1 **Introduction** 1
Nora M. Isacoff and Jennifer Dawes

Part I Constructing History

2 **"Who Are You?": Memory, History, and Nostalgia on the Severed Floor** 13
Jennifer Dawes

3 **The Grim Barbarity of Capitalist Designs: Class Conflict, Corporate Dystopia, and the Sacred Gaze in *Severance*** 27
Dylan Reid Miller

4 **Severed from Reality: The Irrationality of Rationality in Advanced-Stage Capitalism** 43
Nathan Palmer and April M. Schueths

Part II Art & Architecture

5 **Art as an Apparatus of the Invisible Sublime in *Severance*** 63
Bengisu Bayrak Shahmiri

6 **Mapping the Subject Through *Severance's* Corporate Architecture and Design** 81
Christine Prevas

7 **Resisting the Innie/Outie Dichotomy Through Mundane Encounters: In Defense of "Spaces of Transition"** 97
Can Koçak

Part III Agency, Autonomy, and Alienation

8 **An Investigation of Marxist Alienation in the Postmodern Workplace in Apple TV's *Severance*** 117
Mayank Kejriwal

9 **Brain Eugenics: How to Produce an Ideal Worker?** 135
Martin Charvát

10 **"Defiant Jazz": Corporate Rewards as Plantation-Style Oppression in Apple TV's *Severance*** 153
Lauren Shoemaker

11 **The Waffle Party Is Not What It Seems: Sexual, Reproductive, and Labor Exploitation in *Severance*** 171
Kathleen W. Taylor Kollman

Part IV Multifaceted Minds and Bodies

12 **The Aesthetic Virtue of the *Severance* Procedure: Pledging Spectatorial Allegiance to Both Innies and Outies** 193
Heidi Ka-Sin Lee

13 **"Actively Caring for Mankind Since 1866": Nineteenth-Century Medicine, Pain, and the Worker's Body in Season 1 of *Severance*** 215
Sarah Lennox

14 **"The Mystery of Your Youthful Energy": Time, History, and the Representation of Queer Aging in *Severance*** 245
Melanie Cattrell

15 Self-Communication in Severed Minds: Perspectives from Neuroscience, Psychology, and Philosophy 261
Nora M. Isacoff

Index 281

Notes on Contributors

Bengisu Bayrak Shahmiri is a professor in the Department of Graphic Design at Beykoz University, Istanbul, and in Communication Design and Management at Bilgi University, Istanbul. She has authored several articles on contemporary art and co-authored a book entitled *An Essay on the Conceptions of Significance in Contemporary Art*. She is also an independent artist and curator based in Istanbul. She has a doctorate in Fine Arts, an M.A. in Film and Television Studies, and a B.A. in Fine Arts.

Melanie Cattrell holds a Ph.D. in American Studies from the University of New Mexico and an M.A. in English from Bowling Green State University. Her research focuses on the intersection of age, gender, and sexuality in contemporary television. She teaches composition and literature at Blinn College in Bryan, Texas.

Martin Charvát is an associate professor in the Department of Media Studies, head of the Centre for Media Culture Studies at Metropolitan University in Prague, and a researcher at the Film and TV School of the Academy of Performing Arts in Prague. He has published seven scientific monographs and co-authored another eight monographs. He also published fifty book chapters/articles on different topics like media archaeology, contemporary audiovisual culture, and the history of photography. He also translates from English. His upcoming monograph is co-authored work about Gothic mizanscene in contemporary TV

Shows. His latest published work is "Pureness or corruption: Spectres and ghosts between photography and X-rays" in *Philosophy of Photography.*

Jennifer Dawes is a professor and Chair of the Department of Rhetoric and Writing at the University of Arkansas at Little Rock. Her previous edited collection, *Dark Tourism in the American West*, was published by Palgrave Macmillan in 2019.

Nora M. Isacoff, Ph.D., is a cognitive scientist with joint appointments in the Psychology departments at Columbia University and New York University. Her research, writing, and teaching integrate scientific and humanistic approaches to exploring the nature of language, mind, and consciousness.

Mayank Kejriwal is a research assistant professor at the University of Southern California. He holds joint appointments in the USC Information Sciences Institute and the Department of Industrial & Systems Engineering. He is an avid fan of pop culture and fantasy, and recently presented his work on Faustian and Freudian influences on Harry Potter at the Southwest Popular/American Culture Association Conference.

Can Koçak is a lecturer in Media and Cultural Studies in the School of Media, Arts, and Humanities at the University of Sussex, UK. His most recent work is "How I Met Your Fans: A Comparative Textual Analysis of *How I Met Your Mother* and its Reboots," published in *Open Cultural Studies* in 2023.

Kathleen W. Taylor Kollman is a visiting assistant professor at Miami University in Oxford, Ohio, where she serves in the departments of Media, Journalism & Film, and Global & Intercultural Studies. Her scholarship concerns the representation of gender and intersectional identity in popular culture. Kollman has published analyses of sexuality in *Crazy Ex-Girlfriend*, labor exploitation in *Travelers*, and female vampires in music videos. She holds a Ph.D. in American Culture Studies from Bowling Green State University.

Heidi Ka-Sin Lee is a Ph.D. candidate at the Graduate School of International Culture and Communication Studies in Waseda University. The working title of her dissertation is "Lesbianism as Spectacle: Performance, Emotion, and Homosexual Interiority in Contemporary

Popular Cinema," which aims to provide a perceptual-cognitive framework for discussion on recent mainstream lesbian-themed films featuring star actresses in the American spectatorial context.

Sarah Lennox is an assistant professor of English at Massachusetts Maritime Academy. You can find her work on Victorian literature and culture in *Victorian Review*, *Literature Compass*, *The Wilkie Collins Journal*, and *The Journal of Commonwealth Literature*.

Dylan Reid Miller is a Ph.D. candidate in Bowling Green State University's American Culture Studies department studying counterhegemonic temporalities in science and speculative fiction. She previously published "The Unkillable Idea of Benny Russell: Afrofuturist Temporalities and 'Far Beyond the Stars'" in *To Boldly Stay*, the first edited volume devoted entirely to *Star Trek: Deep Space Nine*.

Nathan Palmer is an assistant professor in sociology in the Department of Sociology and Anthropology at Georgia Southern University. He has peer-reviewed articles published in *Sociological Inquiry, American Sociologist*, *Teaching Sociology*, *Journal of Sociology and Social Welfare,* and *Teaching in Higher Education.*

Christine Prevas is a Ph.D. candidate in English and Comparative Literature with a focus on Gender and Sexuality at Columbia University. Their research focuses on architecture, gender, and subjectivity in contemporary American horror media through the figure of the haunted house.

April M. Schueths is a professor of sociology in the Department of Sociology and Anthropology at Georgia Southern University. She has peer-reviewed articles published in *Critical Sociology, Ethnic and Racial Studies, Latino Studies, Journal of Sociology and Social Welfare, Children and Youth Services Review, Journal of Health Care for the Poor and Underserved, Race, Education, and Inequality,* to name a few.

Lauren Shoemaker is an assistant professor of English at Slippery Rock University in the Department of Languages, Literatures, Culture, and Writing. She recently contributed a chapter on the cultural meanings of the Birds Aren't Real conspiracy theory in *Avian Aesthetics in Literature and Culture: Birds and Humans in the Popular Imagination* (Lexington Books 2022).

List of Figures

Fig. 2.1	The sign at the threshold of the severed area	14
Fig. 2.2	Mark, Irving, and Helly in front of Myrtle Eagan's wax figure in the Perpetuity Wing	19
Fig. 2.3	Irving's list of severed workers and map of Kier	24
Fig. 5.1	Lumon lobby from overhead	66
Fig. 5.2	"Kier Invites You to Drink from His Water"	71
Fig. 5.3	Irving and Burt contemplate "The Courtship of Kier and Imogene"	74
Fig. 6.1	Helly on the conference table	82
Fig. 6.2	Lumon lobby as viewed from overhead	90
Fig. 6.3	Petey's map of Lumon's severed floor	93
Fig. 8.1	Minimalist colors, geometric design, and empty space within MDR serve to emphasize the increasingly non-physical nature of work in a technologically driven society	123
Fig. 8.2	The use of shadows, rectangular architectural motifs, and other industrial design elements highlight the impersonal, utilitarian ethos of Lumon	125
Fig. 12.1	Helly at the "severed threshold"	201
Fig. 12.2	Innie Mark reading *The You You Are: A Spiritual Biography of You*	204
Fig. 13.1	Helena's surgery and computer display	230
Fig. 13.2	Helly laid out on the conference table	232
Fig. 14.1	"It's rare to meet a sophisticate" in the halls of Lumon	253
Fig. 14.2	"Are you sweet on this guy?"	255
Fig. 15.1	The Ponzo illusion	264

CHAPTER 1

Introduction

Nora M. Isacoff and Jennifer Dawes

It is not often that a cognitive scientist and an English professor feel compelled to collaborate on a book about the latest bingeable television series.[1] Nor is it common for co-editors to include contributions from scholars in fields as diverse as industrial engineering, anthropology, gender and sexuality studies, and graphic design. And only rarely is such interdisciplinary scholarship accessible to a general audience. That audience, in this case, includes fans of the Apple TV series *Severance* and scholars in any discipline who are interested in a fictional exploration of some of the deepest questions in the arts, sciences, and humanities. The co-editors, whose fields of expertise could not be further apart, met in an online forum for fans of the show and immediately connected over a shared appreciation for *Severance*'s poignancy and significance. We cast

N. M. Isacoff (✉)
Department of Psychology, Columbia University, New York, NY, USA
e-mail: ni2237@columbia.edu

J. Dawes
Department of Rhetoric and Writing, University of Arkansas at Little Rock, Little Rock, AR, USA
e-mail: jdawes@ualr.edu

N. M. Isacoff and J. Dawes (eds.), *Reintegrating Severance*,
https://doi.org/10.1007/978-3-031-57448-1_1

our net far and wide to invite contributions from as many perspectives and orientations as possible. This collection is the result.

Severance centers around the biotechnology company Lumon, which offers employees a voluntary surgical procedure that severs their minds into two distinct personas: The "outie," who can only access memories from outside the Lumon office, and the "innie," who can only access memories from inside the Lumon office. The procedure promises extreme work/life balance: Imagine truly leaving work stress at the office so you can enjoy time with your children at home. Or, envision the kind of singular focus at work that would only be possible without your mind wandering to a recent breakup or an ailing family member. At its core, the series grapples with systemization—with the ways we organize and construct our histories, art and architecture, social orders, and our own bodies and minds. Such systemization may sometimes feel like a welcome reprieve, but this is often too great a detriment, like obscuring the truth, stratifying social classes, or muting our human experiences.

Television shows always reflect the time in which they are produced. Whether they idealize their society or warn against its excesses, television responds to, creates, and dialogues with the important social and cultural values, norms, and events of its time. Naturally, 2022 was the time for a dystopian story about work–life balance. Most ostensibly, the COVID-19 pandemic drastically altered the way people work. For example, one source reports that the percentage of workers in the United States who work from home has tripled since before the pandemic,[2] with numbers much higher when looking exclusively at rates for office employees. This change is welcome by some employees, who appreciate the time saved by not commuting, the opportunity to complete chores during lunch breaks, or the possibility of being home with family members. Other employees resent the reduced separation between work and life, finding that there is an increased expectation to be available at all times and that the lack of a physical transition between work time and home time hinders this psychological transition.[3]

The pandemic also compounded a growing disdain among Millennials and Gen Zers for the "lean in"[4] culture espoused by earlier generations, who often prized ambitiousness and taught their children that with hard work, anything was possible. For complex sociopolitical reasons[5] including the aftermath of 9/11, the 2008 Great Recession, compounding student loan debt, the rising cost of living amid stagnant wages, a reduced social safety net, increased awareness of racial and class injustice, and the rise of fascism and political divisions around the world, younger generations have found that a college degree is not a definite path to basic financial security. This economic reality has shifted values for many younger adults, such as the social psychologist Dr. Devon Price, who advocates for disentangling productivity from self-image in his book *Laziness Does not Exist*.[6] This shift in values has led in part to The Great Resignation which began in early 2021[7] and the practice of "quiet quitting," which is "about divorcing your ego from what you do for a living."[8] A recent *Wall Street Journal* article entitled "The 'Lazy-Girl Job' Is in Right Now. Here's Why" reports that "rather than lean in, young workers say they want jobs that can be done from home, come with a cool boss and end at 5 p.m. sharp."[9] Cross-generationally, the pandemic crystallized life's fragility and unpredictability and forced people to examine their true priorities.[10] *Severance* serves as a commentary on many of these issues.

We *severed* this collection into four sections, each reflecting the series from one of four crucial perspectives. The chapters within each section are written by scholars across disciplines whose work shares a general theme. Each section, and each chapter within, is meaningful in its own right. You are welcome to read the chapters in any order, or to read just a single chapter that speaks to your interest. The collection as a whole also offers its own meaning. In *reintegrating* wisdom from the far corners of scholarship, we hope to offer a rich and multiplicitous approach to understanding the series and the larger questions and ideas that the series sparks.

Constructing History explores identity in the context of historical revisionism and corporate mythology. Chapter 2 (Dawes) uses a cultural history perspective to discuss Lumon's manipulation of nostalgia and pride for the company as a way to supplant individual identity. Chapter 3 (Miller) analyzes these same themes through the philosophies of French social theorists Foucault and Deleuze. Chapter 4 (Palmer and Schueths) introduces the concept of sociological imagination—the interplay between the self, society, and history—by drawing on scholarship from critics of capitalism such as Marx, Weber, and DuBois.

Art and Architecture builds on the first section by exploring the use of visual culture in shaping collective and personal stories. Chapter 5 (Bayrak Shahmiri) identifies uses of a variety of aesthetics within *Severance*, including Romantic, Modern, and Postmodern, and makes comparisons to specific artworks, such as paintings by Hopper, Friedrich, and

Church. Chapter 6 (Prevas) analyzes the effects of corporate architecture and design on workers' subjective experience, such as the numbing effects of precise symmetry and pristine spaces. Chapter 7 (Koçak) argues for the power of spaces of transition—the commute to work, or hallways between offices—as opportunities for resistance and reclamation.

Agency, Autonomy, and Alienation dives deep into the political theories that earlier chapters touched upon. Chapter 8 (Kejriwal) draws on Marxian theory about alienation as a consequence of capitalism and compares *Severance* with fictional works by Kafka and Camus. Chapter 9 (Shoemaker) considers tactics of oppression in the workplace, including productivity incentives and founder worship, and explores how these practices are rooted in the American slavery system. Chapter 10 (Charvát) employs a semiotics lens to shed light on means of taming authentic human emotion in service of efficiency and productivity. Chapter 11 (Kollman) applies feminist, queer, and labor theories to explore sexual and reproductive exploitation.

Multifaceted Bodies and Minds find a way back to our multiplicity as individuals—our complexity as outies and innies and everything in between. Chapter 12 (Lee) discusses the *Severance* viewer's spectatorial allegiance to each character in each of their personas and the cognitive dissonance that comes from trying to understand the contradictions inherent to any person. Chapter 13 (Lennox) draws on the history of anesthesiology, including its uses in childbirth, to explore ways that numbing corporeal pain can lead to deeper existential pain, and the impossibility of harmlessly anesthetizing one part of ourselves. Chapter 14, (Cattrell) explores the intersection of aging and sexuality, underrepresented in the prototypical lenses through which each of these topics is generally investigated. Finally, Chapter 15 (Isacoff) utilizes insights from neuroscience, psychology, and the philosophy of the self to demonstrate how deeply the experiences of each innie and outie shape each other—how their memories and identities stay intact across personas in ways they do not realize—and ultimately celebrates the intraconnection of the self.

In joining the voices of scholars from disparate universities, on several continents, and from a vast number of disciplines, we present you with a reintegrated analysis of *Severance*. As readers, we invite you to think about the ways that the themes in this book map onto your individual experiences and perspectives, and the infinite additional angles from which you might approach the series. It is this interconnected diversity—personal and collective—that empowers flourishing.

List of Season 1 Episodes and Air Dates[II]

Episode 1, "Good News About Hell," February 18, 2022
Directed by Ben Stiller, Written by Dan Erickson and Anna Ouyang Moench

Episode 2, "Half Loop," February 18, 2022
Directed by Ben Stiller, Written by Dan Erickson and Anna Ouyang Moench

Episode 3, "In Perpetuity," February 25, 2022
Directed by Ben Stiller, Written by Andrew Colville, Dan Erickson, and Anna Ouyang Moench

Episode 4, "The You You Are," March 4, 2022
Directed by Aoife McArdle, Written by Kari Drake, Dan Erickson, and Anna Ouyang Moench

Episode 5, "The Grim Barbarity of Optics and Design," March 11, 2022
Directed by Aoife McArdle, Written by Anna Ouyang Moench and Dan Erickson

Episode 6, "Hide and Seek," March 18, 2022
Directed by Aoife McArdle, Written by Amanda Overton, Dan Erickson, and Anna Ouyang Moench

Episode 7, "Defiant Jazz," March 25, 2022
Directed by Ben Stiller, Written by Helen Leigh, Dan Erickson, and Anna Ouyang Moench

Episode 8, "What's for Dinner?" April 1, 2022
Directed by Ben Stiller, Written by Chris Black, Dan Erickson, and Anna Ouyang Moench

Episode 9, "The We We Are," April 8, 2022
Directed by Ben Stiller, Written by Dan Erickson and Anna Ouyang Moench

Cast[12]

Mark: Adam Scott
Helly/Helena: Britt Lower
Dylan: Zach Cherry
Irving: John Turturro
Milchick: Tramel Tillman
Harmony Cobel/Mrs. Selvig: Patricia Arquette
Burt: Christopher Walken
Ms. Casey: Dichen Lachman
Devon: Jen Tullock
Ricken: Michael Chernus
Petey: Yul Vazquez
Alexa: Nikki M. James
Mr. Graner: Michael Cumpsty
Gabby Arteta: Nora Dale
Angelo Arteta: Ethan Flower
Reghabi: Karen Aldridge
Natalie: Sydney Cole Alexander
June Kilmer: Cassidy Layton
Danise: Annie McNamara
Rebeck: Grace Rex
Patton: Donald Webber, Jr.

Notes

1. Faculty working at universities often talk about the "silo" effect of being separated into diverse academic disciplines. Like the Macrodata Refinement and Optics and Design employees on the severed floor at Lumon, we might work for years at the same institution and have little to no contact.
2. Chris Gilligan, "How the Pandemic Boosted Working from Home," *U.S. News & World Report*, 18 May 2023, www.usnews.com/news/health-news/articles/2023-05-18/how-the-covid-pandemic-impacted-working-from-home.
3. Anne Helen Petersen and Charlie Warzel, "Remote Work Is Failing Young Employees," *The New York Times*, 22 November 2021, https://www.nytimes.com/2021/11/22/opinion/remote-work-gen-z.html; Noam Scheiber and David Kasnic. "To Get Ahead at Work, Lawyers Find It Helps to Actually Be at Work," *The New York Times*, 22 October 2021, https://www.nytimes.com/2021/10/22/business/economy/law-firm-return-to-office.html.
4. Sheryl Sandberg, *Lean In: Women, Work, and the Will to Lead*, Alfred A. Knopf, 2013.
5. Derek Thompson, "Millennials Didn't Kill the Economy, The Economy Killed Millennials," *The Atlantic*, 1 November 2019, https://www.theatlantic.com/ideas/archive/2018/12/stop-blaming-millennials-killingeconomy/577408/.
6. Devon Price, *Laziness Does Not Exist*, Atria, 2022.
7. Alexander Serenko, "The Great Resignation: The Great Knowledge Exodus or the Onset of the Great Knowledge Revolution?," *Journal of Knowledge Management*, 2022, 27 (4): 1042–1055.
8. Greg Rosalsky and Alina Selyukh, "The Economics Behind 'Quiet Quitting'—And What We Should Call It Instead," *NPR: Planet Money*, 13 September 2022. https://www.npr.org/sections/money/2022/09/13/1122059402/the-economics-behind-quiet-quitting-and-what-we-should-call-it-instead
9. Katie Mogg, "The 'Lazy-Girl Job' Is in Right Now. Here's Why," *The Wall Street Journal*, 25 July 2023, https://www.wsj.com/articles/the-career-goal-of-the-moment-is-a-lazy-girl-job-f5075c4e?mod=WSJ_ACQ_NA_META_US_CONTENT_DPA_PAID.
10. Heather Long, "Analysis | It's Not a 'Labor Shortage.' It's a Great Reassessment of Work in America," *The Washington*

Post, 10 May 2021, https://www.washingtonpost.com/business/2021/05/07/jobs-reportlabor-shortage-analysis/.

11. "*Severance*: Episode List," IMDB.com, https://www.imdb.com/title/tt11280740/episodes/?ref_=tt_eps_sm.
12. Excerpted from "*Severance*: Full Cast & Crew," IMDB.com, https://www.imdb.com/title/tt11280740/fullcredits/?ref_=tt_cl_sm.

Bibliography

Gilligan, Chris. "How the Pandemic Boosted Working from Home." *U.S. News & World Report*. 18 May 2023. www.usnews.com/news/health-news/articles/2023-05-18/how-the-covid-pandemic-impacted-working-from-home.

Long, Heather. "Analysis: It's Not a 'Labor Shortage.' It's a Great Reassessment of Work in America." *The Washington Post*. 10 May 2021. https://www.washingtonpost.com/business/2021/05/07/jobs-reportlabor-shortage-analysis/.

Mogg, Katie. "The 'Lazy-Girl Job' Is in Right Now. Here's Why." *The Wall Street Journal*. 25 July 2023. https://www.wsj.com/articles/the-career-goal-of-the-moment-is-a-lazy-girl-job-f5075c4e?mod=WSJ_ACQ_NA_META_US_CONTENT_DPA_PAID.

Petersen, Anne Helen and Charlie Warzel. "Remote Work Is Failing Young Employees." *The New York Times*, 22 November 2021. https://www.nytimes.com/2021/11/22/opinion/remote-work-gen-z.html.

Price, Devon. *Laziness Does Not Exist*. Atria. 2022.

Rosalsky, Greg and Alina Selyukh. "The Economics Behind 'Quiet Quitting'—And What We Should Call It Instead." *NPR: Planet Money*. 13 September 2022. https://www.npr.org/sections/money/2022/09/13/1122059402/the-economics-behind-quiet-quitting-and-what-we-should-call-it-instead.

Sandberg, Sheryl. *Lean In: Women, Work, and the Will to Lead*. Alfred A. Knopf. 2013.

Scheiber, Noam and David Kasnic. "To Get Ahead at Work, Lawyers Find It Helps to Actually Be at Work." *The New York Times*. 22 October 2021. https://www.nytimes.com/2021/10/22/business/economy/law-firm-return-to-office.html.

Serenko, Alexander. "The Great Resignation: The Great Knowledge Exodus or the Onset of the Great Knowledge Revolution?" *Journal of Knowledge Management*. 2022, 27 (4): 1042–1055.

"*Severance*: Episode List." IMDB.com. https://www.imdb.com/title/tt1128 0740/episodes/?ref_=tt_eps_sm.

"*Severance*: Full Cast & Crew." IMDB.com. https://www.imdb.com/title/tt1 1280740/fullcredits/?ref_=tt_cl_sm.

Thompson, Derek. "Millennials Didn't Kill the Economy. The Economy Killed Millennials." *The Atlantic*. 1 November 2019. https://www.theatlantic.com/ ideas/archive/2018/12/stop-blaming-millennials-killingeconomy/577408/.

PART I

Constructing History

CHAPTER 2

"Who Are You?": Memory, History, and Nostalgia on the Severed Floor

Jennifer Dawes

In Episode 3, "In Perpetuity," the severed coworkers visit the "Perpetuity Wing" at Lumon where the lives of Lumon's founder and CEOs are immortalized in waxwork-like figures with voiceovers (activated by standing next to the figure) that espouse the company's values. The figures stand upon a base that identifies them, their dates as CEO, and their birth and death years. Standing in front of the figure of Myrtle Eagan (Lumon's first female CEO), Irving describes to Helly the corporate mythology about Myrtle: "She was five CEOs ago. They'd never had a woman before. And she told her father at age seven, she was going to be the first." To which, Helly opines sarcastically: "It almost makes me wish I could remember my own childhood." Irving responds, "It's an unnatural state for a person to have no history. History makes us someone. Gives us a context. A shape." Irving's response captures the value of historical knowledge to an individual as defining the self. Although his comment

J. Dawes (✉)
Department of Rhetoric and Writing, University of Arkansas at Little Rock, Little Rock, AR, USA
e-mail: jdawes@ualr.edu

N. M. Isacoff and J. Dawes (eds.), *Reintegrating Severance*,
https://doi.org/10.1007/978-3-031-57448-1_2

presupposes the harm of Lumon's severance procedure, he does not seem to grasp this implication: that the damage inflicted by the procedure is that separating a person from their past entails separating them from their identity. For Irving, it is enough to know that he works "for a company that has been actively caring for mankind since 1866," as he states the Lumon "party line." For each of the characters, the context, "a shape," that the lives of their outie would provide is replaced by corporate culture and history. The "nostalgia" they feel and that permeates the show is a created sense of home and place that seems to exist only in the confines of the company and is a nostalgia that is actually created and imposed by the company. In this essay, I look at the idea of the incomplete self that is created by the severance procedure and the way that Lumon fills this void with company lore and manipulated nostalgia for Lumon's past, which functions as a stand-in for the severed employees' own personal histories. I also consider how the company's reach extends beyond the severed floor to encompass all of the defined spaces in Kier, P.E. Finally, I look at the way mapping helps the characters to create a context for their lives as well as a method for escape.

The "SVR'D" Self

The motif of abbreviation runs throughout the early episodes of the series. From the characters' shortened names (Mark S., Helly R., Irving B., Dylan G.) to the sign at the entrance leading to the severed floor ("SVR'D ACCESS"), references to incompleteness reflect the larger theme of the divided self (Fig. 2.1).

Fig. 2.1 The sign at the threshold of the severed area

The camera angles in the early scene of Mark in the locker room visually depict this demarcation of self. About eight minutes into the first episode, Mark enters Lumon and begins his daily routine: stopping at the front desk and getting approval to enter from the receptionist, scanning his badge, walking past a wall engraved with a large likeness of Kier Eagan in profile that looks remarkably similar to V.I. Lenin, heading downstairs, and scanning into the SVR'D ACCESS.[1] As he is admitted through the final gray door, the camera angles focus tightly on Mark's actions and body parts. Upon entering the room, an establishing shot reveals nine stainless steel lockers on one side with a pillar bench in front featuring a tufted cushion in "Lumon green." In keeping with the visual symmetry of the camera work, Mark's locker is dead center. The angle and focus of the camera prevent the viewer from seeing the entire room. However at both the beginning and end of this sequence, we see the corner of another matching bench and suspended fluorescent light. Presumably, this room contains 18 lockers, which we find later is unlikely to be enough for all of the workers on the severed floor. Where are the others?

Inside the locker room, he swaps his outside shoes for work ones and leaves his winter coat, keys, wallet, outside ID, and watch in exchange for his inside ID and watch. While exchanging his outer for his inner gear, it appears that the camera is inside the locker as it peers at Mark's face. The intensely horizontal arrangement frames his face with the locker. While the shot only lasts for a few seconds, it is suggestive of the inner/outer dichotomy that is explored in the show. The rest of the scene is composed of a series of tightly focused shots that highlight Mark's hands and feet, visually segmenting his physical self. These shots begin with Mark in profile in the same direction as Kier's silhouette in the engraving, which is followed by individual shots that focus on his hands and feet and the actions of placing items in the locker drawer and tying his shoes. The shots give little overall context for the larger space he inhabits. His actions, memorized to the point of perfection, suggest the routine dailiness of office work. Meanwhile, the camera chops up the work he performs into actions closely inspected individually but without a focus on the whole self, except at the beginning and end of the scene. The camera work in this early scene alludes to the larger theme of incompleteness, an idea that is also developed in the characters' dialogue as they struggle to constitute an identity on the severed floor.

The first words of the first episode—"Who are you?"—as Helly is "born" from the massive womb of the conference room table, establish the primary question ultimately asked by each innie character.[2] The drive to discover the answer to the characters' own individual identities sets in motion the final act of the season. For Mark, at first, the question of identity seems irrelevant. He has to be prodded by the other characters to even consider a response to the question. Dylan, on the other hand, has some of the most fanciful and specific ideas about his own outie self, boasting that he must do "muscle shows."[3] While Irving seems less troubled by questions of identity early in the show, he does notice something black under his nails (paint from his outie's hobby), which causes a brief moment of perplexity. For Irving, the pivotal moment occurs when he learns that his love interest, Burt, is leaving, which causes him to reject Lumon's hold over his identity and to consider what his life is like outside of the severed floor.

Unlike the other characters at the point they are introduced to us, Helly combatively and forcefully asserts her need to understand her identity and self. The other characters have likely already gone through that stage (we learn from Mark that he tried to kill Petey when he first arrived), and when we meet them, they are docile and accustomed to their work at Lumon and to their divided consciousness. Helly, clearly, is not. She has some notably odd responses to her severed state as she tries to figure out who (and what) she is. One of her early suggested possibilities—that she is "livestock" ("Did you grow me as food, and that's why I have no memories?")—seems curious for someone who supposedly has no memories.[4] The concept of humans as food is one derived from horror stories or the rare news headline. Would Helly know about that in her severed form? Later as the MDR workers walk the hallway toward the Perpetuity Wing, another horror movie trope is reflected in her suggestion that she wear Mark's face as a threat to rivals O&D: "If they come back and attack us, I think we should kill Mark. So they think we're crazy with nothing to lose. ... Like I imagine them rounding a corner, and I'm all bloodstained, and I'm wearing your face and they're like 'Whose face is that?' And I'm like 'the last person who fucked with us.' And that's just feeling like a really powerful image to me."[5] This seems like a reference to Jonathan Demme's 1991 *Silence of the Lambs*, as Hannibal Lector wears a severed human face in his escape.[6] How does Helly's severed self have an awareness of this face-wearing trope? Why reference this particular film? Just as the severed workers' identities are fragmented, the antagonist of *Silence*, Jame Gumb, is not fully developed or completely evolved into the final self he hopes to become. Further, both he and the current Eagan CEO

"Jame Eagan" bear an incomplete name, perhaps hinting at something missing in the psychological makeup of the individual.[7]

Other characters are equally incomplete. Mark has no access to the grief that his split self feels on the outside, though vestiges of his sadness are clear to his best friend Petey. Mark is perhaps the most enigmatic character, as he seems to embrace his severed state, accepting his outie's choice and following the rules of Lumon. However, when his perspective is challenged upon encountering a book written by his outie's brother-in-law, Ricken, he begins to reinterpret his severed experience with a defiantly alternative meaning. Ricken's "wisdom" plants the seeds in Mark's mind that lead him to seek the truth.

Dylan and Irving seem to be the most complacent about their severed states. Both embrace the company ethos, but in different ways. For Dylan, the incentives—finger traps, erasers, character portraits, and such—provide adequate compensation for his labor. The juvenile and ridiculous nature of these incentives highlights the fact that these are Lumon-created desires filled by Lumon-created products. Irving mocks Dylan's fascination with the rewards not because they are juvenile or ridiculous but because, in Irving's own reverence for the company, serving Lumon is its own reward. Both characters ultimately challenge the status quo—Dylan in response to inadvertently meeting his outie's son during the "overtime contingency" and Irving when he sees the cavalier way that Burt's retirement is handled despite the fact that it spells doom for Burt's innie. The literal absences of the son and Burt motivate Dylan's and Irving's change in perspective and subsequent actions. Up until they decide to rebel, for everyone in MDR except Helly, the company mythos, deeply entrenched in everything Lumon produces and promotes, has provided sufficient meaning for their lives on the severed floor. Their increasing motivation to rebel begins to match Helly's agitation. In Episode 7, when Irving utters the memorable line "Let's burn this place to the ground," he gives voice to the severed workers' growing sentiment of revolt.[8]

"In Perpetuity"

The layers of meaning created by Lumon as they shape company lore and the nostalgia the workers feel for the company's created history point to the innie workers' own lack of personal identity. They are containers to be filled. Without Lumon, they are nothing. This is fully explored in the Perpetuity Wing scene. Upon closer analysis of this scene, we can see how the overlapping dialogue reveals the pervasiveness of the company's values. As Helly stands in front of the replica of Myrtle Eagan, the figure "speaks."[9]

Myrtle's recorded voice: *I think that to be an Eagan, either a true Eagan or one working in this Lumon family, what you are is a keeper of an ethos, a compact of values that we have long held as precious, and which I do believe will one day save this world.*

[Helly scratches off "Lumon Will Save the World" on her Eagan bingo card as Myrtle keeps talking.]

Myrtle:	*And that ethos goes all the way back through my blood …*
Mark:	Oh, look, you've got one …
Myrtle:	*… to where we all started, with Kier.*
Irving [walks up]:	It's okay if you cry.
Myrtle:	*When I was a girl* [overlapping with Irving] … *my father would make me whisper …*
Irving:	She was five CEOs ago. [Myrtle's muffled speech can be heard in the background.]
Myrtle:	… *until I fall asleep* … [This line is clearly audible but not recorded in the closed captioning.]
Irving:	They'd never had a woman before. And she told her father at age seven, she was going to be the first.
Myrtle:	*Vision. Verve.*
Irving:	Isn't that lovely?
Myrtle:	*Wit.*
Helly [flatly]:	It's beautiful.
Myrtle:	*Cheer.*
Helly:	It almost makes me wish I remembered my own childhood. [Myrtle's muffled speech heard in the background.]
Myrtle:	*Nimbleness. Probity. Wiles.*

As Irving and Helly walk away and Irving begins his speech about history and identity, we can hear Myrtle's muffled voice in the background. Mark, who is standing to the left of Myrtle's figure on screen, lingers with his head down for a moment then joins them. Despite the fact that the "Myrtle" on the screen is not a person (much like the outie "Helena" attests about the innie "Helly"), her voice is prevalent throughout the scene as she recites Lumon's nine core principles. It is notable that the two principles we do not hear her clearly articulate—humility and benevolence—are the qualities least embodied by Lumon's founders and current leadership (Fig. 2.2).

As this scene reveals, memory and how it shapes identity is the central, critical question of the show and is key to the innie characters' struggle. For the innies, the Perpetuity Wing and other Lumon culture (the handbook, the incentives) fill the void created when their outies elected to undergo the Severance procedure. Mark and the Macrodata Refinement crew take Helly to the Perpetuity Wing in the first place because, as Irving says, she is "starved for meaning," implying that the company culture, history, and lore will provide this meaning she lacks. Nostalgia for the

Fig. 2.2 Mark, Irving, and Helly in front of Myrtle Eagan's wax figure in the Perpetuity Wing

company's past as it celebrates Lumon's "values" will fill the hole in her awareness of her own personal history and make her life at Lumon (the only life this version of Helly has) more meaningful.

Just as the innies would not know whether or not the "history" that is imparted in the Perpetuity Wing is accurate, they would also have no concept of the innate "weirdness" of the display. The aesthetics of the Perpetuity Wing give it an ominous feel, but the innies would have no reason to understand how creepy the waxwork figures might be to an audience outside of Lumon. In his study of wax museums in Scandinavia, *Living Pictures, Missing Persons: Mannequins, Museums, and Modernity*, Mark B. Sandberg writes:

> The "THINGNESS" inherent in the idea of display is nowhere more evident than in the wax museum. After all, mannequins provide a particularly fleshy sort of simulation; even as they seem to transport viewers into the presence of fame, or celebrities to the spectator's feet, wax figures provide continual reminders of that display's material means: staring eyes, the immobility of the pose, the embalmed sheen of wax. Sensations of visual mobility and variety play off the scandalous physicality of the figure, leaving behind a vague discomfort, a whiff of seediness that clings to wax figures to this day.[10]

This "vague discomfort" a viewer might feel in seeing the human form replicated in wax is not echoed by the characters (with the exception of Helly) as they approach the display either worshipfully (Irving) or at the very least unquestioningly (Mark and later Dylan). The choice of a wax display for the founder and former CEOs is notable for the history of the wax form as well as the mutually reinforcing nostalgic and eerie feelings it evokes. Wax displays are an old art form with early examples of funeral effigies dating back to the fourteenth century. Wax museums grew in popularity in the nineteenth century. The most famous and arguably the best is Madame Tussaud's in London, which opened its doors in 1835.[11] In recent years, contemporary museum displays have moved away from waxworks to incorporate digital/video displays that do not have the uncanny impact of viewing the human form doubled in a wax effigy. The fact that the executives at Lumon chose the wax museum format (as opposed to video and or photographic displays of the historical figures) underscores the intentionally eerie feeling of the display itself. It also emphasizes the nostalgic nature of the message and the visual representations of the founders. The "Perpetuity Wing" feels like an elaborate roadside attraction one might encounter in a 1950s family vacation.

Leaving the wax figures, the characters move on to a display of mouths disconnected from faces, which Dylan calls "The Mouth Wall," emphasizing again the fragmented nature of their experience. Finally, they come to the most important display—Kier Eagan's home, nostalgically and meticulously recreated, frozen in time, a building inside a building, the home, a temple to the company founder. The "building inside a building" can be seen as reflecting the containment of the severed workers. The void of the workers' selves is filled with the company's primary tenet that the workers and founders are family, and their container is a maze of surveillance where they are continuously watched but their attention is perpetually directed away from this control. When any of them voice concerns about the company control, the company representative and handler, Mr. Milchick, assures them of their own outies' compliance with and embrace of company policy. The innies have been "severed" from the knowledge of their true selves (the outies) with only the understanding that their outies have embraced their current state. With everything of their history and "selves" sucked out, Lumon can fill them with allegiance and love for the company.

The characters embrace Lumon's message to varying degrees. In Kier's replica house, we see this disparity: Helly refuses to acquiesce to her role at Lumon, flees the scene, and tries to escape the severed floor. While Mark seems to accept Lumon, he also makes light of the company lore in "Eagan bingo." And, in the house, Irving calls him out for his attempt to "bedsit" as he crosses a rope in an attempt to sit on Kier's bed. While Irving, the most "devout" of the severed employees, chastises Mark for giving Helly the bingo card and for his transgressive behavior in Kier's house, Dylan's response is the most ambiguous. He loves the company incentives but mocks the displays in the Perpetuity Wing. His response to Kier Eagan's house: "I hate this place. It smells like 19th century ass." It is, however, notable in all of the characters' reactions that none of them seem to question the validity of the history presented to them. While they might mock the company displays or try to escape their "imprisonment," they don't ever seem to question the historical accuracy of the reality presented to them. This leads us to the questions: Who is Kier Eagan? How and where might he have existed in the outside world? Why is his house so important? What, in fact, is this outside world?

Mapping Kier, P.E.

Like the consciousness of the severed workers, the show is divided between the brightly lit spaces of Lumon and the moody gray world outside. Kier, P.E. seems to be a company-created town located in the northern United States. Stepping away from the severed floor of Lumon, we are given a view of the area through the key locations of Mark's and Mrs. Selvig's neighborhood (strangely occupied by seemingly only themselves); Mark's sister and brother-in-law's house; Pip's restaurant; the Damona birthing cabins; and Petey's greenhouse, among other places. Later, in the final episode, we get a better sense of the mapping of the larger town when Irving attempts to reach Burt.

In addition, the created spaces both inside and outside Lumon point to the way nostalgia functions in the show on two levels—the characters' nostalgia for the Lumon creators' past and the viewers' nostalgia for elements of their own personal and collective past in the old cars, outdated technology, and vintage clothing. Like Lumon, the city of Kier appears to be a container that reflects a not-too-distant past. From Mrs. Selvig's funky 70s-style clothing to the dated 80s and 90s cars the characters drive, Kier seems to exist in another time, but one within living memory. We see the cars and the clothes and recognize these cultural touchstones of our own past, which causes us to question not only where we are but *when* we are. This is particularly notable given the emphasis on the nineteenth-century past of the company's founding.

The naming of places in the town suggests the corporation's influence. Mark lives at Baird Creek Manor (after Baird Eagan, the fourth Lumon CEO), while we learn later that Irving's apartment is part of the Leonora Lake housing development (seventh CEO). Pip's is obviously named for Phillip Eagan, the sixth CEO. Careful viewers will also note the Swab Girl Bathhouse and Soapery and Imogene's Clothing in downtown Kier reflecting, of course, the name and profession of Kier's wife.

While the town of Kier is clearly dominated by the company, there are several spaces that appear to be outside the influence of Lumon. Petey's choice of a greenhouse on Half Loop Road suggests that he is potentially outside the reach of Lumon in that location.[12] Reghabi chooses to hole up in an abandoned space in Ganz College in neighboring Ganz. Some viewers have speculated that Devon and Ricken's house is potentially closer to Ganz than to Kier and, therefore, also removed from the Lumon sphere of influence. Likewise, the Damona Birthing Retreat seems to be outside of town. However, it also (somehow) serves as a severed space for Gabby Arteta as she gives birth.

Even though Lumon clearly owns the town of Kier, the main characters reject the idea that the company is a threat. Mark and Alexa go on two dates at a restaurant in downtown Kier, Gerhardt's, named after fifth Lumon CEO Gerhardt, where they encounter protestors from the "Whole Mind Collective" in front of the ironically named "Hall of Records" upon leaving the restaurant. In addition, the alley spaces where June's band performs their pointed "Fuck You Lumon" song is clearly in downtown Kier.

The tertiary characters' protest of Lumon suggests that the company's hold over the town is not absolute. The protests combined with the fact that State Senator Angelo Arteta has to lobby for the legality of the severance procedure implies that it is not yet widely accepted. In addition, while the innies' lives inside Lumon are carefully monitored, and Mrs. Selvig keeps a close eye on Mark on the outside, Irving's nocturnal activities at home—drinking copious cups of coffee and painting the entrance to the break room over and over—are unobserved by Lumon overseers.

The viewer must piece together the clues in the show about the locations and how they relate to Lumon, creating their own "maps" of the spaces in and around Kier. It is not until the final episode that the town is seen on a broader scale as Cobel and Irving race toward their destinations, crossing paths briefly. By this point, the act of mapping has become both a gesture of defiance and a practical strategy. We learn early on that mapping is forbidden on the severed floor ("Render not my creation in miniature") and that Petey's map is contraband.[13] Mark's destruction and later recreation of the map signals a change in his innie's perception not only of place and space but also of his own identity and worth. While "old" innie Mark is fearful of transgression, "new" innie Mark, still fearful, is emboldened to try to understand his place in the company's space. Mapping becomes a signal for the characters' growing need to understand their own identities. Irving's outie had begun the process of mapping as he collected the names and addresses of the severed workers and kept a map with the information. When innie Irving discovers this list and map, it gives him the tools to find the answers he seeks about Burt (Fig. 2.3).

The defiant act of mapping also helps Dylan to find the control room where he is able to activate the Overtime Contingency. As the characters prepare to meet the world their outies inhabit, Mark warns them that they

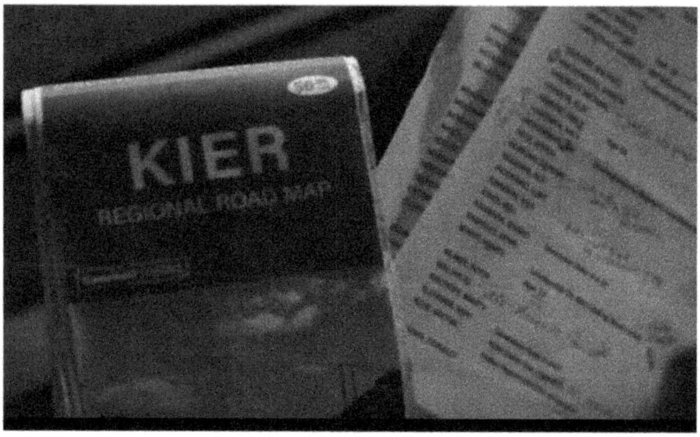

Fig. 2.3 Irving's list of severed workers and map of Kier

must quickly figure out how to navigate the spaces and people they will encounter. Whether they will be successful in their attempts remains to be seen as the show ends with a cliffhanger.

Conclusion

The mapping of space in the world of *Severance* as well as the scenes on the severed floor, notably in the "Perpetuity Wing," point to the larger implications of the show and its relation to our own world. *Severance* can be read as both a corporate response to worker fatigue in the company's actual severance procedure and, simultaneously, an indictment of capitalism and corporate culture. It is no surprise that workers become numb to repetitive, meaningless work. The simple truth of human nature is that work needs to "mean something," and the more repetitive and meaningless the work (as in the number sorting in Macrodata Refinement), the more the workers need a sense of larger meaning. While the outies never have to experience the tedium that is their daily work life, the innies are "held captive" for eight hours a day and filled with "meaning" created by the company in the form of an origin myth that provides both the backstory of the company and its ethos.

Part of Lumon's lore is that the workers and the Eagans are "family." How different is this from corporate rhetoric in the U.S. today? In a quick Google search of the phrase "workers as family," the first 10 hits point to the toxicity of this corporate construction. A growing number of workers are rejecting these ideas and leaving their positions, especially for remote work. In a TikTok in 2022, corporate recruiter Bryan Creely popularized the phrase "quiet quitting," the act of doing just enough at your job but no more. Creely talks about the "great resignation" in response to "hustle culture" and offers the third option of backing off from overwork instead of completely leaving a job.[14] However, on the severed floor, there is no backing off, there is only work and more work. If they slack off or are insubordinate, they are tortured in the Break Room. Retirement seems to be an option for some characters, but, even then, the workers can only leave at the peril of losing their own innie identities. Their employment literally defines and creates their work selves as they will effectively cease to exist outside of the workplace. As cultural critique, *Severance* forces us to consider how our work shapes our own sense of self and at what cost. We must also reckon with the powerful and profound impact of corporate culture on the American work landscape.

Notes

1. *Severance*, "Good News About Hell."
2. *Severance*, "Good News About Hell."
3. *Severance*, "In Perpetuity."
4. *Severance*, "Good News About Hell."
5. *Severance*, "In Perpetuity."
6. *Silence of the Lambs*, directed by Jonathan Demme, 1990.
7. While "Jame" is a perfectly legitimate name as a derivative of the name "James," it is unusual enough to be noted when it is used in television and film. See: https://www.mynamestats.com/First-Names/J/JA/JAME/index.html. According to ourbabynamer.com, it means "supplanter." See: http://www.ourbabynamer.com/meaning-of-Jame.html.
8. *Severance*, "Defiant Jazz."
9. *Severance*, "In Perpetuity."
10. Mark B. Sandberg, *Living Pictures, Missing Persons: Mannequins, Museums, and Modernity,* Princeton UP, 2003. 18.
11. "Our History," Madame Tussauds London. https://www.madametussauds.com/london/information/our-history/. Accessed November 21, 2023.

12. The name of the road underscores the incompleteness reflected in other elements of the show. Petey will only begin the journey but, as it's a "half loop," he won't come full circle.
13. *Severance*, "The You You Are."
14. Bryan Creely, @alifeafterlayoff, "More People Are 'Quiet Quitting' Instead of Leaving," TikTok, March 4, 2022. Accessed November 21, 2023.

Bibliography

Creely, Bryan. @alifeafterlayoff. "More People Are 'Quiet Quitting' Instead of Leaving," TikTok, March 4, 2022.

"First Name JAME." *Mynamestats.com*. https://www.mynamestats.com/First-Names/J/JA/JAME/index.html.

"Meaning of Jame." *ourbabynamer.com*. https://www.ourbabynamer.com/meaning-of-Jame.html.

"Our History." Madame Tussauds London. https://www.madametussauds.com/london/information/our-history/.

Sandberg, Mark B. *Living Pictures, Missing Persons: Mannequins, Museums, and Modernity*. Princeton UP, 2003.

Silence of the Lambs. Directed by Jonathan Demme, 1990.

CHAPTER 3

The Grim Barbarity of Capitalist Designs: Class Conflict, Corporate Dystopia, and the Sacred Gaze in *Severance*

Dylan Reid Miller

The cult at the heart of the megacorporation Lumon Industries, the primary antagonist of the 2022 Apple TV+ show *Severance*, is founded on the carefully constructed scripture surrounding its first CEO, Kier Eagan. The protagonists are a group of Lumon employees who have been given medically induced dissociative identity disorder (DID) by the company using a procedure called "Severance." Severance creates "alters" (the DID community's term for individual people within their systems) with total dissociative amnesia who can only "front" (take conscious control of the body) when on the controlled "Severed Floor" they are assigned to work on. These alters have minimal information about the world outside their workplace, with tight security preventing unintended breaches, and neither the working nor non-working alters retain memories from the

D. R. Miller (✉)
American Culture Studies, Bowling Green State University, Bowling Green, USA
e-mail: dylan.reid.miller@gmail.com

N. M. Isacoff and J. Dawes (eds.), *Reintegrating Severance*,
https://doi.org/10.1007/978-3-031-57448-1_3

other person. This allows the company to indoctrinate the working alters into a form of governance—and self-governance—by a set of rules in the *Compliance Handbook*, claimed to be the word of Kier, and to keep this a secret from the non-working alters and the public at large.

The show is aware of capitalism's precarity that "sharply and frequently returns in forms of suffering that plague the public and provoke cracks in [its] defenses and its social acceptance,"[1] and considers a potential dystopian resolution to the problem of its innate instability by injecting the social and temporal realities of feudal life into its economic materiality. Namely, Lumon reintroduces religious institutions, a cornerstone inherent to myriad facets of peasants' social lives, into its systems. Hinging the governance of its working alters on the mythologized life of a historical figure turns their worldview into an encompassing form of "civil religion," wherein the structure of a nation or other "imagined community"[2] is regarded as an expression of "divine will, natural law, or the destiny of a particular people."[3] The imagined community of Lumon supersedes nation, as corporations are not bound to territories or states and the explicit goal of current CEO Jame Eagan is to expand the Severance program worldwide,[4] which would normally bring with it a loss of control as global capitalism transforms religious tradition into something that "must be 'sold' to a clientele that is no longer constrained to 'buy'"[5]; however, the addition of this feudal social control is intended to dissolve the "free market" of ideas without disrupting the bourgeoisie's economic dominance that brought it about. This speculative ideological formulation articulates how various strains of late capitalism can and do function as civil religions, attempting to alienate the global proletariat so thoroughly that they can be entirely dehumanized and transformed into a permanent and unseen underclass without the capacity to leverage resistance.

Lumon's administration knows that the scripture of the *Compliance Handbook* alone is not enough to ensure worker belief and loyalty, and so creates cultural objects that root the handbook in a historiographical narrative of Lumon's past. This essay addresses the visual culture of Lumon's civil religion, centering on the collection of paintings hung by the Optics and Design (O&D) department throughout the otherwise sparse and sterile severed floor. Providing a visual culture helps to concretize the company's self-determined collective memory in the minds of the Severed labor force, using the power of images to construct and maintain the social order of imagined communities to generate belief in the working alters. Yet no system has a totalizing effect on the ideological perspectives of the communities they are integrated into; even looking devoutly offers a range of understandings negotiated between the viewer and the image. I argue that the character arc of Irving B., initially a true believer who becomes disillusioned when the managers of the severed floor curtail his nascent romantic relationship, represents the power of the gaze to repress but also how his changing needs and perspectives transform the action of looking with belief into a mechanism for structural resistance.

Religious visual and material cultures are an important part of constructing faith-based social realities. As religious art history scholar David Morgan has argued, studying the objects intended to be the targets of a "sacred gaze," or "the particular configuration of ideas, attitudes, and customs that informs a religious act of seeing as it occurs within a given cultural and historical setting,"[6] can also illuminate the behaviors that rely on these objects and the attitudes that inform vision as a cultural act. Seeing is not merely the observation of an object's qualities, but "an operation that relies on an apparatus of assumptions and inclinations, habits and routines, historical associations and cultural practices."[7] The spiritual meaning of religious images goes beyond the depiction of the sacred and extends to the way they are used by the viewer to affirm and perform belief. It becomes a crucial part of indoctrination into a belief system to provide contextualized objects to be gazed at and a framework of understanding that orients them as sacred, and to analyze sacred images must also include an understanding of their functions in these contexts. In the case of Lumon this orientation is meant to convince alters who view the institutionally sanctioned art to perpetuate the system they live in through a capitalist realist perspective, demanding belief that this ontology is the correct one and, further, that there can be no other.[8]

Kier and the Tempers

Severance does not open immediately with Lumon's religious and cultic elements, though it is clear from the start that it is not an ordinary office. Mentions of service to Kier, the unsettling nature of the Severance procedure and the ritual induction of the new employee Helly R., and the abrupt and unexplained disappearance of Helly's predecessor Petey, build tension about the true nature of the company, but the first episode does not directly show the tactics of reward and punishment used to ensure compliance. What it does establish is that Lumon is a "society of control," as defined by Giles Deleuze, through highlighting the way its processes "modulate" to adapt to developing threats against its power. A network of cameras turns the workplace into a panopticon, the audience left just as unsure as the laborers whether someone is watching at any given moment and requiring constant self-regulation based on fear. In the Macrodata Refinement office, where the four protagonists work, the first piece of artwork explicitly produced by Lumon for the purposes of indoctrination can be seen on the wall during Episode 1, "Good News About Hell." The sole decoration in the room apart from a pair of clocks is a portrait of Kier Eagan that sits above a small nook that houses the department's volumes of the *Compliance Handbook*. In a closely cropped frame that focuses attention on the face, a professionally dressed Kier makes direct eye contact with observers so that this portrait, like the omniscient Abrahamic God, can watch over the "Refiners" as they work. Kier's gaze functions as an extension of the cameras by reminding them of the rules they are expected to follow and why, particularly the department head who is expected to ritualistically acknowledge it every morning.[9]

Episode 2, "Half Loop," features this portrait more prominently as the show begins to bring the cult of Kier to the foreground. Here, it is established that Irving is the protagonist most concerned with following Lumon's ideology to the letter. When Mark S. removes the department's group photos from the desks before the new ones arrive, Irving prints off the relevant handbook passage to chide him for breaking protocol. At Helly's ritual welcoming party, the portrait is conspicuously kept in frame over the head of their supervisor Seth Milchick while they play an icebreaker, which drives Mark to confess his "sins" regarding the photos. When the game concludes and the alters mingle, another conspicuous shot shows Irving deliberately seated with the portrait over his shoulder to solidify his adherence to the doctrine of Lumon and the respect that he pays to its visual culture. That Irving's non-work alter is a painter, shown at the beginning of the eighth episode "What's For Dinner?", suggests that Irving already had a well-developed sense of the gaze as a practice that can determine "the conditions under which the visible is visible, the rules governing visibility and the credibility of images, and what power an image may assert over those who see it,"[10] predisposing him to adoption of the sacred gaze within the material conditions of Lumon even absent his memories.

Later in "Half Loop," Irving is sent to the Wellness department to meet with the counselor after falling asleep on the job and dreaming of a viscous black substance consuming his workspace, which turns out to be the paint his non-work alter uses. Hanging in the Wellness waiting room is a neoclassical style painting depicting a handbook passage wherein Kier lays out his theory of the Four Tempers, Woe, Frolic, Dread, and Malice. Like the antiquated and scientifically debunked notion of the Four Humors, he wrote that a person's character is defined by the balance of the Tempers and that "should you tame the tempers as I did mine, then the world shall become but your appendage."[11] Kier appears in the mouth of a cave brandishing a whip similar to a cat o' nine tails representing Lumon's nine "Core Principles" (Vision, Verve, Wit, Cheer, Humility, Benevolence, Nimbleness, Probity, and Wiles) at the cowering figures of an old woman, a bride, a humanoid ram, and a court jester, the canonical representations of the Tempers. Professor of Christian theology Joerg Reiger writes in the introduction to the book *Religion, Theology, and Class: Fresh Engagements After Long Silence* that "Christian images of God's power have shaped up in the context of the Roman Empire,"[12] with early images produced of the Christian God closely resembling the contemporary Emperor. He further argues that this relationship between ruling classes and the notion of God as king has led to the power of the successful CEO entering the contemporary Christian imaginary as a new way to envision Godlike power. This painting makes use of the connective tissues that link power and divinity by framing Kier as a Biblical prophet, dressing him in a belted tunic and sandals in the style of the Roman Empire and setting the light source behind him to create a halo effect. The image as a whole is designed to represent mastery over the base instincts of human nature as a path to piety and demonstrates the spiritual self-flagellation that the working alters are expected to perform to properly embody their "immutable" roles in the preordained hierarchies of the company's internal society. Its placement in Wellness, one of the primary spaces specifically delineated for punitive ritual on the severed floor, reminds them of this duty in a place and time where they are already primed to consider their subaltern positionality as subjects of the Lumon social strata.

Perpetuity and the "Lumon Legacy of Joy"

Before it was in Wellness, the painting of Kier taming the tempers hung in the Perpetuity Wing. Perpetuity is a museum-like space devoted to the Eagan family that Irving calls the "living soul of Lumon,"[13] which includes wax figure replicas of each past CEO and a complete recreation of Kier Eagan's home. At Irving's prompting, the Refiners take Helly to Perpetuity in Episode 3, "In Perpetuity," to help her settle in; he believes that she struggles because she does not feel a connection to the world around her, and that showing her their visual culture will give her a sense of purpose. While Helly refutes this connection, the sequence is useful for establishing the importance of visual culture in the indoctrination process through formalizing a "Cultural Memory"[14] with ostensibly fixed meanings that working alters can be taught to "read" in the Lumon produced artwork. This kind of cultural literacy, learned through interaction with objects of Cultural Memory, "assimilates newcomers and reinforces its conception of social order"[15] by using the Severance procedure to eliminate the more flexible "Communicative memory" of lived experience.[16] It ingrains a hermeneutic that forecloses on the possibility of other representations and subsequently the possibility of other forms of understanding. "To know something is to be able to represent it"[17] and vice versa, so limiting what the alters see and how they see it necessarily limits their knowledge and imagination. There is a great diversity of events shown in the paintings and other art, many of them blatantly atemporal and metaphorical like Kier taming the Tempers, and they are rendered in styles from across art history, but this is merely another extension of the encompassing quality of the visual culture. It forms the facade of a coherent cultural lineage that has produced its own art across time and posits the alters as its inheritors. Therefore, the past becomes a site unable to materially render potentiality outside of the Lumon Cultural Memory.

This restriction is reinforced by a strict ban on producing art, including maps of the severed floor ("render not my creation in miniature"[18]). The MDR refiners' scope is so limited that when Mark uncovers a map made by Petey before he disappeared, they discuss if the drawings on the right side are "how houses look."[19] Accepting the ordained hermeneutic grants the alters a sense of community by way of the "culturally institutionalized heritage of [their] society,"[20] as Irving explains to Helly in front of a photo wall of smiles called the "Lumon Legacy of Joy:"

> *Irving*: It's an unnatural state for a person to have no history. History makes us someone. Gives us a context. A shape. But waking up on that table, I was shapeless. But then I learned that I work for a company that has been actively caring for mankind since 1866. Look. Each of these is

a real smile from someone on the outside. Someone Lumon Industries has helped... you're part of a history now.
Mark: A noble one.[21]

He uses the Legacy of Joy to interpellate Helly into the alters' collective "sacralized identity," sacralization being "the inevitable process that safeguards identity when it is endangered by the disadvantages of the infinite adaptability of symbol-systems... protect[ing] a system of meaning, or a definition of reality, and modif[ying], obstruct[ing], or (if necessary) legitim[izing] change."[22] He hopes that she will be repaid as he was with the sense of belonging that all Lumon produced art promises in return for faith[23] that it possesses and displays "truth."

Her rejection of the controlling self-image, and embrace of the suffering the system causes her, uniquely allows her to see differently from the start; even the irreverent fourth protagonist Dylan G. has sublimated his lack of genuine belief to a desire for the "perks" offered for hard work such as finger traps, caricature art, and "waffle parties" in which the highest performing Refiner of the quarter reenacts the taming of the Tempers in a sexual ritual. He willingly assimilates to earn these perks, at one point asserting that a painting existing is "ironclad proof" that the events depicted are part of a real history.[24] Symbols commonly stand for an entire national and ideological history as a mechanism of assimilation. For example, Protestants in the antebellum United States closely bound their values to the country's flag and the concept of national unity, particularly as the Civil War broke out in the 1860s. Clergyman Henry Ward Beecher endorsed the flag, claiming it was not merely a "painted rag" but "a whole national history... It is the NATION." As the law shifted to prohibit Bible readings in public school, the flag became the preeminent means of "imposing a civilizing piety on the impressionable minds of the nation's youth to counter the perceived menace of difference and division based on religion and ethnicity."[25] In a fitting echo of Beecher's words, Irving tells Mark that Perpetuity is not just "a lot," but "everything."[26]

It is clear that the art is designed to call the alters toward an affinity of their shared imagined community (Macrodata Refinement) within Lumon society. Helly's refutation of the sacred gaze and the identity it demands is thus not enough on its own to undermine the functioning of the bio- and necropolitical rule of law on the severed floor. Working alters are kept in a state of social death to the wider world, treated as non-existent—Mark's non-work alter insisting that he does the job and there is no "other one"[27]—or non-human—Helly's non-work alter telling her "I am a person, you are not."[28] This traps them in the process of slow death, "the physical wearing out of a population and the deterioration of people in that population that is very nearly a defining condition of their experience and historical existence,"[29] awaiting the "retirement" of their non-work selves that will invariably end their lives. As long as Helly's fellow workers, refiners and otherwise, see the portrait on the wall as a symbol to be venerated, her isolated resistance does not mount a genuine threat to the "full spectrum dominance"[30] of Lumon's hegemony. Without the disruption of the sacred gaze she hits the negative ontological limit of biopower, suicide that damages the dominating power[31]; she unsuccessfully attempts to hang herself in the elevator that initiates a "switch" (the term for when a different alter begins to front) to make her non-work alter suffer and die at the cost of her own life.[32] Mark and Dylan's path to class consciousness emerges from reading an external text, a book written by Mark's brother-in-law Ricken Hale, and by Dylan meeting his child when he briefly fronts outside of work, experiences that offer them new representations and new knowledge. Irving, on the other hand, has his faith breached by Lumon's own visual culture.

"The Grim Barbarity of Optics and Design"

Irving's arc is fittingly facilitated by the head of O&D, Burt G., whom he meets in Wellness during "Half Loop." Over the course of the season, they develop romantic feelings for each other, a taboo in the handbook because it creates a networked bond between the departments outside of the sacralized identity shared by the majority of working alters. The first crack in the ideological horizon ironically comes when Milchick "runs a 266" on Irving,[33] code for the weaponization of visual culture to create division among the departments. This invokes an abstracted form of real-world counterinsurgency strategies that "focus on… internal contradictions, trying to keep the different subjects separate and exacerbate their ideological differences in order to prevent a political recomposition."[34] In the case of Irving, a painting titled "The Grim Barbarity of Optics and Design" is sent to the Macrodata Refinement printer as he attempts to scan a small map with directions to Burt's workspace after another nightmare featuring the black paint. It graphically depicts nondescript O&D workers killing and eating equally nondescript Refiners in the style of Francisco Goya's Black period, the departments distinguished by the colors of their badges—green and blue, respectively. This painting is meant to demonstrate the dangers of socializing outside one's department and thus breaking the social order Kier demands, playing off an existing rumor among the Refiners about this event's occurrence. Dylan brings up this rumor earlier in the show to discourage Irving from befriending Burt, but since the painting has never been a part of the hallway rotation it is not a formal part of the religious canon. Its sudden appearance affirms Dylan's belief in the massacre and that Kier sorted the departments by virtue, with Macrodata Refinement being "clever and true" and O&D being "cruelty centered."[35] Irving remains unsure since Milchick tells him that it did not happen and the necropolitics of the severed floor have led him to think of death as an impossibility for working alters. The 266 is effective in sowing doubt about Burt's character, yet at the same time, these conflicting messages shake Irving's heretofore devout application of the sacred gaze to every painting on the floor.

He is further disabused of his faith upon Burt's revelation that "The Grim Barbarity of Optics and Design" has a twin painting titled "The Macrodata Refinement Calamity," identical in every way except the colors of the badges, reframing the event with the Refiners as the aggressors and O&D as their victims. Up to this point, the origin of the paintings is deferred. The O&D department receives the paintings in frame and is tasked only with upkeep and placement. This obfuscation of the artistic agent is intentional, allowing the instillation of a visual practice wherein workers focus only on the meaning of the images in the context of the handbook without thinking about their source or the intent of their creator. The events surrounding "Grim Barbarity" and "The Macrodata Refinement Calamity" enable Irving to recognize the art as having a social function and a motive beyond objectively depicting events in Lumon's past. Exposed to ambivalent and contradictory information from paintings that claim to refer directly to the handbook, Irving begins questioning the communicative contract that reading with the sacred gaze infers and the images fail to reliably impart the Cultural Memory he depends upon. He is not yet ready to disavow the handbook's divinity and infallibility, but it introduces insecurity into his understanding of the collective identity he has embraced. This is where Irving's study of visual culture turns away from the maintenance of order and toward its eventual destruction.

"The Courtship of Kier and Imogene"

At several points in the show, Burt challenges Irving's "understanding of communication media as a univocal, unidirectional transmission of information from a sender to a receiver."[36] While Irving having this understanding sounds paradoxical with earlier claims that the sacred gaze makes the viewer an active participant in the production of religious meaning, it is important in cases of ideologically restrictive systems that believers are unaware of their role. The disempowerment of the devout is crucial to upholding these systems of control, so the power they hold must be obscured from them. Burt has been severed for almost seven years[37] compared to Irving's three[38] and has access to more of Lumon's material and visual culture because of his job including an older, first edition of the handbook, a window into the power of the working alters resulting in a different perspective on Kier's expectations.[39] His work is more explicitly a form of immaterial labor than Irving's (though it is unclear exactly what the Refiners are doing, keeping them alienated from the product of their labor), giving him a different role in the fabric of Lumon's society; "the production of ideas, knowledges, and affects... does not merely create means by which society is formed and maintained; such immaterial labor also directly produces social relationships... the production involved here is the production of subjectivity, the creation and reproduction of new subjectivities in society."[40] Beyond simply hanging art in the halls and producing the appropriate sacralized identity, Burt actively develops a relationship with Irving and encourages Irving to evolve his understanding of his place in Lumon society through interactions with its visual culture. The first instance that demonstrates this is before the 266:

Burt: I know the handbook, old man. I'm more of a first edition guy. The original word of Kier: "And I shall whisper to ye dutiful through the ages. In your noblest thoughts and epiphanies shall be my voice. You are my mouth, and through ye, I will whisper on when I am ten centuries demised."

Irving: I don't understand.

Burt: He doesn't just speak to us through the handbook or the paintings. He finds other ways.

Burt is a believer less constrained by his sacred gaze; the additional representations and thus knowledges he has access to, such as the first edition of the handbook and the presumably complete library of "canon" paintings, empower him to take independent action in the name of Kier in a way that Irving cannot.

Burt's agency through access to the paintings emerges amidst discovering the existence of "The Macrodata Refinement Calamity." Burt shows Irving another painting titled "The Courtship of Kier and Imogene," which Irving has never seen, illustrating how Kier met his wife when they worked together at an ether factory. Contemporary printings of the handbook are vague about their relationship, only saying that they were "bonded by the spirit of industry." This alternate interpretation of their love that Burt has access to opens Irving's mind to the idea of acting upon his feelings: "They met as colleagues. Took heart to each other as colleagues. Makes you wonder how something could be wrong if Kier..."[41] Though this line is cut off by Dylan, this scene once again shows the adaptation of Irving's sacred gaze. "Grim Barbarity" gave him the tools to recognize the social construction of the meaning of images, and the contiguous introduction of "The Courtship of Kier and Imogene" is his first foray into changing that meaning. "Images do what their users require of them,"[42] and the change in his needs from fitting into a society to exploring his relationship with Burt transforms how he reads a new piece of art. He still carries the burden of piety to Kier, and the gaze that accompanies that still constructs his relationship with the painting as one that requires Kier-as-God to endorse an idealized capitalist "state" molded by the handbook that might allow him to act on his romantic feelings. That said, he is now able to question the authority of the existing "state" of Lumon administration. So, in "Defiant Jazz," when Burt is forcibly "retired" to punish Irving for his disobedience, Irving realizes that there are ingrained inequities inherent to the structures he lives within. Kier fell in love at work, yet Irving is denied the opportunity. The authority of images he has subscribed to lacks reality at its foundations; the paintings are "systems of representation that defer to yet other signifiers and systems,"[43] like the handbook and the rituals of reward and punishment, which in turn refer back to the paintings for legitimization, and the truth that Lumon's visual culture is only an extension of their control over them manifests. Burt's mediated, reformist gaze that had him believe Kier would want the working alters to be "true partners in his teachings"[44] collapses under the material reality of their oppression.

Irving's final act of looking returns him to the portrait in the Macrodata Refinement office. Instead of sitting beneath it, he stands to meet

Kier's gaze. What before was an image that iconically signified the righteous order of Kier's word is now a representation of the reality that those words make manifest, where Kier serves as a cruel God whose domain (the capitalist workplace) was designed for biopolitical exploitation.[45] It is not that Irving no longer looks with a sacred gaze; he is still contextualizing the painting by way of the civil religion of the severed floor. Rather, the cultural and historical setting of the religion has come into focus, making the painting unintelligible in the familiar language of devotion. If "the power of images … consists of seeing the countenance of the otherwise intangible,"[46] the power of Lumon's images has always been seeing capitalist class exploitation, with the goal of conveying a sense of this social order as just. By holding onto his sacred gaze instead of abandoning or refuting it, Irving is able to watch the mask fall away and leave bare the actual truth it conveys. He opens the handbook stored beneath the portrait and reads out a passage: "endow in each swing of your axe or swipe of your pen the sum of your affections, that through me they may be purified and returned. No higher purpose may be found than this. Nor any higher love." Then, without breaking eye contact, he places a deviled egg in the handbook and slams it shut, punctuated by a final close-up of Kier's face as it looks back, robbed of the control that accompanied its power in the eyes of the devoted. Irving then joins his fellow Refiners in their plan to use Lumon's technology to switch to their working alters outside of work and tell the world what has been done to them. Though it may result in all of their "retirements" and thus deaths, their solidarity produces the threat to Lumon's hegemonic dominance that Helly as a single alienated worker was unable to generate on her own.

Conclusion

The first season of *Severance* evokes well-trod Marxist understandings of combatting alienation from the self, others, and one's labor as part of the path to class consciousness and effective resistance to the oppression of the proletariat. Irving's character arc adds to this a complex consideration of the way workers under capitalism engage with visual culture in their societies. Images have a powerful influence on human sociality, a fact demonstrated across innumerable cultures throughout the Anthropocene. In modern capitalist nations, bourgeois institutions can claim exclusive ownership of images and other creative endeavors under the legal construct of intellectual property, to be mass-produced and disseminated via consumer markets; in such cases, these projects become tools to further the bourgeoisie's material and ideological interests, namely the suppression of class consciousness among the proletariat. However, this does not preclude the possibility of those same images being a vessel for communicating the reality of the social control they carry. As capitalist-made visual culture generates ideology it reveals its capacity to do so, leaving the ideology vulnerable to recognition that can awaken a political consciousness in the viewer.

The show itself also functions as a self-reflexive example of this possibility, as a product made under capitalism that mounts a substantial critique of the system that produced it. The show vividly and unsparingly depicts the horrors of worker alienation under late capitalism and resolutely asserts a clear need for worker organization and collective action in the face of repressive hegemonic power structures. These criticisms could be dismissed as a manifestation of political "interpassivity"[47] associated with capitalist realism that "performs our anti-capitalism for us, allowing us to continue to consume with impunity,"[48] since the season concludes with the working alters successfully contacting the outside world which provides some level of catharsis to viewers despite the associated cliffhanger. Additionally, the knowledge that the show's creators and production company intend to create follow-up seasons may give the audience further hope that their defiance will bring about change. That said, *Severance* includes in the potentially interpassive act a demand to view the show itself critically through the plot I have analyzed in this essay. Irving's nightmares featuring the paint his non-work alter uses to make art unsanctioned by Lumon—and the clay sculpture Mark's work alter makes in Wellness that resembles the one from his wife's car accident—succinctly represent the show's perspective that creative expression is central to human experience and can never be entirely subordinated to corporate control, encouraging the viewer to look beyond and outside of the meanings served to them by ideologically sanctioned sources. This depiction of a budding left-wing revolutionary struggle, hard-fought by its severed workers but not without some sense of optimism, develops over the show's first season, and the importance of visual culture in how the character of Irving expresses this working-class political positionality is uniquely poised to help foster class consciousness among the proletarian subset of its audience.

Notes

1. Richard D. Wolff, "Religion and Class," in *Religion, Theology, and Class: Fresh Engagements After Long Silence*, ed. Joerg Rieger, New Approaches to Religion and Power (Palgrave Macmillan US, 2013), 36.
2. Benedict Anderson, *Imagined Communities: Reflections on the Origin and Spread of Nationalism*, New Edition (Verso, 2006).
3. David Morgan, *The Sacred Gaze: Religious Visual Culture in Theory and Practice*, First Edition (University of California Press, 2005), 220.
4. *Severance*, "The We We Are."
5. Peter L. Berger, *The Sacred Canopy: Elements of a Sociological Theory of Religion*, Reprint (Open Road Media, 2011), 138.
6. Morgan, *The Sacred Gaze*, 3.
7. Ibid.
8. Mark Fisher, *Capitalist Realism: Is There No Alternative?* (Zer0 Books, 2009).
9. *Severance*, "Half Loop."
10. Morgan, *The Sacred Gaze*, 5.
11. *Severance*, "In Perpetuity."
12. Joerg Rieger, *Religion, Theology, and Class: Fresh Engagements after Long Silence*, First Edition, New Approaches to Religion and Power (Palgrave Macmillan US, 2013), 6.
13. *Severance*, "In Perpetuity."
14. Jan Assmann, *Cultural Memory and Early Civilization: Writing, Remembrance, and Political Imagination*, First English Edition (Cambridge University Press, 2011).
15. Ibid., 221.
16. Assmann and Czaplicka, "Collective Memory and Cultural Identity," 126.
17. Morgan, *The Sacred Gaze*, 79.
18. *Severance*, "The You You Are."
19. Ibid.
20. Jan Assmann and John Czaplicka, "Collective Memory and Cultural Identity," *New German Critique*, no. 65 (1995): 130.
21. *Severance*, "In Perpetuity."
22. Hans Mol, *Identity and the Sacred: Sketch for a New Social Scientific Theory of Religion* (Blackwell, 1976), 6.

23. Morgan, *The Sacred Gaze*, 82.
24. *Severance*, "The Grim Barbarity of Optics and Design."
25. Morgan, *The Sacred Gaze*, 233.
26. *Severance*, "In Perpetuity."
27. *Severance*, "Good News About Hell."
28. *Severance*, "The You You Are."
29. Lauren Berlant, "Slow Death (Sovereignty, Obesity, Lateral Agency)," *Critical Inquiry* 33, no. 4 (June 2007): 754.
30. Michael Hardt and Antonio Negri, *Multitude: War and Democracy in the Age of Empire*, First Edition (Penguin Press, 2004), 53.
31. Ibid., 54.
32. *Severance*, "The You You Are."
33. *Severance*, "The Grim Barbarity of Optics and Design."
34. Hardt and Negri, *Multitude*, 72.
35. *Severance*, "In Perpetuity."
36. Morgan, *The Sacred Gaze*, 97.
37. *Severance*, "Defiant Jazz."
38. *Severance*, "Half Loop."
39. *Severance*, "The You You Are."
40. Hardt and Negri, *Multitude*, 66.
41. *Severance*, "The Grim Barbarity of Optics and Design."
42. Morgan, *The Sacred Gaze*, 73.
43. Ibid., 100.
44. *Severance*, "Hide and Seek."
45. Morgan, *The Sacred Gaze*, 259.
46. Ibid., 260.
47. Robert Pfaller, *Interpassivity: The Aesthetics of Delegated Enjoyment*. Incitements (Edinburgh University Press, 2017).
48. Fisher, *Capitalist Realism*, 12.

Bibliography

Anderson, Benedict. 2006. *Imagined Communities: Reflections on the Origin and Spread of Nationalism*. New Edition. Verso.

Assmann, Jan, and John Czaplicka. 1995. "Collective Memory and Cultural Identity." *New German Critique*, no. 65: 125–33. https://doi.org/10.2307/488538.

Assmann, Jan. 2011. *Cultural Memory and Early Civilization: Writing, Remembrance, and Political Imagination*. First English Edition. Cambridge University Press.

Berger, Peter L. 2011. *The Sacred Canopy: Elements of a Sociological Theory of Religion*. Reprint. Open Road Media.

Berlant, Lauren. 2007. "Slow Death (Sovereignty, Obesity, Lateral Agency)." *Critical Inquiry* 33, no. 4 (June): 754–80. https://doi.org/10.1086/521568.

"Defiant Jazz." 2022. *Severance*. Apple TV+, March 25.

Deleuze, Gilles. 1992. "Postscript on the Societies of Control." October 59: 3–7.

Fisher, Mark. 2009. *Capitalist Realism: Is There No Alternative?* Zero Books.

"Good News About Hell." 2022 *Severance*. Apple TV+, February 18.

"Half Loop." 2022. *Severance*. Apple TV+, February 18.

Hardt, Michael, and Antonio Negri. 2004. *Multitude: War and Democracy in the Age of Empire*. First Edition. Penguin Press.

"Hide and Seek." 2022. *Severance*. Apple TV+, March 18.

"In Perpetuity." 2022. *Severance*. Apple TV+, February 25.

Mol, Hans. 1976. *Identity and the Sacred: Sketch for a New Social Scientific Theory of Religion*. Blackwell.

Morgan, David. 2005. *The Sacred Gaze: Religious Visual Culture in Theory and Practice*. First Edition. University of California Press.

Pfaller, Robert. 2017. *Interpassivity: The Aesthetics of Delegated Enjoyment*. Incitements. Edinburgh University Press.

Rieger, Joerg. 2013. *Religion, Theology, and Class: Fresh Engagements After Long Silence*. First Edition. New Approaches to Religion and Power. Palgrave Macmillan US.

"The Grim Barbarity of Optics and Design." 2022. *Severance*. Apple TV+, March 11.

"The We We Are." 2022. *Severance*. Apple TV+, April 8.

"The You You Are." 2022. *Severance*. Apple TV+, March 4.

Wolff, Richard D. 2013. "Religion and Class." In *Religion, Theology, and Class: Fresh Engagements After Long Silence*, edited by Joerg Rieger, 27–42. New Approaches to Religion and Power. Palgrave Macmillan US.

CHAPTER 4

Severed from Reality: The Irrationality of Rationality in Advanced-Stage Capitalism

Nathan Palmer and April M. Schueths

When *Severance* premiered in 2022, many cultural critics described the show as a terrifying dystopia,[1] where work is hell.[2] *Severance*, however, is not a horror story in any conventional sense; there are no jump-scares, monsters, or gore. If watched on mute, the show would appear fantastically mundane and banal. Nevertheless, *Severance* is unnerving because it feels familiar; it depicts the logic of capitalism taken to an extreme that is simultaneously shocking yet recognizable. It is arresting to see the modern office transformed into a forced labor camp where knowledge workers, typically spared the full brutality of capitalism, are dominated by their managers, and forced into being as close to a purely rational actor as possible. And yet, many viewers find the show disconcerting precisely because it is rooted in reality. The audience can relate to the innies grieving their loss of agency, their futile search for meaning within

N. Palmer · A. M. Schueths (✉)
Georgia Southern University, Statesboro, GA, USA
e-mail: aschueths@georgiasouthern.edu

N. Palmer
e-mail: npalmer@georgiasouthern.edu

N. M. Isacoff and J. Dawes (eds.), *Reintegrating Severance*,
https://doi.org/10.1007/978-3-031-57448-1_4

alienation, and their desperate need to make sense of their place within a world that operates outside their view. In many ways, the plight of the innies is, to varying degrees, the plight of all workers in advanced-stage capitalist societies. Like the innies of *Severance*, workers today are often forced to live through the consequences of decisions made by distant nameless bureaucrats.

Analyzed with a nearsighted understanding of history, *Severance* appears to be a rumination on the ills of the post-Covid workplace and the modern struggle to find "work–life balance." Taking the long view, however, *Severance* depicts the logical extremes (or perhaps the most recent conclusion) of social phenomena that began with the Industrial Revolution and the rise of capitalism. To a student of history and the social sciences, the Severance Procedure is merely another example of capitalism further metastasizing. Industrial capitalism began by severing the economy from the rest of society and the worker from that which they produce, both of which Marx believed made society unsustainable; ever since, capitalists have been severing everywhere they can to postpone the inevitable consequences of attempting to live unsustainably.

This chapter provides context to *Severance's* critique of capitalism by reviewing the works of social theorists, Karl Marx and Max Weber. In addition to expounding on the contradictions inherent to capitalism, we will point readers to avenues for liberation and change. Before you can address a social problem, you must first understand it. The sociologist C. Wright Mills argues that for an individual to understand both their personal experiences and the events unfolding in society, that individual must be able "to grasp the interplay of [human] and society, of biography and history, of self and world."[3] This intellectual reflexivity between the self, society, and history is what Mills called the sociological imagination. The innies find their lives to be inscrutable because the Severance Procedure prevents them from placing their lived experiences within the larger societal and historical context beyond Lumon's doors. Outside of the show, in reality, workers everywhere can develop their sociological imaginations to understand their lives better, their capitalist societies, and their moments in history. And in doing so, they can devise strategies of action to address the harms created by capitalism.

The Severance Procedure

For readers who may need a review or those new to the television series, severance is a fictitious procedure that allows workers at Lumon Industries to bifurcate their consciousness so that the person who works at Lumon, called an "innie" in the show, has no knowledge of the outside world or the person they are when not at work. The outside-of-work person is referred to as an "outie." Innies only come into existence through the severance procedure. Their entire universe begins and ends within the confines of Lumon. The innies perceive their problems as isolated from more compelling social issues even though the macro system, including Lumon, a part of corporate America, has ties to government and politics, and profoundly impacts the direction of their lives. Severance is the ultimate solution to creating a so-called work–life balance.

Mark, the main protagonist in *Severance*, was recently promoted to Lumon Industries Macrodata Refinement Chief after his supervisor and close work friend, Petey, mysteriously left Lumon without explanation. Mark now leads the MDR team of Dylan, Irving, and, most recently, Helly. Electing to undergo the Severance Procedure for Mark was an attempt to avoid the pain of losing his spouse, Gemma, who was allegedly killed in a car accident, or at least divide his pain in half as he only experiences this loss as an outie. During a conversation between outie Mark and his sister, Devon, she pokes a hole in his attempt to escape his suffering. Devon tells him, "I feel like forgetting about [Gemma] for eight hours a day isn't the same thing as healing."[4] The paradox is that Mark would likely never have agreed to the severance procedure if he believed Gemma was alive.

By undergoing severance, Mark lives a lonely life of pain, devoid of meaning, arguably worse than if he had faced the cards he was given. Initially, he cannot break free from Lumon's exploitation, which maintains and exacerbates his agony. For example, Mark fails to recognize his wife, Gemma, who is actually alive, and that she is, in fact, Ms. Casey, his colleague as his innie sees her. Mark cannot see the complete picture of his life; he is oblivious that Mrs. Selvig, his outie neighbor and eventual lactation consultant for his sister, is really his superior, Ms. Cobel, and is conspiring with Lumon. Outside of Lumon, Mark cannot recognize his work friend, and previous supervisor, Petey. He only sees him as "a businessman," even though Petey has been unsevered and has details about the corruption of their company that can save Mark's life all at the expense of Petey's life.

Helena Eagan, on the other hand, daughter of Jame Eagan, CEO of Lumon, agreed to the Severance Procedure to help Lumon's public image, to normalize the procedure as ethical, and to reassure the public by showcasing that even an Eagan is willing to be severed. Helena Eagan and others at Lumon did not anticipate that Helly, her innie, a Macrodata Refiner, would be so insubordinate, combative, and dead set on escaping. Helly says, "I quit. I don't wanna do the file-sorting thing or the never-seeing-the-sun-thing or the disappearing-friends thing. I just don't want any of it."[5] After being tortured by Milchick, a supervisor, Helly watches a video of Helena that Lumon prompts her to make. In the video, Helena says to her innie, Helly, "I am a person. You are not."[6] Helena's statements confirm that Lumon does not see innie workers as people but as commodities. Perhaps because of this dehumanization, Helly attempts suicide by hanging herself with an extension cord but is rescued by Mark, her supervisor, and Graner, a Lumon security officer.

Unlike Helly's and Mark's stories, the background of other Lumon MDR workers Dylan and Irving are not presented to the viewers nor is the reason they decided to undergo the Severance Procedure. Perhaps it was Dylan's confidence about the goodness of the world or Irving's former military connections, however, the reasons are never fully revealed. Ultimately, capitalism is challenged by what matters most in their lives: social connections. When Dylan learns that he has a son during an Overtime Contingency Protocol, his mood shifts to anger and he eventually responds violently toward Milchick. Dylan states, "I wanna remember my fucking kid being born."[7] Similarly, when Burt from the Optics and Design Department retires from Lumon, Irving's heart is broken as he realizes he may never see Burt, the man he loves, again. Eventually, Irving, who had formerly been a loyal company man, joins the other MDR workers and says, "Let's burn this place to the ground."[8]

As the series progresses, we see the Lumon workers begin to break free, reintegrate themselves, and disrupt Lumon Industries. To better understand the eventual upheaval at Lumon, let us start at the beginning of the original severance, where the economy was severed from the rest of society, as we apply classical theory to the show.

The Original "Severance"

The work of Karl Marx, a prominent philosopher, economist, and critic of capitalism, provides greater insight into *Severance*. According to Marx, capitalism, specifically industrial capitalism, was the impetus for the original severance, which disconnected the economy from the larger society, spread worldwide, and people experienced misery at all levels except for the direct benefactors.[9] With the rise of industrialization, the economy shifted from an economy based on agriculture and physical labor to an economy predicated on production and manufacturing. Capitalism emerged as a profit-focused economic system based on the private ownership of production that operates in a laissez-faire competitive market system in which the owners of capital employed free-wage labor. Capitalism seeks to maximize exchange value (i.e., the monetary value something can command in an economic market), often at the expense of use value (i.e., the utility something has to humans).

Industrial capitalism is a type of capitalism used to represent a cadre of co-occurring social phenomena, the first half of the term denotes the shift from an economy based on working the land to one based on mechanized production in factories. According to most historians, the industrial revolution began in England toward the end of the eighteenth century, before rapidly spreading through Europe, and the Americas, eventually becoming the dominant system of production globally.[10] Industrialization created dramatic increases in productivity, producing unprecedented material and economic surpluses.

The emergence of industrial capitalism in Europe upended centuries of social order based on tradition, duty, and mutuality. Prior to the appearance of industrial capitalism, feudalism was the socio-economic system of most European countries. Feudalism was a hierarchical system in which serfs, who were bound to the land, provided labor and tribute to lords in exchange for protection and the right to cultivate the land. This was a deeply unfair system, where power and resources were concentrated in the hands of a ruling elite. However, lords were paternalistically bound to their serfs, serfs were bound to the land, and the prosperity of the community was to the benefit of all involved parties. Landlords could not seek workers from other communities and serfs could not seek employment in other labor markets. Under feudalism, the laborer and the employer were bound together. In pre-industrial societies labor was often bounded by slavery, serfdom, or bonded service (the fact that forced labor continues to this day[11] demonstrates that capitalism did not bring an end to bounded labor).

Marx criticized capitalism as an exploitative and dehumanizing system that created class conflict between the Bourgeoisie, the owners of the means of production, and the Proletariats, the wage workers. He understood industrial capitalism, as a dialectal form of social change; where the tension between opposites (i.e., contradictions) can be leveraged to create change, but ultimately these contradictions cannot last and thus this form of change must either adapt or give way to another form of change. Marx believed that capitalism had many inherent contradictions and that, eventually, despite the Bourgeoisie's best efforts to perpetually adapt the economic system, industrial capitalism would fall to the Proletariat's communist revolution.

One of the key societal shifts Marx believed facilitated the emergence of industrial capitalism was the Enclosure Movement in Europe, which describes the efforts to convert lands that had been held in common ownership for centuries into privately owned tracts.[12] This movement began the process of severance by separating the land from the people. The separating of the economy from the rest of society was the initial severance brought about by industrial capitalism. In contrast to feudalism, industrial capitalism shredded the social ties and obligations between lord and serf and replaced the feudal social contract with the profit motive. The emergence of industrial capitalism in Europe upended centuries of social order based on tradition, duty, and mutuality and eventually replaced it with a social order based on rationality, wage labor, and privatization.

The term free market is used in conjunction with capitalism, as freedom, or free doom as Marx would argue, was the promise of capitalism. The "free" in free markets and free labor denotes freedom from all social obligations beyond profit maximization. When proponents of capitalism use the word free, they almost always mean something is unbounded, disentangled, or severed. Marx believed that the so-called freedom brought about by capitalism was a thin rhetorical veneer used by capitalists to conceal the advantage they stood to gain from profoundly reshaping the social order and severing the economy from the rest of society. Free labor means workers can choose their place of employment, and employers are free from the burden of caring for and protecting their workers. Markets are said to be free when individual buyers and sellers transact voluntarily, free from the concerns of the rest of society (i.e., free from government regulation). Industrial capitalism "freed" individual self-interest from the concerns of the whole of society.

Instead of being free, Marx argued that the Proletariats were alienated and exploited, treated like machines, and blocked from fulfilling and humanizing labor by the capitalist system. "They sell not only their labor power, but also their souls. They have no control over the product they are producing while their work is devoid of any redeeming human qualities."[13] Additionally, Marx argued that workers end up internalizing capitalism through the internalization of the market. The Severance Procedure, then, is a radical form of the internalization of capitalism. Marx might say that with the enslavement of capitalism, workers can now enslave parts of their fractured selves. The worker can now externalize their work to their innie self as the Lumon workers can. Marx would have likely argued that the dehumanizing aspects of capitalism focused on profits also harm worker's personal lives creating a disparity between work and home that should not be tolerated.

The Myth of the Work–Life Severance

At the heart of the modern discussion over work–life balance is the idea that work and life are separate and antagonistic. This perceived divide is a relatively modern invention. In the pre-industrial United States, for instance, when the economy was predominantly agrarian, the primary economic unit was a household, and the primary workplace was the family farm.[14] Work and life commingled on the family farm and every member of the family worked together.[15] On the family farm, there was a level of equality between men and women as coworkers (even if patriarchy dominated the relationship, on the family farm, women were treated as capable workers and the "domestic labor," as we call it today, that they contributed was recognized and compensated in so much as the returns from the farm were shared with the entirety of the household).

The shift to industrial production shocked the sensibilities of many at the time.[16] They were horrified by the brutish conditions of factories and the rampant squalor of the cities that grew up around them. Either out of a sense of chivalry or as a move to hoard resources, men at the time promoted the idea that only they could withstand the brunt of capitalism, concluding work is no place for women. Of course, women have always contributed to the economy both inside and outside the home (this is especially true for poor women and women of color). However, the idea that women needed to be spared from the horrors of paid labor was built on the idea that the home needed to be a refuge from the factory. If the ideal capitalist workplace was ruthlessly concerned with efficiency and did not care at all about the well-being of their workers, then the idealized home needed to be the space where one was loved and nurtured regardless of their output. Unlike the work done by men outside of the home, domestic labor went financially uncompensated and was said to be a "labor of love." The first iteration of the work–life divide was the bifurcation of domestic and paid labor.

> If the workplace was ruthless and competitive, the home would be kind and cooperative. If the workplace rewarded individualism and self-promotion, the home would be a place for togetherness and selflessness. If work was about profit, home was about care. And if women did anything resembling work in the home ... it was no longer work, it was a labor of love.[17]

Yet, the idea that work and life can be separated ignores their interconnections in both directions. There would be no workers showing up to the factories without the "domestic labor" required to keep them fed, clothed, and recuperated. It is also a myth that people can separate their personal lives from who they are at work, as well as a fallacy that workplaces want workers without personal lives (the work they do at Lumon requires that humanity). Life doesn't impede work at Lumon, it facilitates it.

Severance in the Modern Workplace

Adding to our analysis and extending the work of Marx, we turn to Max Weber,[18] a German sociologist and prominent classical theorist. Although Weber criticized capitalism, he rejected Marx's idea of a communist revolution and viewed capitalism as merely a flawed system with an undetermined end.[19] Weber helps us understand work in terms of bureaucracy, culture, religion, and rationality tied to capitalism and which creates disconnection in the modern workplace.

Severance in the contemporary workforce can be traced back to Weber's idea of rationality that developed in tandem with capitalism and the increase of bureaucracies, or impersonal stratified structures, where labor is specialized and protocols are formal. Rationality focuses on efficiency, calculability, predictability, and control; Weber saw rationality as leading to bureaucracy, where modern society is a powerless "iron cage" devoid of meaning and freedom.[20] Weber argued, "Rational calculation... reduces every worker to a cog in this bureaucratic machine and, seeing himself in this light, he will merely ask how to transform himself... to a bigger cog... The passion for bureaucratization at this meeting drives us to despair."[21] Like Marx, Weber sees dehumanization within the alleged rationality of capitalism.

The opposite side of the rationality coin is irrationality; it illustrates how at the micro-level, some choices and behaviors from the top may appear ridiculous yet also aid the larger macro-bureaucratic systems. George Ritzer pulled together Weber's work and coined the term, the irrationality of rationality, highlighting the strain between these two dialectics.[22] For example, in *Severance*, the Lumon divisions, including Macrodata Refinement, Optics and Design, Disposal, Reclamation, and other unknown divisions, are not permitted to fraternize. Some believe that other division members are dangerous (e.g., Dylan threatens Burt with a stapler when he comes to MDR as he feels threatened but realizes he is not in danger)[23] Workers like Irving and Burt, who are instantly connected, risk being punished for exploring other departments; this and other minor rule violations can result in being sent to the break room. The isolation of Lumon divisions is irrational to workers, including Irving and Burt, yet Lumon Industries purposefully creates division as a rational tactic to keep their operations moving forward. Ultimately, the contact between Lumon divisions becomes a genuine threat to their covert operations.[24]

Weber's concept of the Protestant work ethic can also help us understand another alarming aspect of Lumon, their ode to the secular religious fervor of capitalist workplaces. The Protestant work ethic is "a religiously based, severe, ascetic approach to life that stresses unremitting hard work, refraining from sensual enjoyment, and success in the eyes of God."[25] Although not as dominant in modern-day workplaces, cultural remnants of the Protestant ethic remain; we see the vestiges in *Severance*. For instance, Lumon's policy manual reads like a religious text studied diligently by Irving. Kier Eagan, the creator of Lumon Industries, allegedly uncovered the four tempers found in the human soul which are meant to be balanced: woe, frolic, dread, and malice.[26] Mastering the four tempers seems to be the key to becoming a successful worker, therefore, they have monitoring systems to ensure the balance. "When Lumon managers sense that their team members are struggling with the unnatural state of permanent work, they send them for 'wellness check' with an in-house counselor, much as Amazon reportedly sends its exhausted warehouse workers to 'AmaZen' stations for guided meditations and other well-being activities."[27] Lumon Industries is "a kind of nineteenth-century L. Ron Hubbard–whose koans the employees are trained to accept as gospel."[28]

The Protestant Ethic also discussed Weber's understanding of callings, which is a secular vocational drive to achievement, loosely tied to its religious origins. Many middle-class workers, especially in the United States, have sought purpose through their vocations. Ms. Cobel appears to see her work at Lumon as a calling, even being fired for "going above and beyond" for intruding in the life of Mark, her outie staff member.[29] Cobel says, "I'll take care of Helly. I'll fix it like I fix everything." Even after being terminated from Lumon, Ms. Cobel tries to stop Helly from telling the truth at the Lumon Gala.[30]

Similarly, managers often push the idea that their team of employees operates like a family. Therefore, workers are encouraged to treat their coworkers like family, to put their heart and soul into their job, to sacrifice or "take one for the team," to do uncompensated/unrecognized work for the greater good. However, when workers seek to be treated like family members, they are almost always denied because work will not love you back. Although Kier Eagan met his wife Imogene at work and can be seen in the painting, "The Courtship of Kier and Imogene," Lumon workers, in particular, Irving and Burt, and others will be punished for crossing this line.[31]

Beyond Weber, modern workers sever themselves for their jobs in various ways. Some workers use dissociation, a mental coping mechanism to address feelings of alienation from alienating work or labor. Workers may space off during their workday by mentally leaving the present moment, from time or "the clock," separating themselves from the drudgery of work. Even workers who purport to enjoy their work have the ability to get lost in their tasks, losing a sense of time.

Emotion management, as sociologist Arlie Hochschild[32] calls emotional labor, is another disconnection tactic and requires workers to conform to "feeling rules" whereby they shift their facial expressions and body language to demonstrate the expected feelings while suppressing their true emotions. For example, in the opening scene, Mark demonstrates emotion management by remaining calm and following his work script when Helly wakes up as an innie and curses at Mark and tries repeatedly to escape Lumon.[33]

Professionalism is another way that workers sever themselves in the workplace and is what sociologist Erving Goffman would call impression management, a technique centered on the idea of providing a performance, where behaviors are used to manage how others perceive them; this takes place on what he called "the front stage."[34] Goffman explains that the backstage is where individuals can let their hair down and be their authentic selves. We see Mark backstage at work when he finds, shares, and dares to read *The You You Are*, a book written by Dr. Ricken Lazlo Hale, who is actually his brother-in-law, unrecognizable to Mark's innie self.[35]

Workplace severance strategies help workers tolerate the daily grind. Yet, workers must continually negotiate the internal push and pull between their agency, that is their own sense of influence and control, and the need for their paycheck. Innie workers at Lumon, however, likely do not know their salary and cannot calculate whether their severance is worth the sacrifice, even financially.

The Promise of Sociology and the Innies Need for a Sociological Imagination

Humans are inherently social beings; their understanding of the self and the world, such as larger social structures, including family, religion, government, and economic systems, mutually shape one another. Social connections are a basic psychological need for human survival,[36] which illustrates that the individual cannot be separated from the social because it is a reciprocal process. The absence of social networks leads to more superficial and less fulfilling relationships for both the innies and the outies. The Severance Procedure, however, removes the connective tissue joining the self and society, a bridge that is required for being fully human. The workers at Lumon must abandon part of their humanity to compete in the marketplace. In other words, the severance process attempts to degrade workers.

Ironically, we see a contradiction as Lumon needs aspects of workers' humanity (e.g., motivation, emotion, perception) to complete work in the Macrodata Refinement (MDR) division. For example, as Mark trains Helly he explains, "Each category of numbers presents in such an order as to elicit an emotional response in the refiner." He goes on to say, "They'll be sort of disconcerting, scary."[37] Later, it's discussed that the numbers can also be "comforting."[38] The MDR teams must have access to their emotions to do their work, this is an essential part of being human.

How can the MDR workers find change and even liberation from the contradictions of severance? The answer is the sociological imagination. In recent years, scholars have pushed toward making sociology more public and seek to share the sociological imagination as an analytic tool beyond the discipline and academy into the lives of everyday people to aid collective well-being and empowerment.[39] C. Wright Mills coined the term and defined the Sociological Imagination, and it is a seminal concept in the discipline of sociology which helps people critically understand the "quality of mind essential to grasp the interplay of [humans] and society, of biography and history, of self and world."[40] In other words, the sociological imagination provides a framework for connecting the micro and macro by allowing one to see their individual problems as not separate from others but within the context of larger social problems and issues. The sociological imagination is "a method that can be applied to better provide a critical lens to dismantle the hegemonic nature of social structures and decolonize what is considered common knowledge."[41] Even without the Severance Procedure, the sociological imagination can be a complex perspective to grasp, given the dominant values of "American individualism" in the United States, where individuals are seen as having more control over their life chances than the impact of social forces.[42]

Socialization in the United States tends to assess life through an individual lens. Using only an individual lens tends to "blame, dehumanize, and other the victim, thereby inhibiting the understanding and application" of the sociological imagination.[43] Moving beyond the individual-level analysis may lead to an increase in empathy, which is "the ability to know, understand, and perceive what other people feel, think, or experience."[44] Increased empathy allows stereotypes to be challenged and has been found to decrease victim-blaming and may increase the sociological imagination.

Embracing a sociological imagination better equips people to deal with modern problems. Critical thinking skills are often viewed as one of the main benefits of the sociological imagination. For example, Grauerholz and Bouma-Holtrop argue that sociological critical thinking differs from standard critical thinking and must include "sociological knowledge and awareness."[45] Sociological critical thinking begins with the sociological imagination and is "the ability to evaluate, reason, an idea and information while demonstrating awareness of broader social and cultural contexts."[46]

Reunification of personal troubles and public issues is required for liberation. People can only demand change if they are in touch with their sociological imagination; severance prevents this. The severed Lumon employees need their sociological imagination, and it is only when they access it can they understand Lumon's manipulation and move toward "illumination above all,"[47] the very motto Lumon professes to follow.

Notes

1. Sophie Gilbert. "When Work Is a Terrifying Dystopia." *The Atlantic*. (2022). https://www.theatlantic.com/culture/archive/2022/02/severance-makes-workplace-eerily-dystopian/622883/.
2. Alan Sepinwall. "Work Is Hell in *Severance*." *Rolling Stone*. (2022). https://www.rollingstone.com/tv-movies/tv-movie-reviews/severance-review-1294293/.
3. C. Wright Mills. *The Sociological Imagination*. Oxford University Press, 1959: 3.
4. *Severance*, "Good News About Hell."
5. *Severance*, "Half-Loop."
6. *Severance*, "The You You Are."
7. *Severance*, "The We We Are."
8. *Severance*, "Defiant Jazz."
9. Karl Marx and Friedrich Engels. *The Communist Manifesto: Selected Works by Karl Marx and Friedrich Engels*. New York: International Publishers, 1848.
10. Stephen Edgell. *Sociology of Work*. Thousand Oaks, CA: Sage, 2006.
11. U.S. Department of Homeland Security. "What Is Forced Labor?" (2022). https://www.dhs.gov/blue-campaign/forced-labor.
12. John Bellamy Foster, Brett Clark, and Hannah Holleman. "Marx and the Commons." *Social Research: An International Quarterly* 88, no. 1 (2021): 1–30.
13. Laura Desfor Edles and Scott Appelrouth. *Sociological Theory in the Classical Era: Text and Readings*. London: Sage, 2005: 23.
14. James A. Henretta. "Families and Farms: Mentalite in Pre-industrial America." *The William and Mary Quarterly: A Magazine of Early American History* 35, no. 1 (1978): 3–32.

15. Lisa Wade. *American Hookup: The New Culture of Sex on Campus*. New York: W. W. Norton, 2017.
16. David Rosner and Gerald Markowitz. "A Short History of Occupational Safety and Health in the United States." *American Journal of Public Health* 110, no. 5 (2020): 622–628.
17. Lisa Wade. *American Hookup: The New Culture of Sex on Campus*. New York: W. W. Norton, 2017: 57.
18. Max Weber. *The Protestant Ethic and the Spirit of Capitalism*. Translated by Talcott Parsons. New York: Charles Scribner's Sons, 1904–1905/1958.
19. Laura Desfor Edles and Scott Appelrouth. *Sociological Theory in the Classical Era: Text and Readings*. London: Sage, 2005.
20. Ibid.
21. Max Weber. *The Protestant Ethic and the Spirit of Capitalism*. Translated by Talcott Parsons. New York: Charles Scribner's Sons, 1904–1905/1958.
22. George Ritzer. *The McDonaldization of Society*. Thousand Oaks, CA: Pine Forge Press, 1993.
23. *Severance*, "The You You Are."
24. *Severance*, "Hide and Seek."
25. Charles E. Hurst. *Living Theory: The Application of Classical Social Theory to Contemporary Life*. New York: Routledge, 2005: 157.
26. *Severance*, "In Perpetuity."
27. Sophie Gilbert. "When Work Is a Terrifying Dystopia." *The Atlantic*. (2022). https://www.theatlantic.com/culture/archive/2022/02/severance-makes-workplace-eerily-dystopian/622883/.
28. Naomi Fry. "*Severance* Is Sci-Fi for the Soul." *The New Yorker*. (2022). https://www.newyorker.com/magazine/2022/04/25/severance-is-sci-fi-for-the-soul.
29. *Severance*, "What's for Dinner?"
30. *Severance*, "The We We Are."
31. *Severance*, "The Grim Barbarity of Optics and Design."
32. Arlie Russell Hochschild. "Emotion Work, Feeling Rules, and Social Structure." *American Journal of Sociology* 85, no. 3 (1979): 551–575.
33. *Severance*, "Good News About Hell."
34. Erving Goffman. *The Presentation of Self in Everyday Living*. New York: Doubleday and Company, 1959.
35. *Severance*, "The Grim Barbarity of Optics and Design."

36. Debra Umberson and Jennifer Karas Montez. "Social Relationships and Health: A Flashpoint for Health Policy." *Journal of Health and Social Behavior* 51, no. 1 (2010): S54–S66.
37. *Severance*, "Half-Loop."
38. *Severance*, "In Perpetuity."
39. Michael Burawoy. "Open Letter to C. Wright Mills. Practicing Public Scholarship: Experiences and Possibilities Beyond the Academy." *Antipode* 40, no. 3 (2008): 18–28; Michael Burawoy. "For Public Sociology." *American Sociological Review* 70, no. 1 (2005): 4–28.
40. C. Wright Mills. *The Sociological Imagination*. Oxford University Press, 1959: 4.
41. Jacob Kelley, Andrea Arce-Trigatti, and Ada Haynes. "Beyond the Individual: Deploying the Sociological Imagination as a Research Method in the Neoliberal University." In *The Handbook of Critical Theoretical Research Methods in Education*, edited by Cheryl E. Matias, 284–302. New York: Routledge, 2021: 299.
42. Lawrence M. Eppard, Mark Robert Rank, and Heather E. Bullock with Noam Chomsky, Henry A. Giroux, David Brady, and Dan Schubert. *Rugged Individualism and the Misunderstanding of American Inequality*. Bethlehem, PA: Lehigh University Press, 2020: 1.
43. Marcia Ghidina. "Deconstructing Victim-Blaming, Dehumanization, and Othering: Using Empathy to Develop a Sociological Imagination." *Teaching Sociology* 47, no. 3 (2019): 231.
44. Ibid., 234.
45. Liz Grauerholz and Sharon Bouma-Holtrop. "Exploring Critical Sociological Thinking." *Teaching Sociology* 31, no. 4 (2003): 493.
46. Ibid.
47. *Severance*, "Hide and Seek."

Bibliography

Burawoy, Michael. "Open Letter to C. Wright Mills. Practicing Public Scholarship: Experiences and Possibilities Beyond the Academy." *Antipode* 40, no. 3(2008): 18–28.

———. "For Public Sociology." *American Sociological Review* 70, no. 1 (2005): 4–28.

Edgell, Stephen. *Sociology of Work*. Thousand Oaks, CA: Sage, 2006.

Edles, Laura Desfor, and Scott Appelrouth. *Sociological Theory in the Classical Era: Text and Readings*. London: Sage, 2005.

Eppard, Lawrence M., Mark Robert Rank, and Heather E. Bullock with Noam Chomsky, Henry A. Giroux, David Brady, and Dan Schubert. *Rugged Individualism and the Misunderstanding of American Inequality*. Bethlehem, PA: Lehigh University Press, 2020.

Foster, John Bellamy, Brett Clark, and Hannah Holleman. "Marx and the Commons." *Social Research: An International Quarterly* 88, no. 1 (2021): 1–30.

Fry, Naomi. "*Severance* Is Sci-Fi for the Soul." *The New Yorker*. (2022). https://www.newyorker.com/magazine/2022/04/25/severance-is-sci-fi-for-the-soul.

Ghidina, Marcia. "Deconstructing Victim-Blaming, Dehumanization, and Othering: Using Empathy to Develop a Sociological Imagination." *Teaching Sociology* 47, no. 3 (2019): 231–242.

Gilbert Sophie. "When Work Is a Terrifying Dystopia." *The Atlantic*. (2022). https://www.theatlantic.com/culture/archive/2022/02/severance-makes-workplace-eerily-dystopian/622883/.

Goffman, Erving. *The Presentation of Self in Everyday Living*. New York: Doubleday and Company, 1959.

Grauerholz, Liz, and Sharon Bouma-Holtrop. "Exploring Critical Sociological Thinking." *Teaching Sociology* 31, no. 4 (2003): 485–496.

Henretta, James A. "Families and Farms: Mentalite in Pre-Industrial America." *The William and Mary Quarterly: A Magazine of Early American History* 35, no. 1 (1978): 3–32.

Hochschild, Arlie Russell. "Emotion Work, Feeling Rules, and Social Structure." *American Journal of Sociology* 85, no. 3 (1979): 551–575.

Hurst, Charles E. *Living Theory: The Application of Classical Social Theory to Contemporary Life*. New York: Routledge, 2005.

Kelley, Jacob, Andrea Arce-Trigatti, and Ada Haynes. "Beyond the Individual: Deploying the Sociological Imagination as a Research Method in the Neoliberal University." In *The Handbook of Critical Theoretical Research Methods in Education*, edited by Cheryl E. Matias, 284–302. New York: Routledge, 2021.

Marx, Karl, and Friedrich Engels. *The Communist Manifesto: Selected Works by Karl Marx and Friedrich Engels*. New York: International Publishers, 1848.

Mills, C. Wright. *The Sociological Imagination*. Oxford University Press, 1959.

Ritzer, George. *The McDonaldization of Society*. Thousand Oaks, CA: Pine Forge Press, 1993.

Rosner, David, and Gerald Markowitz. "A Short History of Occupational Safety and Health in the United States." *American Journal of Public Health* 110, no. 5 (2020): 622–628.

Sepinwall, Alan. "Work Is Hell in *Severance*." *Rolling Stone*. (2022). https://www.rollingstone.com/tv-movies/tv-movie-reviews/severance-review-1294293/.

Umberson, Debra, and Jennifer Karas Montez. "Social Relationships and Health: A Flashpoint for Health Policy." *Journal of Health and Social Behavior* 51, no. 1 (2010): S54–S66.

U.S. Department of Homeland Security. "What Is Forced Labor?" (2022). https://www.dhs.gov/blue-campaign/forced-labor.

Wade, Lisa. *American Hookup: The New Culture of Sex on Campus*. New York: W. W. Norton, 2017.

Weber, Max. *The Protestant Ethic and the Spirit of Capitalism*. Translated by Talcott Parsons. New York: Charles Scribner's Sons, 1904–1905/1958.

PART II

Art & Architecture

CHAPTER 5

Art as an Apparatus of the Invisible Sublime in *Severance*

Bengisu Bayrak Shahmiri

In *Severance*, the Apple TV+ series, art and design are integral to the creation of the uncanny feeling of the spaces the characters inhabit. The eerie atmosphere of the show is achieved through a variety of art and design styles extending from twentieth-century Modern to nineteenth-century Romantic to 1980s Postmodern. With its cold color scheme, large empty spaces, references to minimalist and abstract painters such as Joseph Albers and Kazimir Malevich, as well as the uncanny landscapes of Edward Hopper, the show refers to modernist aesthetics to underline the solitary nature of the individual. It also appropriates and transforms the Romantic style of the nineteenth-century painters such as Caspar David Friedrich and Francisco Goya to achieve a sense of alienation from time and space, and of the sublime. With this stylistic palimpsest, the series creates a narrative that culminates in a sense of what we can call the invisible sublime.

B. Bayrak Shahmiri (✉)
Beykoz University, Istanbul, Turkey
e-mail: bengisubayrak@beykoz.edu.tr

Istanbul, Turkey

N. M. Isacoff and J. Dawes (eds.), *Reintegrating Severance*,
https://doi.org/10.1007/978-3-031-57448-1_5

Abstract Minimalist Aesthetics, and the Sublime of the "Black Square"

In the opening scene of the first episode ("Good News About Hell") we see Helly lying on an office table in the middle of a conference room. A male voice (that of Mark S.) comes from the speaker on the table: "Who are you?" … "I wonder if you'd mind taking a brief survey." Helly is awakened by the voice, quite disoriented and anxious, tries to open the door, and shouts "Open the door! Let me out!" As she wakes up, we see the walls of the room, divided into gray square units made of some sort of fabric, floor to ceiling, similar to those isolation rooms in mental hospitals. As she accepts the fact that she cannot get out of the room, she decides to take Mark's questionnaire. However, she cannot answer the questions and notices that she does not have any memory. She does not recall anything, even her own name. As Helly finds out more about Lumon, the viewers also get more information. Later on, she watches herself on a previously recorded video, stating that she gave consent for her "perceptual chronologies to be surgically split," separating her memories between her work life and her personal life.

In the next sequence, the viewer is introduced to the surroundings and inside of Lumon Industries, respectively. The company is in a very horizontal and relatively shallow building located in a beautiful landscape. The photography of the scenery is reminiscent of Andreas Gursky's large-scale photographs, which are often commentaries on consumerism and global capitalism. His subjects are often human-made landscapes, such as supermarkets, stock exchanges, luxury hotels, and warehouses. For example, his work titled "Amazon" (2016) demonstrates an almost infinite number of goods in the storeroom of Amazon. The overwhelming scenery portrays the power of capitalism. Gursky's works might inspire fascination, but the after-effect of such works is discomfort. What Gursky gets at are the relentless, cruel forces of global capitalism, people are lost in a world of excesses of mass production and waste. The sublimity achieved through the repetition of the visual elements in Gursky's art can be associated with Kant's mathematical sublime.[1] Similar to Gursky's art, the car park scene in this sequence underlines the vastness of the space, creating a sense of technological sublime which is an early twentieth-century replacement of Kant's nature-appreciating sublime.

In his *Analytic of Sublime*, Kant defines sublime as "absolutely great," something that is "beyond all comparison great,"[2] "the mere capacity of thinking which evidences a faculty of mind transcending every standard of the senses."[3] Kant first differentiates the beautiful and the sublime with regard to our judgment of taste:

> The beautiful in nature is a question of the form of the object, and this consists in limitation, whereas the sublime is to be found in an object even devoid of form, so far as it immediately involves, or else by its presence provokes, a representation of *limitlessness*, yet with a super-added thought of its totality. Accordingly the beautiful seems to be regarded as a presentation of an indeterminate concept of the understanding, the sublime as a presentation of an indeterminate concept of reason. Hence the delight is in the former case coupled with the representation of *quality*, but in this case with that of *quantity*.[4]

Here, two significant points with regard to the difference between the beautiful and sublime come forward: their relationship with forms and the way they bring pleasure out. Unlike the beautiful, the sublime is not concerned with the form of an object, it is either related to formless things or things with forms beyond our ability to contemplate due to their sizes or infinity. "... true sublimity must be sought only in the mind of the judging subject."[5]

The distinction between the two is elaborated further when defining the sublime. Kant's natural sublime is defined in two categories: the "mathematical sublime" and the "dynamic sublime." The mathematical sublime relates to "magnitude" such as experiencing the immense view from the top of a high mountain or contemplating the number of stars in the infinitely great universe. The dynamic sublime is related to "might," an overpowering force such as a storm at the ocean or a volcanic eruption. In both cases, as nature gets bigger and irresistibly stronger, the observer feels overwhelmed and insignificant. That it is awe-inspiring and overpowering are the main characteristics of the sublime which appear in various ways in *Severance* throughout the episodes.

As Mark walks into the Lumon building, we are introduced to the indoor design of the premises: The very large main lobby of Lumon Industries is shown from a high angle so we see the size of the space and the gigantic carpet giving a direct reference to the "Homage to Square" series of Joseph Albers (Fig. 5.1).

Associated with the Bauhaus and minimalist art, Albers explored geometric forms and color interactions. His geometric abstractions

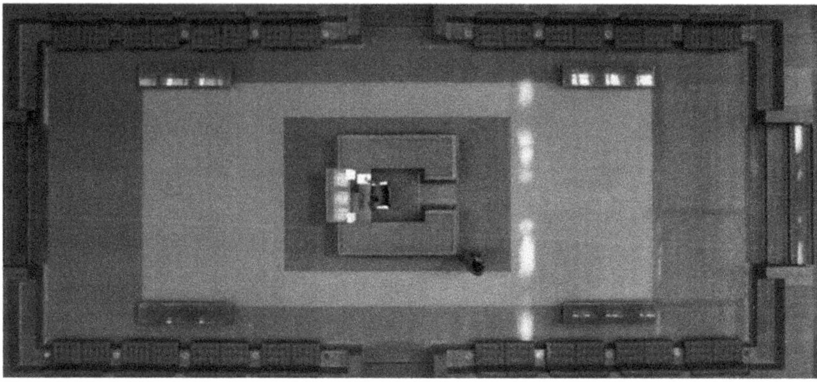

Fig. 5.1 Lumon lobby from overhead

and studies in color investigated the relationship between design and psychology. The obvious resemblance between this scene and Albers is achieved through the nested rectangles, the color scheme, and the symmetrical composition. In the opening scene of the series, we see a similar carpet underneath the office table where Helly was sleeping. The symmetrical and geometrically arranged compositions of these scenes are another linking element of the connection between *Severance* and minimalist art. Emerging in the mid-twentieth century, particularly in the United States, minimalist art is characterized by the elimination of representational and figurative elements and the reduction of visual forms in order to achieve extreme simplicity as well as a minimum level of emotional content. Creating a sense of purity, minimalist works typically employ a limited color palette, favoring neutral colors, grays, black and whites. Minimalists tend to use industrial materials (steel, aluminum, glass, and so forth) with flat surfaces, often avoiding surface texture. Minimalist art is exhibited with a great emphasis on the space and the relationship between the work of art and the space around it. Hence, the negative space around the work of art is considered as important as the works themselves. The vast emptiness in the office spaces of Lumon Industries, such as the large space around a quartet of connected desks, refers to these qualities and to the way minimalist art was installed indoors.

Not only the opening scene but almost all scenes in *Severance* have strong, symmetric compositions. One of the main reasons that makes a symmetric composition powerful is the sense of balance and stability, which minimalist art often exhibits. Visual harmony is created by aligning the elements to the central axis, as well as by the reduction of clustered visual elements. As the aesthetics of the series is a mixture of different movements of abstract art (including Bauhaus, mid-twentieth-century Minimalism, and its preceder Suprematism, which had a significant influence on the development of abstract art, and modern art in general), these styles can be seen in the series in a multilayered fashion. Abstract art is non-representational and non-objective by the nature of its philosophy. It does not engage in mimetic conventions, therefore there are no references to the "real" visible world that we comprehend with our senses. Instead of depicting the visible world surrounding us, abstract art communicates through the elements of design such as line, shape, texture, tone, and color. This way of modern abstraction goes back to Paul Cézanne. In 1904, in a letter to Emile Bernard, Cézanne wrote: "Everything in nature is formed upon the sphere, the cone, and the cylinder. One must learn to paint these simple figures and then one can do all that he may wish." Here Cézanne proposes the reduction of nature's infinite number of amorphous forms to a finite number of geometric forms. In some scenes, these modernist ideas are used in a combinational way, such as the one in the 5th episode ("The Grim Barbarity of Optics and Design"), when Helly and Mark walk through the corridors of Lumon after Mark gives her the hand-drawn map. As Helly walks ahead toward the dark and the motion sensor-controlled white lights follow her, it looks like there is a dynamic black rectangle behind her, and together with the light they move with Helly as Helly walks. This looks like Kazimir Malevich's renowned painting the "Black Square" (1913).

In the "Manifesto of Suprematism," Malevich (originally published in 1916 by Bauhaus Bücher), states: "When in the year 1913, in my desperate attempt to free art from the ballast of objectivity, I took refuge in the square form and exhibited a picture which consisted of nothing more than a black square on a white field, the critics and, along with them, the public sighed, 'Everything which we loved is lost. We are in a desert… Before us is nothing but a black square on a white background."[6] The Black Square has no reference to the known, visible world yet the viewer continues to seek meaning. As the art critic Will Gompertz explains, the Black Square might appear quite simple yet confusing: "Once it had escaped from a rationalist prison, the unconscious mind would be able to 'see' that the artist was presenting the entire cosmos, and all life within it, in his small, square, simple painting."[7]

The creation of abstract-concrete existence in abstract art is the creation of a new reality that transcends the world of objects, as opposed to the interpretation of the natural scale of the world of objects. The concepts of real and abstract are often considered opposite to each other because, while the world around us can be perceived empirically, the abstract is comprehended by the mind, therefore "abstract-concrete" or "abstract-real" may sound paradoxical. However, the representation of the abstract visually and the contemplation of it is as follows: the thing which is conceived as abstract is objectivized in a form, and then that form is cognized as a reality on its own. One of the pioneers of abstract art, Piet Mondrian explains how we reach to this concept:

> The new plastic can be called abstract not only because it is the direct expression of the universal but also because its expression excludes the individual (or naturalistic concreteness). We can call its exact expression of relationship abstract – in contrast to oppression through natural appearance, which it *abstracts*. If we call the new plastic abstract, the question arises whether the abstract can be represented visually.... Through the very culture of representation through form, we have come to see that the abstract –like the mathematical*[8]– is actually expressed in and through all things, although not determinately. ... [The artist] learned to represent exactly what is vaguely perceptible in nature, he reduced and destroyed the concreteness of appearance (by simplification), yet he did no more than carry the conception of art to its logical conclusion. And so, our age arrived at abstract-real painting.[9]

In this context, the sublime of the modern era comes to the fore again with abstract art. This modern sublime, in Kantian thinking, is a spiritual sublime grounded in the subject. "The presentation of the unpresentable," which Lyotard (1985) articulates in *The Sublime and the Avant Garde* through Kant's concept of *dargestellt* (presented/represented/described) which Kant used to describe the way in which concepts or objects are presented or represented in human cognition, finds existence in abstract art. The abstract art originated in *Severance* is a tool to create a connection to the sublime. In contrast with the very tangible and robust devices such as the toy-like computers used by the employees of Lumon, the *real* technology itself and how the real technology functions such as "the text readers" disallowing them to take any sort of text out of the office premises for their "outies," remains invisible. The employees of Lumon change their outfit—even their watches, which functions as a metaphor for a different time and space—in the section of Lumon named "Svr'd Access" before entering the elevator that empowers the shift from the non-work consciousness to work consciousness. In the first episode, we see that the shape of Mark's face changes (achieved by changing the lens of the camera with a different focal length) as the elevator takes him to the severed floor.

As the American cultural historian David E. Nye pinpoints in his book *Seven Sublimes*, "unlike the traditional sublime which dealt with objects the senses can apprehend (whether natural or technological or a combination of the two) many objects of contemporary biology, physics, and astronomy cannot be sensed."[10] As Lumon Industries claims to be the "pioneers in biotechnology," the "mysterious and important work" they perform already incorporates the sublime. Nye calls this sort of sublime "intangible" and highlights that it needs to be "mediated": "Because we cannot sense them directly, these objects must be represented through mathematics, images, graphs, diagrams and descriptions."[11] Exemplifying Nye's term, let's reflect on our perception of the news about the Webb Space Telescope, which is working to find out about the first galaxies in the early universe. This is incredibly fascinating yet not easy to fully comprehend. This sort of sublime experience is mediated on two levels: The first one is in a denotative way; it should be mediated by a high technology device, and, in this example, it is the space telescope itself. The second level of mediation is the interpretations of the scientists. Some experts must "translate" and interpret those images for non-experts to make sense out of what they see. Otherwise they may count as merely beautiful sceneries for them. This point is where the narrative starts. In recent history, some of these sorts of narratives, such as the Apollo 11 mission (the moon landing), turned into contemporary myths. There are many narrative elements in *Severance* which work to construct the myth of Lumon and elevate Kier to Christ-like status. One of the connotations of the sublime is made through the name of the company, which is like a parapraxis: "lumen" is "the standard unit for measuring the brightness of a light, equal to the amount of light hitting one square foot of surface one foot away from the light."[12] This linguistic similarity adds a divine quality to the company. Historically, in the late nineteenth century, electricity was a sublime phenomenon, and electric lighting was a spectacle on its own and a promising invention. Going back to the scene of Helly and

Mark walking through the corridor, our attention is constantly drawn to the way light is used. Throughout the scene Helly and Mark's movements are traced by the lights, generating the feeling that the Black Square itself is in motion.

Nature-Originated Sublime Transforming into the Invisible Sublime

The paintings and the dialogues describing the painting in the 4th and 5th episodes are particularly important in constructing Lumon's sublimity. The first painting appearing in the 4th episode is "The Youthful Convalescence of Kier." The painting depicts the story of the founder Kier Eagen's recovery from illness. It portrays a sick child lying in bed, surrounded by five people, of which a female figure seems to be praying to a supreme power for the child's recovery. The candle in the hand of one of the maids gently illuminates the center of the dark room and emphasizes the central figure by using light and dark values that are generated by a single light source. First coined in the late fifteenth century during the Renaissance, the technique "chiaroscuro" ("chiaro" meaning "light," and "scuro" meaning "dark" or obscure) allows painters and other creatives to achieve drama in their works and also to generate more depth on the image surface. It was also widely used in the seventeenth century by painters such as Rembrandt and Caravaggio. We see this painting, while awe-inspired Irving and Burt talk about it. Burt reads from his memory the biblical-like lines from the handbook:

Burt: The original word of Kier: "And I shall whisper to ye dutiful through the ages. In your noblest thoughts and epiphanies shall be my voice. You are my mouth, and through ye, I will whisper on when I am 10 centuries demised."

Irving: I don't understand.

Burt: He doesn't just speak to us through the handbook or the paintings. He finds other ways.

This painting makes clear that Kier, in fact, does not need any tool to address the employees of Lumon. He has mysterious ways, just like God.

The second painting we see in the fourth episode is "Kier Invites You to Drink from His Water," which is an interpretation of the renowned painting “Wanderer Above the Sea of Fog” (aka “Sea of Mist,” 1818) by Caspar David Friedrich (Fig. 5.2).

It portrays beautiful scenery with a pastel color scheme: round mountains and flat lowlands depicted in soft shades of green and royal blue-colored ponds against a pinky background during sunset. There is a subtle contrast between the original painting and the interpreted version. Painted in cold shades of grays, blues, and dark browns, “Wanderer Above the Sea of Fog” is one of the most iconic works of Romanticism, which was characterized by a deep appreciation for nature, and a perfect example of Romantic fascination with the nature-oriented sublime. With its themes of the sublime and transcendence, the spirit of Romanticism is known for favoring the individual’s emotions over the rationalism of Enlightenment. The solitary figure portrayed in the painting stands on a rock and gazes out over the sea of fog and the partially hidden sharp mountains. Overwhelmed by the vastness of the landscape, he admires the power of nature. The powerful emotional impact of the painting evokes the feeling of wonder and makes the viewers reflect on the idea of seeking higher values and truths, the insignificance of humans, and in general, the sublimity of nature. In the interpretation of the original painting, there is no feeling of the sublime in terms of the insignificance of the human, on

Fig. 5.2 “Kier Invites You to Drink from His Water”

the contrary Kier looks like a proud man who owns all those lands and offers the waters to his people. The dialogue between Irving and Burt makes the painting less important than the other paintings:

Irving: Is it awful to say I don't care for that one?
Burt: No. Honestly, it makes me nervous too. Such a lovely vista, but I keep thinking…
Irving: He could slip.

At this point, the nature-originated sublime loses its value and leaves its place to the invisible sublime to come. Another interpretation of "Wanderer Above the Sea of Fog" is seen one more time, in the 8th episode ("What's for Dinner?"), while Helly, working on sorting her numbers, reaches 100% on "Siena." A 1980s style-animated video clip appears on the computer screen taking the viewer between the high mountains with some snow on their tips. Then we see a cartoon Kier Eagan standing upon a rocky precipice with his back to the viewer, watching the vast foggy landscape with high mountains ripping into the clouds. Kier turns toward the viewer and speaks to Helly:

> I knew you could do it, Helly R. Even in your darkest moments, I could see you arriving here. In refining your macrodata file, you have brought glory to this company and to me, Kier Eagan. I … I love you. But now I must away, for there are others who need me around the world. Goodbye, Helly R., and thank you.

In the video clip, the cold colors of the painting are replaced with warm colors dominated by the color pink, and instead of the shallow mountains and the smooth color transitions we see in the painting in the fourth episode, this time we see sharp mountains, and rough-edged shapes like those in the mid-1980s 8-bit video games. This time, the source of the sublime effect is withdrawn from nature to Kier, not only because he flies over the mountains just like Superman, but also by his Jesus-like utterance of "I love you."

The third painting we see in the fourth episode is a portrait of Kier in uniform, and the last two paintings are "Aurora Borealis" (1815) by Frederic Edwin Church depicting a beautiful scenery with the fascinating green north lights (which is the only original painting shown in the series), and "Encounter with the Stony Guest," a small painting, we see sideways which makes it hard to recognize its details. These paintings are only seen for a very short time when Burt carries the paintings put together next to each other on a trolley. The way they were carried gives an impression of some sort of unimportance, as if they have completed their mission of constructing the existing narrative and from this point onward, the myth of Kier should be something more abstract, greater than what it was before. This can be compared to the iconoclastic controversy that occurred in the eighth and ninth centuries during the Byzantine Empire era, when there was an intense rejection of religious icons (whether through removal, defacement, or destruction) in the Orthodox Church. From this moment in the show and onward, Kier's sublimity reaches an intangible and invisible level, which is much higher than before.

In the fifth episode, the painting "The Courtship of Kier and Imogene" portrays Kier as an ordinary worker standing by a huge boiler. Imogene stands by him, holding a piece of cloth and looking directly at his face (Fig. 5.3).

Similar to "The Youthful Convalescence of Kier," the central single source of light illuminates the subject of the painting. The conversation between Burt and Irving highlights that even the feeling of love is divine when it is somehow work related.

Burt: He met his wife while a stewman in an ether factory.
Irving: The handbook just says that they were bonded by the spirit of industry.
Burt: I know, but if this interpretation is correct.
Irving: They met as colleagues. Took heart to each other as colleagues.

Another important narrative element is the substance "ether." It is a colorless, highly flammable, liquid chemical that is used as an anesthetic and also as a solvent in various industrial processes. With regard to the substance ether, several historical facts are relevant to this discussion. In Ancient Greek, "aether" was believed to occupy space beyond the atmosphere of the Earth. During the early modern era, scientists such as Isaac Newton claimed that light waves required matter for the propagation of light. In the late nineteenth century, the Michelson–Morley experiment sought to identify the motion of the Earth through ether. Until the

Fig. 5.3 Irving and Burt contemplate "The Courtship of Kier and Imogene"

advancements in the early twentieth century stating that the speed of light is constant, the misconceptions carried over. Other connotations might be the fact that the words "anesthetic" and "aesthetic" share linguistic roots. Going back to the painting, ether works like an alchemistic and mysterious substance that carries Kier to a higher position and status, which is infinite, omnipresent, and universal. This is the last painting about this narrative and a connection point to the invisible qualities of the sublimity that is associated with Kier.

The Dark Matters

In the fifth episode, the style and narrative of the paintings change: there is a clear shift from nature-appreciating Romanticism to dark Romanticism. "The Grim Barbarity of Optics and Design" (and the same painting with differently colored badges, "The Macrodata Refinement Calamity") is a dark painting, not only because of its color scheme, but also because of its subject matter. The painting depicts the employees of the Optics and Design Department as brutal cannibals. The painting pays homage to Francisco Goya's "Black Paintings," "Saturn Devouring His Son" (1820–1823) in particular. Incorporating social commentaries, Goya's paintings focus on human nature and the reality surrounding humans. Goya is a renowned painter of the Romantic era, who used a variety of styles, yet he is more known in popular culture for his series, "Black Paintings." This series depicts haunting themes and delves into the darker aspects of human nature, including madness and violence. "Saturn Devouring His Son" portrays Saturn (in Roman mythology, the Titan Cronus in Greek mythology) eating his offspring because of his fear of being overthrown by his sons. Interpreting the destructive nature of power, the painting seems to be an inspiration for "The Grim Barbarity of Optics and Design," as there are not only visual stylistic similarities between the two but also content connections. The painting in the fifth episode is used as a propaganda tool in order to separate and isolate the employees of the two departments, Macro Data Refinement and Optics and Design, and make them believe that the other department's employees are dangerous and violent. That's why there are two versions of the same painting with only different colored badges. Lumon is arguably pitting the two departments against each other by actively promoting paranoia in each. By separating the two departments, Lumon can better keep them under control.

As the employees of Lumon start to realize that "nothing down there [on the severed floor] is what they say" (as Petey says in the first episode) and the darker side of Lumon starts to be revealed, the darker paintings appear more frequently. In the fifth episode, Irving has a hallucination of some dark, petrol-like greasy looking unidentified matter coming down from the office ceiling. The hallucination Irving had in the fifth episode prefigures the events of the eighth episode. In the opening scene of the eighth episode, Irving reads a book. As the sun goes down, he takes his dog and moves toward his house. We see Irving entering into a house very similar to those depicted in Edward Hopper's paintings. Hopper is known for his paintings depicting urban and rural life mostly in the suburban regions in the United States. The railroad is one of the themes that is often seen in his paintings as a metaphor for the effects of modern life on individuals. Hopper's works explore the themes of alienation and the solitariness of the individual. In most of his works, there is a spatial separation achieved through the use of contrasting color schemes for indoors and outdoors. This contrast also aligns with the alienation of the individual. The reminiscence in the scene is enhanced by the sound of the horn of a train approaching (of which the image is not shown), as Irving moves toward his house.

As soon as he gets in, he pours himself a cup of black coffee and takes a moment in tranquility. Then he moves toward his studio space and takes one of the several copies of the same painting of the "testing floor" he painted before from the tripod aside and puts an empty wood panel on it. He puts "Ace of Spades" by Motörhead on, and adds lots of black paint on his palette. He paints with a painting knife aligned with the rhythm and pace of the dynamic song. This scene creates ambiguous feelings in the viewers. On one hand, the unknown things about Lumon are revealed bit by bit; on the other hand, things get darker (as Irving puts paint on the panel, our vision of him gets smaller and smaller, a visual representation of this ambiguity). Darkness corresponds with the way the intrusion of reality is visually represented. The mood gets darker as things beneath the surface disturb the constructed myth of Lumon Industries.

Conclusion

One of the most fundamental subjects in *Severance* is the idea of the invisible sublime. Since the sublime is generally related to an experience of nature, rather than an artistic interest, its reflections in art are embodied not as a literal depiction of the sublime, but as expressions of the experiences of the sublime. It is not surprising that the manifestations of Romantic taste in the eighteenth and nineteenth centuries emerged as various depictions of the transcendence of nature. Many painters including Caspar David Friedrich, J. M. W. Turner, and Théodore Géricault used nature, which they depicted as powerful and transcendent, as a means of expression of human thoughts and feelings. In the early nineteenth century, Romanticism's convergence with the sublime led to the emergence of some specific motifs, such as high mountains, ships struggling in stormy raging seas or shipwrecks succumbing to the struggle, and themes such as the surrender of the soul to unknown forces at night in Black Romanticism, as well as formal features such as high contrast light and shadows, and dramatic compositions. These images and formal features were often used by artists, poets, writers, and other intellectuals. Certain clichés of Romantic manifestations of the sublime emerged because of the repeated usage of the motifs and themes. After the industrial revolution, the natural sublime was replaced by the spectacles of technological sublime, the creations of the human. These include skyscrapers, bridges, canals, zeppelins, railroads, and so forth. As technology evolved, some other sublime things such as electron microscopes, space telescopes, holograms, microchips, and other inventions which were not necessarily huge in size or tangible have appeared. Their sublimity is due to the new perspectives they provide on new worlds such as the micro-cosmos and macro-cosmos that are not necessarily visible to the naked eye. The advancements in technology led to the emergence of the intangible sublime. The mediated and intangible sublime (in Nye's terms) has as its foundation scientific evidence and rational reasoning. One of the reasons that I prefer to use the word "invisible" sublime is because, in the series, the employees (and the viewers) *accept* the rules of the game and are not informed about how the *real* technology operates. In addition to this, there is the spiritual approach to the sublime (let's remember Irving in the 8th episode asking Mark whether standing behind Helly and chanting her name would help Helly to accomplish the task).

To arrive at this fundamental subject, the series establishes a relationship between the idea of abstraction and the idea of the sublime. A metaphorical analogy is created between the world of abstract art and the employees of Lumon with their severed memories. As abstract art leaves the real visible world surrounding us aside and creates its own world based on geometrical forms, colors, and other design elements, the employees of Lumon leave their outies and switch to their innies as they get into the elevators. The innies can only live in the world of abstraction that Lumon creates as they do not inhabit the concrete visible world outside Lumon. Abstraction means that comprehension of existence takes place outside the real world. This, in itself, requires the formation of an abstract system of values. In this way, one moves away from the empirical world and involves oneself in an abstract world. The office spaces we see throughout the episodes of the first season are designed with a modernist, abstract, and minimalist aesthetic. This aesthetic design creates a continuous ground for Lumon employees that disconnects them from the real world and actual time outside the severed floor. Starting from the very first scene of the series, this aesthetic is clearly reflected in the visual style of the building spaces, as well as the liminal spaces such as the labyrinth-like corridors and the elevators.

One of the prominent art movements in the series is Romanticism which is utilized as a tool emphasizing human emotions. The relationship between modernism and Romanticism may look distant, however, the origins of abstract art date back to the nineteenth century. This is particularly true of Romanticism, as it challenged the preceding centuries' imitation and idealization of previous works and re-evaluated the relationship between human and nature. As the nineteenth century's dominant objective materialist understanding of reality was replaced by a subjectivist understanding of reality at the beginning of the twentieth century, a new interpretation of reality and existence related to the abstract emerged. In science, the loss of the solidity of matter and its approach to an abstract essence through new studies on energy drew the existence of nature into a field of abstract intellectual interest.[13] In philosophy, the naturalistic universe was replaced by a subjectivist-idealistic universe that was based on the subject at hand. The changes in science and philosophy were reflected in the field of art in the form of shifting interests from the empirical comprehension of the object to its meaning as an entity of consciousness. Although the object is a sensory reality, "it is an abstract intellectual being, an ideality,... abstract intellectual being is a being opposed to sensory reality." [14] *Severance* makes use of the abstract as a base for the alienation and Romanticism in order to achieve the invisible sublime in a gradual fashion.

The series is loaded with linguistic and visual connotations, and subliminal references as seen in the names of the company and the characters as well as the artworks that symbolize themes such as alienation and the insignificance of the individual, and sanctity of work and the so-called work–life balance. The themes are visualized and narrated through the use of art, the interpretations of some iconic artworks, and the use of certain art and design movements, Romanticism, abstract art, and minimalism in particular.

Notes

1. Julian Bell, "Contemporary Art and the Sublime," in Nigel Llewellyn and Christine Riding, eds., *The Art of the Sublime*, Tate Research Publication, January 2013, https://www.tate.org.uk/art/research-publications/the-sublime/julian-bell-contemporary-art-and-the-sublime-r1108499, accessed 28 October 2023.

2. Immanuel Kant, *Critique of Judgment* (Oxford: Oxford University Press, 2007), 75.
3. Ibid., 81.
4. Ibid., 75.
5. Ibid., 256.
6. Kazimir Malevich, *The Non-Objective World* (Chicago: Paul Theobald and Company, 1959), 8.
7. Will Gompertz, *What Are You Looking At?* (New York: Penguin Group, 2012), 112.
8. Mondrian adds a footnote here: "*Aristotle already identified the abstract with the mathematical."
9. Piet Mondrian, *The New Art—The New Life: The Collected Writings of Piet Mondrian (1917-1924)*, ed. and trans. by Martin S. James (Massachusetts: G.K. Hall & Co., 1986), 35–36.
10. David E. Nye, *Seven Sublimes* (Massachusetts: The MIT Press, 2022), 91.
11. Ibid., 91.
12. "Lumen," Cambridge Dictionary, https://dictionary.cambridge.org/dictionary/english/lumen.
13. See İsmail Tunalı, Felsefenin Işığında Modern Resim (İstanbul: Remzi Kitabevi, 1996).
14. Ibid., 122.

Bibliography

Bell, Julian. "Contemporary Art and the Sublime." In Nigel Llewellyn and Christine Riding, eds., *The Art of the Sublime*, Tate Research Publication, January 2013. https://www.tate.org.uk/art/research-publications/the-sublime/julian-bell-contemporary-art-and-the-sublime-r1108499. Accessed 28 October 2023.

Cézanne, Paul. Edited by John Rewald. *Paul Cezanne Letters*. 4th edition, 1946.

Gompertz, Will. *What Are You Looking At?* New York: Penguin Group, 2012.

Kant, Immanuel. *Critique of Judgment*. Oxford: Oxford University Press, 2007.

Levine, Caroline. "Gursky's Sublime." *Postmodern Culture* 12, no. 3 (2002). https://doi.org/10.1353/pmc.2002.0017.

"Lumen." Cambridge Dictionary. https://dictionary.cambridge.org/dictionary/english/lumen.

Lyotard, Jean-François. 1985. "The Sublime and the Avant Garde." *October*, Vol. 6, pp. 1–18.

Malevich, Kazimir. *The Non-Objective World*. Chicago: Paul Theobald and Company, 1959.

Mondrian, Piet. *The New Art—The New Life: The Collected Writings of Piet Mondrian (1917–1924)*. Edited and translated by Martin S. James. Massachusetts: G.K. Hall & Co., 1986.

Nye, David E. *Seven Sublimes*. Massachusetts: The MIT Press, 2022.

Tunalı, İsmail. *Felsefenin Işığında Modern Resim*. İstanbul: Remzi Kitabevi, 1996.

CHAPTER 6

Mapping the Subject Through *Severance's* Corporate Architecture and Design

Christine Prevas

The first episode of *Severance*, "Good News About Hell," begins with a striking visual image: an overhead shot of a corporate boardroom, its perfect symmetry broken only by the sprawled body of a woman lying on the table, discordantly out of place (Fig. 6.1).

This woman, the audience shortly learns, is Helly R., a new recruit to the "Severed" floor of Lumon Industries, who has undergone a procedure that "severs" her mind and memories, creating two distinct people sharing a body and mind—an "outie" and "innie" whose memories, personality, and experiences are spatially locked away from one another, such that one exists only on the severed floor, and the other only exists outside of it.

From this opening shot, and from the insistent spatiality of its central conceit, *Severance* communicates its interest in the relationship between the self and space. Who are we when we are at work? The show's speculative premise quite literally asks. And who are we when we leave? Perhaps

C. Prevas (✉)
Columbia University, New York, NY, USA
e-mail: cap2260@columbia.edu

N. M. Isacoff and J. Dawes (eds.), *Reintegrating Severance*,
https://doi.org/10.1007/978-3-031-57448-1_6

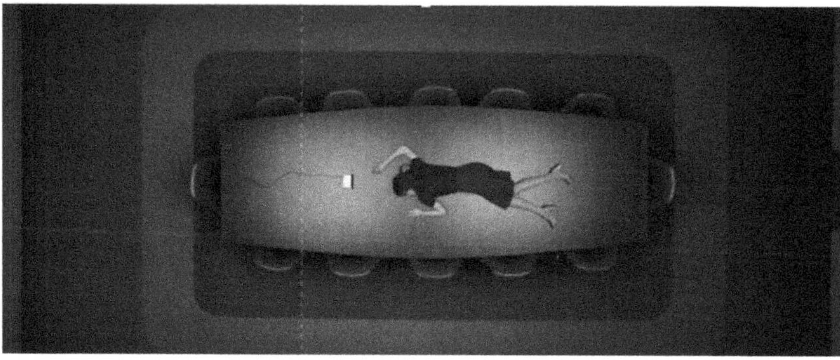

Fig. 6.1 Helly on the conference table

more pertinently, how do the shapes of the spaces we occupy at work and at home inform the answer to those questions?

Severance addresses these questions in a variety of ways, the foremost of which is through its set design and cinematography, which highlight the stark differences between the brightly lit, colorful, and carefully organized design of the severed floor and the more muted colors and naturalistic atmosphere of the world outside. The almost absurd artificiality of the severed floor's unsubtle design principles make the severed floor feel otherworldly in contrast to the world beyond its walls.

Severance also addresses these questions in the structure of the plot and narrative through the ways characters interact with one another and with those same spaces. As Helly R. undertakes an initiation survey designed to test the effectiveness of the Severance procedure, the disembodied voice on the other end—later revealed to be her department chief and the show's protagonist Mark S.—reads from a script in the manual: "I can sense that the questions made you feel afraid or disoriented." Here, the show once again reveals its fascination with spatial metaphor. "Well, the good news is, you're *at* an *orientation*."[1] Beyond the bounds of this scripted joke, orientation and disorientation become central conceits through which *Severance* addresses questions about the nature of subjectivity, and its susceptibility to outside influence—in particular, outside influence through space and architectural design.

The severed floor, for Helly R., Mark S., and the show's other "innies," is inescapable. Severed from their memories and unable to leave without activating the neurological chip that makes their existence possible, it is the only world they have ever or will ever know (until the end of the first season). As such, the architectural design of that space is pivotal to their engagement with the world at large. It shapes them in profound and undeniable ways. And once the show sets those questions up in this isolated environment, it reaches beyond the severed floor to ask those same questions of who the characters are outside. How much, the show asks, are *we* shaped by the design principles of the spaces we occupy? And is there a way out?

Severance's striking visual engagement with corporate architecture and design, then, serves to make concrete the way architecture designs and produces certain subjectivities. Through visualizing the production of a "Severed" corporate subjectivity via corporate architecture and design, *Severance* reaches beyond just the severed floor to interrogate the quotidian architectural practices which shape us every day in ways beyond our recognition, questions how much of ourselves is shaped by the capitalist environments we navigate every day, and gestures toward possibilities for resisting them.

Architecture and Subjectivation

To consider that the architecture of the severed floor plays an integral and transformative part of the Severance procedure unavoidably recalls Michel Foucault's description, in *Discipline and Punish*, of "an architecture that would operate to transform individuals: to act on those it shelters, to provide a hold on their conduct."[2] While space is often made to appear value-neutral, and, as architect Joel Sanders notes, "we tend to think of architecture as unencumbered by politics and ideology," to the contrary, the built spaces we occupy and navigate organize the way we live and the way we think, constructing and regulating racial, gendered, and sexual subjectivities in a variety of ways.[3]

In *Severance*, the power of architecture to inculcate specific behaviors and subjectivities is seen most obviously through the architecture and design of the severed floor. While the clean, minimalist design of the Macrodata Refinement office recalls, in many ways, the soulless sameness of much real-world corporate design, the winding, twisting windowless hallway that connects these office spaces together bears less resemblance to an office and more, in some ways, to the design principles of a casino. As architects Robert Venturi, Denise Scott Brown, and Steven Izenour observe in *Learning From Las Vegas*, the typical casino floor plan is that of an "intricate maze," which "never connects with the outside light or outside space. This disorients the occupants in space and time. One loses track of where one is and when it is."[4] In her book *Addiction by Design*, Natasha Dow Schüll investigates the common architecture of Las Vegas casinos as one part of a larger project—part aesthetic and part technological—to transform customers into gamblers. The "casino's 'commercial vernacular style,'" Schüll writes, "responds to popular needs or desires for escapism as part of a larger effort to *guide* those needs and desires."[5] The aim of the maze-like internal structure of the casino, Schüll demonstrates, is "to steer [the customer's] behavior in accordance with the extractive aims of the larger operation."[6] The architectural choices of the space act to inculcate in the customer certain behaviors, certain modes of being, and certain ways of thinking—much like the architectural choices of the severed floor guide not only the movements but also the beliefs and desires of the workers in accordance with similar extractive aims, taking from them labor rather than money.

However, architecture does not only work to encourage certain behaviors, but to produce subjectivities—that is, to transform *who we are* through the way it moves us. As queer theorist Paul Preciado highlights, a new "grammar" of subjectivity "is produced performatively through the repetition of architectural conventions: the creation of frameworks of visibility, access denial, or permission, spatial distribution, and segmentation of the public and the private."[7]

By "subjectivity," here, I follow media studies scholar Cameron Kunzelman, who usefully articulates the difference between the "stable" or "imperial" subject of much Western philosophy, and Félix Guattari's concept of "subjectivation." While, as Kunzelman lays out, the Lockean subject has a stable originary core that gains characteristics through experiences, for Guattari the subject itself is always in flux, mutable and changing, shaped constantly and continually by its external encounters. Subjectivation for Guattari, then, is "not merely the process through which subjectivity is formed at an early age but instead a baseline process that is always happening in each moment."[8] As Kunzelman writes:

> the activity of capitalism is such that we are built over and over again, minute to minute, day to day. It is not that I gain or lose properties in Lockean way, with a stable core being maintained throughout. That central core of the self, and the way it interacts with the world, is radically altered moment-to-moment. Its stability is only an illusion. Who I am does

> not depend on the disposition I have toward a particular experience, but instead how the materials around me are decoding my subjectivity and remaking it in the moment.[9]

Myriad systems of power influence the shaping of this subjectivity, from media to technological interfaces to architecture, among others. And through this process of subjectivation, each designed space produces its own ideal subject.

As such, in *Severance* it is not only the literal medical procedure of "severance," nor the technological intervention of the neurological chip inserted during that procedure, but a broader product of aesthetics, architecture, and design which produces what we might think of as "severed subjectivity." Lumon's architecture and design principles work to produce a new type of subjectivity, that of the severed worker, the subject who is nothing *but* worker.

Lumon's Corporate Architecture and Severed Subjectivity

Through what kinds of architectural practices does Lumon produce this severed subjectivity? In her book *Framing Places: Mediating Power in Built Form*, architectural critic Kim Dovey explores the ways in which built spaces allow for the exertion of power over the people within those spaces through both force—for instance, those strategies common to confinement and incarceration—and coercion. Dovey outlines three different types of coercion operating at the spatial dimension: manipulation, which "operates primarily by keeping the subject ignorant," as "power is made invisible to its subject and the possibility of resistance is thereby removed"; seduction, which "manipulates the interests and desires of the subject"; and authority, which "is integrated with the institutional structures of society such as the state, church, private corporation, school and family."[10] Through a combination of these strategies of coercion, and along a number of different dimensions including orientation and disorientation, and segregation and access, Dovey writes that architecture "evokes and enables certain forms of life while constraining others with both walls and sanctions."[11]

There are several broad strategies apparent in Lumon's architecture that make its severed workers susceptible to the influence of its design. As Dovey writes, quoting sociologist Barry Barnes' *The Nature of Power*:

> A fragmented experience of space and time with the loss of a sense of orientation and community can be conducive to coercive control. The ideal subjects of coercive power "should live as atoms, wholly in the public realm, under surveillance, but as far as possible without social relationships."[12]

The sprawling empty hallways of the severed floor, the long distance between departments—which are discouraged from interacting with one another—and the expressly forbidden status of owning or producing maps or any other representation of the spatial logic of the floor work together to keep the departments isolated from one another, and to keep the severed workers both segregated *and* disoriented. And the presence of security cameras throughout the floor points to a high degree of surveillance—not to mention the disciplinary apparatus of the Break Room, which could easily generate a chapter-length Foucauldian analysis of all on its own.

While the set design of the Macrodata Refinement office is influenced by mid-century American office design, especially, as production designer Jeremy Hindle notes, by architects such as Eero Saarinen and Kevin Roche, the design is also intentionally anachronistic, and each desk, computer, and chair was specifically manufactured to avoid association with any real-world design.[13] The Macrodata Refinement office apes the design of an "open-plan" office, with all four of its employees in a shared space, their desks divided by partial partitions that give them the illusion of privacy while also keeping their work (their screens, their desks, and their bodies) in full view of outside observers, unlike the closed off layout of a cubicle or individual office. The "open-plan" office layout, architectural theorists Bill Hillier and Julienne Hanson observe, is a layout which, despite its' "openness," counterintuitively restricts the motion of bodies within it, preventing freedom of movement within the space. They write that this "has the effect of converting the distributed system from a permissive circulation system, neutral with respect to categories of inhabitants, into a control system by which those dependent on it become fixed to their places."[14] As well, the "open-plan" "synchronizes" the workers within it, and flattens status differences between them, especially relative to those workers whose status nets them a separate office or space. In the case of Macrodata Refinement, this means a flattening of the hierarchy between Mark S. as MDR's "department chief" and the rest of this team, as well as a drastic heightening of the hierarchy between the MDR team and those in management positions, supervisor Seth Milchick and manager Harmony Cobel, who are either shown to have their own office, in the case of Cobel, or who seem to float unrestricted through the space of the entire severed floor, in the case of Milchick. This creates quite a drastic power differential between the severed workers in MDR and the non-severed management class: "the open-plan is a means of converting what were status differences between inhabitants into what is virtually a class difference within the inhabitant structure of the building."[15] As well, the unusual arrangement of the desks within the MDR office's "open-plan," grouped closely together at the center of a large open room, privileges space for the circulating supervisor to surveil the workers and de-emphasizes the individuality of each desk by clustering them into a single, undifferentiated unit.

In addition to these broad architectural influences, smaller design principles that organize office life on the severed floor work equally to subjectivate the severed workers. In fact, Lumon's use of the three forms of coercion Dovey outlines—manipulation, seduction, and authority—map relatively cleanly onto the effect of Lumon's architecture and design on three of the show's severed protagonists.

Mark S. is defined by his manipulation through ignorance: given the responsibility of becoming the new department chief at the beginning of the season, after Petey leaves, Mark S. is constantly discouraged from questioning why things are the way they are. Though he is given the illusion of being in control through his new position, in that position he is given literal scripts to follow, keeping him from charting his own path. Less through architecture itself and more through the design of documents like the training manual from which Mark S. conducts Helly R.'s introductory survey, Mark S. is kept on track through a kind of manufactured tunnel vision that encourages him not to look too closely at the operations of power that surround and influence him.

Dylan G., in contrast, is defined by his seduction by Lumon's productivity incentives: he is motivated by collecting finger traps, caricature portraits, and waffle parties—the latter of which, a late season episode reveals, involves a more literal form of seduction in the guise of a disturbing burlesque performance and, presumably, a sexual experience. Dylan is taken in by the promise of Lumon's rewards for his hard work, a fulfillment of the economic common-sense idea that incentives increase productivity, but moreover his desire *for* these ultimately meaningless rewards is also designed by Lumon itself—a construction made all the more clear by the ridiculousness and childishness of the rewards themselves. Lumon tells him what he should want, and then leverages those artificial desires to encourage desirable behaviors. These prizes are designed to fill gaps left intentionally by the severed floor's architecture: they take the place of personal effects, occupying the space on desks and in desk drawers where one might ordinarily put family photos or personal items. And yet they all share the same powder blue color, a color visually associated with the Lumon brand throughout the show. Even the sexual experience of the "Waffle Party" involves Lumon's brand via its mythologization of Kier Eagan. Where individuality would usually enter to fill the spaces around the infrastructure of office life, Lumon's incentives fill that same space with more of itself, and offer nothing else in its place.

Irving B., meanwhile, is defined by his deference to Lumon's authority, both at the level of the law—shown through his strict adherence to the Lumon Employee Handbook—and the "church"—through his semi-religious worship of Kier Eagan and the Eagan family as made manifest on the severed floor through the Perpetuity Wing and the paintings hung throughout the floor by Optics and Design.[16] Quasi-religious, often Baroque-looking art, for instance, punctuates the otherwise entirely plain white halls of the severed floor, filling the need for visual stimulation with the insistent repetition of Lumon's self-mythologizing. In the Perpetuity Wing, Irving explains the importance of this self-mythologizing. He is presented to the audience as out of touch: "It's okay to cry," he tells Helly, as she crumples up one of Dylan's "Lumon Bingo" cards, telegraphing that Irving is the only one of the four who takes this church-like trip seriously.[17] But Irving's reverence for the religiosity of Lumon, for the biblical handbook and the iconography of Optics and Design, makes him no more a dupe to Lumon's propaganda than Dylan or Mark. In fact, in the Perpetuity Wing, Irving quite clearly articulates a commonality that all of the innies share, which makes them especially susceptible to their subjectivation as workers. "It's an unnatural state for a person to have no history," he tells Helly. "History makes us someone. Give us a context. A shape. But waking up on that table, I was shapeless."[18]

The shapeless, empty self recalls Guattari's subject and its mutable, ever-changing core. This core, in the real world, is shaped by "processes of overlapping subjectivation," as Kunzelman writes: "The family, home, school, and office molds you down into a particular subjectivity, *but that subjectivity exists only so long as those structures can hold you in those ways.*"[19] By removing those other spaces and systems of power which have already subjectivated the outie, by taking away the overlapping subjectivities produced by those real-world spaces, the innie is left to interface *only* with the designed spaces which will produce the desired Severed subjectivity. Because the innies never experience a space outside of the severed floor, they are held permanently within the process of subjectivation via Lumon's architecture, as a Severed subject no longer in flux.

Innies and Outies: Subjectivation Outside the Severed Floor

After its sinister, disorienting *in media res* opening scene, *Severance* introduces its audience more clearly to the functioning of the Severance procedure through a long sequence which follows Mark Scout/Mark S. through the beginning of his workday: crying alone in his car in the Lumon parking lot; entering the mirrored[20] Lumon building; checking in; trading out his personal effects for a blue badge, dress shoes, and a nondescript watch; riding the elevator down to the severed floor; and finally following a long series of undifferentiated white hallways through a number of twists and turns from the elevator to what we will come to identify as the Macrodata Refinement office where Mark S. works.[21]

After Mark Scout leaves his car, this sequence is predominantly composed of wide and extreme wide shots as the camera tilts to show the audience the Lumon parking lot, the outside of the building, and the lobby of the building, all of which are presented as grand in scale, dwarfing Mark Scout's small figure. These wide shots, and a notable overhead extreme wide shot (see below), orient the viewer in a building that is familiar to Mark Scout; any strangeness, including a large engraving of the bust of Kier Egan on one wall, is rendered commonplace, and the viewer is oriented by what amounts to a series of establishing shots familiarizing them with the building. In contrast, Mark S.'s long walk down the hallway on the severed floor is presented primarily as a nearly continuous medium or medium close-up dolly shot, with Mark S. walking directly into the camera as it tracks backward. This tighter shot, combined with the uniformity of the white-walled hallway, has the opposite effect: it disorients the viewer, who can neither get a sense of Mark S.'s surroundings, nor see where he is going. Rather than the mostly still shots that cut from room to room in the building upstairs, this extended one-shot as Mark S. navigates the hallway is dizzying and feels never-ending: we have no idea how far he has walked, nor which relative direction his many turns have taken him.

The composition of this sequence initially presents a stark difference between the outside world and the severed floor. As we move from wide establishing shots to disorienting tracking shots, from the brutalist architecture above to the bland white sameness of the hallway below, the two halves of the building feel like alien worlds to one another. However, the stark symmetry of the architecture in the first half of the sequence—parking spots, seating areas, and staircases are all mirrored along the center axis of the screen—gestures toward a larger symmetry, that of the effects of architecture and design principles on those who navigate these spaces. In fact, Lumon's headquarters as a whole mirror the logic and design of the severed floor. This symmetry builds a visual and architectural consistency between the outside world and the "inside" world of the innies—down to the color of the carpet, and the shots which frame Mark Scout entering the building and Helly R. on the conference table (Fig. 6.2).

As below, these shots emphasize, so above: while the operations of corporate architecture and design on the innies who have never experienced a world *not* designed by Lumon's deliberate aesthetic and architectural choices are hardly subtle, their correspondent outies interface with architecture, and are impacted by it, in much the same way. The

Fig. 6.2 Lumon lobby as viewed from overhead

architectural subjectivation of the innies, therefore, serves not as an especially susceptible exception to the rule, but as a heightened exaggeration of a process to which all are subject, even if less obviously so.

Lumon, after all, designs more than just its own office spaces. Mark Scout lives in Lumon-owned housing,[22] and the Severance procedure is revealed to be used on people outside of Lumon's corporate interests, including a Senator's wife who uses Severance to avoid experiencing childbirth.[23] For Peter Kilmer/Petey, who has undergone a process of "reintegration" of his Severed self, the commonalities between the severed floor and the outside world blur: he experiences both simultaneously, and as he does, the cuts between the two emphasize the echoes that ripple between them, the structural similarity between the severed floor's long hallway and the road and bridge he walks along in the world above.[24] In the transition between this scene and the next, dialogue from the severed floor begins to intrude upon the scene, further blurring the defined boundaries between one space and the other.

With this blurring of spaces, and with the monumental quasi-religious architecture that characterizes Lumon's headquarters, the impact of corporate design and power on the show's outies manifests in addition to its impact on the innies. While the Severance procedure ostensibly promises a freedom from work for the outie, who need no longer experience or remember the drudgery of their own labor, this blurring reveals that the opposite may be true: through severing the worker from the self, Lumon manages some amount of control of both halves, mirroring real-world corporate architecture's structural marriage of work, family, and religion which characterizes our particular moment of extreme neoliberal capitalism.

Fugitive Mapping and Collective Resistance

Is Lumon's architecture inescapable, then? The final episodes of the season see three of the four innies temporarily escape the severed floor through their use of the "overtime" protocol, which wakes them up outside of the severed floor. However, on the outside, none of them find themselves free of Lumon's influence: Helly finds herself at a Lumon gala, where she realizes that she is really Helena Eagan; Mark S. finds himself at a party attended by his boss Harmony Cobel in the guise of his neighbor Mrs. Selvig; and Irving finds that his outie has been obsessively painting images of a dark hallway and an elevator from the severed floor, and seemingly investigating Lumon's operations and other severed workers.

But much of the season does chart their progressive resistance against the architecture which subjectivates them, not only presented as a desire to physically escape the severed floor, but also a yearning to understand it. To return to Dovey, the operation of manipulation relies upon power being "made invisible to its subject," which in turn removes the possibility of resistance. One of the primary ways Lumon keeps its severed workers ignorant is through a sort of literal invisibility: not only have none of them seen the world outside of the severed floor, but none of them have seen the entirety of the severed floor itself. By the book, the severed workers are meant to stay in and around their offices, with the exception of the Break Room—a disciplinary apparatus—and the Perpetuity Wing—a monument to Lumon—which they need permission to go to. More than that, characters mention several times throughout the season that maps are forbidden, and that they are not supposed to provide directions to the other offices. While this is masked as another quasi-religious decree from the handbook—"Render not my creation in miniature"[25]—the inaccessibility of maps keeps the larger operation of Lumon's architecture invisible. It keeps the workers disoriented, alienated, and prevents them from understanding their place as a part of a larger totality, except as a cog with a defined function.

Maps, then, take on a central place in the show as a form of resistance. As an illicit activity, the creation, discovery, and following of maps and directions allows the severed workers to temporarily escape or resist the subjectivation of Lumon's architecture. This is most obvious in the character of Petey, who, after being reintegrated, has been mapping the halls of the severed floor. There is a clear connection, here, between the act of mapping and the refusal of his Severed state: mapping enacts a form of fugitivity that leads him toward escape, both physical escape from the severed floor and freedom from the manipulation of the architecture as he comes to understand it more (Fig. 6.3).

However, Petey's escape is ill-fated as his reintegration fails and he dies only days later. And what's more, his map is incomprehensible, of no real use to Mark S. to whom he leaves it, except as a sort of symbol, a gesture toward the idea that this kind of mapping, this kind of resistance, is possible. While Helly and Mark S. agree to work together to recreate Petey's map after Mark S. destroys it, we never see their attempts to do so, or the product of this work. The importance of the map, it seems,

Fig. 6.3 Petey's map of Lumon's severed floor

is less in its physical existence and more in the promise it provides, or understanding the architecture which entraps them and its effect on them, and in connecting them to what's beyond: not a literal map, but, to use a term from Frederic Jameson, a *cognitive* map.

Jameson proposes cognitive mapping in *Postmodernism, or, the Cultural Logic of Late Capitalism*, as a new cultural model and aesthetic practice specific to the spatial organization of late capitalism. Drawing on Kevin Lynch's description of the "alienated city... a space in which people are unable to map (in their minds) either their own positions or the urban totality in which they find themselves," cognitive mapping provides an antidote to this disorientation.[26] It not only combats disorientation, but also allows for subjects to "regain a capacity to act and struggle which is at present neutralized by our spatial as well as our social confusion."[27] Cognitive mapping is not literal mapping, however; it is not a mimetic representation of space, like the map Petey draws. Instead, Jameson emphasizes, cognitive mapping is "a pedagogical political culture which seeks to endow the individual subject with some new heightened sense of its place in the global system."[28] It is a project of disalienation that works to situate the subject within the totality of society as a whole—and, too, in relation to a collective.

In *Severance*, Petey's attempts to literally map the severed floor create a mimetic representation of space which is not only practically incomprehensible, but ultimately does little to help him. Following his own map of the severed floor as he hallucinates after his reintegration leads him down unproductive paths and, eventually, to his own death. Mark S.'s interest in the map he finds on the back of Petey's photo does not lead him to any real revelations. The creation of a map, or the giving of directions, is presented not as a useful individual action, but instead as one which connects people. When Burt, from Optics & Design, provides directions from Macrodata Refinement to O&D, it is in the effort to build connections—to build upon the connection he's already formed with Irving, and to extend the invitation to the rest of Irving's team. Mapping, then, becomes a means of connection as much as it becomes a tool of orientation: the fact that it is forbidden is a part of the larger effort to isolate the workers from one another, to prevent any feelings of collectivity or comradery among the different teams that work on the severed floor.

As such, it is only when the severed workers begin to undertake this project *together* that they make any meaningful progress toward resisting Lumon's influence—not necessarily in creating a comprehensive literal map, but in creating a cognitive one, an understanding of themselves in relation to the world beyond the severed floor that allows them to plot their escape. If *Severance* frames mapping as an illicit activity which enacts a fugitive relationship to corporate architectural space, then this mapping cannot be successfully undertaken at the level of the individual, but only ever as a collective action which deliberately resists the production of the idealized hyper-individual worker-subject represented by the "Severed" self. The power of mapping lies not in its ability to render a complexly designed space understandable, or in its ability to allow those subject to that space to manipulate that space in return. Instead, mapping is a means toward a larger end: an awareness of the way space is subjectivating us, and a subsequent recognition of our relationship not as an individual, but as a part of a collective with the ability to resist not the process of subjectivation itself, but the very terms of those designing these spaces in the first place.

Notes

1. *Severance*, "Good News About Hell."
2. Michel Foucault, *Discipline and Punish*, 172.
3. Joel Sanders, "Introduction," in *Stud: Architectures of Masculinity*, 10.
4. Robert Venturi and others, *Learning From Las Vegas*, 49.
5. Natasha Dow Schüll, *Addiction by Design: Machine Gambling in Las Vegas*, 37.

6. Ibid., 40.
7. Paul Preciado, *Pornotopia: An Essay on Playboy's Architecture and Biopolitics*, 130.
8. Cameron Kunzelman, *The World Is Born from Zero: Understanding Speculation and Video Games*, 69.
9. Kunzelman, 71.
10. Kim Dovey, *Framing Places: Mediating Power in Built Form*, 13–14.
11. Ibid., 18–19.
12. Ibid., 13.
13. Jackson McHenry, "The Stories Behind *Severance*'s Eerie Office Design," *Vulture*, https://www.vulture.com/article/severance-office-design-explained.html.
14. Bill Hillier and Julienne Hanson, *The Social Logic of Space*, 195.
15. Ibid., 195.
16. Lumon also blurs the lines between law and religion through the employee handbook, as well, which is seen to be printed in a format resembling a traditional Christian bible ("What's For Dinner?", 24:22). Further, though Irving is not the only one to draw upon the familiar trope of coworkers being "like family," his repeated refrain, "What's for dinner, kids?" frames him as particularly invested in the dynamic, yoking together family and all of its associated authority into the authority of law and religion as well.
17. *Severance*, "In Perpetuity."
18. Ibid.
19. Kunzelman, 71–72, my emphasis.
20. I mean "mirrored" here both in reference to the mirrored windows which cover the building's entire facade, and the near-perfect symmetry that characterizes its architecture.
21. *Severance*, "Good News About Hell."
22. In discussing the set design for Mark's house in an interview with *Vulture*, production designer Jeremy Hindle commented that "The architecture of his place is so perfectly wrong," pointing in particular to the surveillance-like quality of his side-by-side house with Mrs. Selvig/Harmony Cobel's house, which is elevated slightly "so she can peer down into his life."
23. The conflation between "work" and "childbirth" implied by this plotline opens up interesting questions for further analysis in productive conversation with Marxist-Feminist work on social

reproduction theory and gestational labor (see, for instance, Sophie Lewis' *Full Surrogacy Now: Feminism Against the Family.*).
24. *Severance,* "In Perpetuity."
25. *Severance,* "The You You Are."
26. Frederic Jameson, *Postmodernism, or, the Cultural Logic of Late Capitalism*, 51.
27. Ibid., 54.
28. Ibid., 54.

Bibliography

Dovey, Kim. *Framing Places: Mediating Power in Built Form*. London: Routledge, 2014.
Foucault, Michel. *Discipline & Punish: The Birth of the Prison*. Translated by Alan Sheridan. New York: Vintage Books, 1995.
Hillier, Bill, and Julienne Hanson. *The Social Logic of Space*. New York: Cambridge University Press, 1984.
Jameson, Fredric. *Postmodernism, or, The Cultural Logic of Late Capitalism*. Durham: Duke University Press, 1992.
Kunzelman, Cameron. *The World Is Born from Zero: Understanding Speculation and Video Games*. Boston: De Gruyter Oldenbourg, 2022.
McHenry, Jackson. "The Stories Behind Severance's Eerie Office Design." *Vulture*, April 1, 2022. https://www.vulture.com/article/severance-office-design-explained.html.
Preciado, Paul. *Pornotopia: An Essay on Playboy's Architecture and Biopolitics*. New York: Zone Books, 2019.
Sanders, Joel. "Introduction." *Stud: Architectures of Masculinity*. Edited by Joel Sanders. 2nd edition. New York: Princeton Architectural Press, 1996.
Schüll, Natasha Dow. *Addiction by Design: Machine Gambling in Las Vegas*. New in Paper edition. Princeton: Princeton University Press, 2014.
Venturi, Robert, Steven Izenour, and Denise Scott Brown. *Learning from Las Vegas: The Forgotten Symbolism of Architectural Form*. Revised edition. Cambridge: MIT Press, 1977.

CHAPTER 7

Resisting the Innie/Outie Dichotomy Through Mundane Encounters: In Defense of "Spaces of Transition"

Can Koçak

Introduction

Severance, the Apple TV+ show which aired its first season in 2022, takes place in a setting where people can shift at ease between two different surgically divided selves: a work self ("innie") and a non-work self ("outie"). This service, also referred to as the severance procedure, is offered to the employees of Lumon Industries, a mysterious establishment for which the characters of the show are working. While there is a mystery surrounding the actual work carried out within the company, and specifically within the Macrodata Refinement (MDR) Department where the show spends most of its runtime, the technologies and goods manufactured there are deemed important and Lumon itself is hailed as widely successful and influential.

C. Koçak (✉)
University of Sussex, Brighton and Hove, UK
e-mail: can_kocak@hotmail.com

N. M. Isacoff and J. Dawes (eds.), *Reintegrating Severance*,
https://doi.org/10.1007/978-3-031-57448-1_7

One of the most notable aspects of the severance procedure is that neither of the selves knows about the experience of the other self. Every morning the outies go to the headquarters of Lumon Industries, located in the fictional town of Kier, PE, much like how a regular employee would go to work. They go into the building, step inside the elevator, and transform into their innie selves as the elevator goes up. Dan Erickson, the creator of the show, refers to this as a threshold that one passes, which causes the chip in the severed mind to activate and switch into an innie.[1]

Following their shift into an innie, the outie is no longer aware of what the workday entails. Until the innie walks back in the elevator and returns up to the main floor at the end of the day, everything inside the building of Lumon Industries' headquarters is a complete mystery to the outie. Similarly, the innie has no idea about what the outie's life is like, including such things as their hobbies and relationship status, and whether they have children or not. This lack of knowledge creates a profound sense of disconnect between the innies and outies, highlighting the extent to which their lives are compartmentalized and emphasizing the boundaries imposed by Lumon Industries.

If one is to consider the use of spaces in the narrative, they would see a disorienting and uncanny depiction. Lumon is the kind of workplace where employees lack precise knowledge about the nature of their work, the existence of departments beyond their own, and the layout of the building. The corridors, with their identical design and monotonous arrangement, only amplify this unsettling atmosphere. As employees navigate through the labyrinthine hallways, they become enveloped in a sense of sameness and repetition, as if trapped in an unending loop of familiarity. The lack of distinguishing features or unique elements further adds to the eerie ambiance, leaving a lingering feeling of unease and confusion.

As the innies begin to experience unease regarding their limited knowledge concerning the company they work for and grow curious about what lies beyond their department, their perception of work undergoes a change, and the dubious politics of Lumon gradually unfold. This awareness is initiated by the arrival of Helly R., who desperately tries to get out, revealing the exploitative nature of the whole severance procedure.

As this dichotomy between innie and outie is emphasized, not much room is left for what this chapter identifies as "spaces of transition"—coffee breaks, corridors, the everyday commute—, which provide mundane encounters that are valuable for individuals and communities as a way of reclaiming their "right to the city,"[2] as well as providing a form of resistance against "conspicuous production."[3] The convenient nature of this transition between work and non-work states in *Severance* is precisely what creates the disorientation of the worker, sense of uncanniness, and the capitalist exploitation that permeates the narrative universe. The near absence of these spaces of transition on the severed floor not only reinforces the isolation and confinement experienced by the characters but also reflects a broader critique of the dehumanizing effects of modern-day work culture, where the blurring of boundaries between work and personal life erodes the potential for genuine connection, autonomy, and collective resistance.

What Are "Spaces of Transition"?

Following the lockdown measures against the COVID-19 pandemic, life, for many, turned online. Lectures and seminars in universities, meetings in professional working environments, or gatherings among friends were no longer held in person, but recreated in front of digital screens. The use of "recreated" is important in this sense as it provides an idea of how online settings have been, and are being, discussed in academic and interpersonal contexts. So far, the dichotomy between these spaces has solely been examined in terms of whether online forms of sociality could provide a substitute for offline social interactions.[4] And, for better or for worse, they do. Academics can still deliver the lecture's content, employees can provide updates about their work or hear from management about their company, and people can catch up with friends or acquaintances. Whether the focus is on how lecturers could get students to turn on their videos[5] or how digital tools could foster collaboration in remote working environments,[6] the discourse seems to be trapped in the debate over whether these online meetings foster a genuine connection or not, and there is a prevailing colloquial consensus that they rarely do.

Then again, as soon as online lectures, meetings, or informal gatherings finish, people close their screens and are immediately confronted with being back in their everyday lives. They transition from an "on" state, meaning being present and engaged in an academic, professional, or personal environment, to an "off" state, where they are present in their domestic spaces and possibly engaged in leisurely activities or household chores, all with a single click. While this convenience enhances accessibility, it also signifies what is lost in the attempt to recreate offline settings within online spaces.

This chapter discusses spaces of transition as settings that offer opportunities for ordinary and chance encounters, such as corridors, thresholds, corners near water coolers, bathrooms, interior areas of transportation vehicles, or streets. Whether one is involved in pre- or post-meeting discussions, exchanging greetings with acquaintances, taking a momentary break, commuting, or simply enjoying a leisurely walk, these spaces provide opportunities for interaction, connection, and engagement.

Since they break the strict dichotomy between home and away, or work and leisure, occupying the space between one's point of origin and destination,[7] these transitional environments can be seen as liminal spaces,[8] not fully conforming to either an "on" or an "off" state. The inherent sense of uncertainty often linked to liminal spaces plays to the advantage of spaces of transition, as it allows for the elusive nature of these environments to flourish. Because of their temporary and transitory characteristics, these spaces influence one's thinking, conversations, and behaviors, injecting a touch of spontaneity amidst strict divisions.

Spaces of transition have a potential to fit within the discourse around access to public spaces, and around claiming the city itself as a setting of co-creation through negotiation.[9] While based on mundane and random encounters, the very fact that they provide opportunities for diversity and togetherness turns spaces of transition into a necessary tool for civic participation, and simultaneously, a threat to exert control over in the eyes of authority.[10] When one gives up on these encounters as they swiftly shift back and forth between work and non-work settings, they inevitably give up on novel experiences offered by urban contexts. Spaces of transition are valuable simply because they disrupt the stiff, yet still confusing on-or-off flow of everyday life, which has come to dominate professional and interpersonal settings.

According to David Harvey, Professor of Anthropology and Geography at The Graduate Center, CUNY, the concept of the right to the city extends beyond simply having the individual freedom to access urban resources.[11] It encompasses the right to transform ourselves by bringing about changes in the city. Additionally, this right is not limited to individuals but is a collective right, as the ability to reshape urbanization processes requires the exercise of collective power. Harvey argues that "The freedom to make and remake our cities and ourselves is... one of the most precious yet most neglected of our human rights."[12] By underscoring the significance of this right, its potential to empower individuals and communities to reimagine and reconstruct their urban environments in ways that align with their needs and aspirations is also highlighted.

Having established this as a collective act, one can also think about the solitary movement of people through the city, and how spaces of transition affect individuals' experience of urban settings. In his 2005 study, Michael Bull, Professor of Sound Studies at the University of Sussex, examines the utilization of iPods and explores how users, while having control over the music they listen to, also strive to "inhabit" the spaces they navigate.[13] The use of such technologies seems to connect various aspects of urban movement, effectively filling the spaces in-between communication or meetings and organizing the occupied spaces in the process.

Spaces of transition can also provide an escape from the "always on, always available" politics of our time. These liminal spaces have a potential to change the nature of the transition from "off" to "on," especially by making it further complicated than the click of a button. If one has more time for everyday contexts and mundane ways of being, they will have less time for contributing to "conspicuous production," which is a term coined by Michael Polanyi, the Hungarian-British physical chemist and sociologist, to explain how people's status within society have come to be defined by how hard they work.[14]

Psychoanalyst Josh Cohen, in his book *Not Working: Why We Have to Stop*, delves into the prevailing cultural norms that prioritize work, connectivity, and an incessant influx of information.[15] Cohen highlights how a perpetual state of busyness infiltrates even our most tranquil moments. With regard to the increasing prevalence of burnout among individuals, he puts forth the following argument that sheds light on this phenomenon: "Not working has almost always been valued only to the extent that it serves the cause of work. It is time we spoke up for not working, in all its creative possibilities, as its own value.... The art of doing nothing is disappearing. Little wonder so many of us are burning out."[16] With their potential for ordinary and serendipitous encounters, spaces of transition exemplify the framework presented here. These spaces offer opportunities for individuals to momentarily step away from the constant demands of work and embrace the value of simply being present and engaging in unproductive activities, fostering a much-needed respite from the burnout-inducing culture of constant busyness.

It should be noted that none of these environments inherently resist work or disrupt labor relations. For example, past studies have shown the significance of commuting in maintaining an efficient labor market,[17] which suggests that commuting actively contributes to work rather than being considered as part of an "off" or an in-between state. Nevertheless, this does not negate the possibility of these spaces transforming into such contexts, and it is precisely this potential that this chapter seeks to examine.

Another inquiry regarding spaces of transition revolves around their exclusivity to offline environments or if they can be replicated in online settings. Despite efforts made with collaboration apps like Donut and Watercooler or by exploring the possibility of generating similar effects through one-on-one conversations in Zoom calls, the prevailing agreement suggests that capturing serendipity in the virtual realm remains challenging.[18] This challenge highlights the inherent difficulty of fully recreating the unpredictable and spontaneous nature of offline spaces in online environments. It suggests that while technological advancements have provided avenues for connection and communication, the organic and unforeseen encounters commonly experienced in physical spaces of transition may be more elusive to replicate virtually.

All Space, No Transition: *Severance*

In labor law, a severance package is provided to employees whose employment contracts are involuntarily terminated or severed from a company.[19] This process is designed to safeguard the recently unemployed by facilitating their shift from a consistent income to a phase that may entail uncertainty or hardship. It is intended to offer financial support, access to benefits, and necessary resources to aid in their reintegration into the job market or during a period of career transition. A well-designed severance package not only offers immediate financial assistance but also provides practical support and resources to empower individuals in navigating job loss and career transitions, aiming to mitigate the impact of unemployment and foster a more equitable approach to labor relations.[20] Ironically, the "severance" procedure in the show takes on a different meaning than the way it provides legal reassurances to workers within the corporate world, symbolizing the company's power over employees' livelihoods. This service provided by Lumon Industries can be seen as a reflection of capitalism's way of managing, and in some cases, taming,[21] various forms of resistance and dissent within the workforce.

The premise of *Severance*, which is promoted as an "allegorical twist"[22] or a "dystopian take"[23] on work–life balance, spins this idea around, simultaneously recreating the on/off dichotomy rejected by spaces of transition by clearly separating an innie from an outie.[24] The elevator in Lumon's headquarters is important in this sense, as it is the space where this shift from outie to innie, and from innie to outie, happens.

At first glance, it might be tempting to refer to Lumon's elevator as a space of transition. Indeed, it marks a change; both from a non-work self to a work self, and from a non-work setting to a setting of work. However, much like the shift from an online meeting to a domestic space, this shift happens with a single click, caused by the activation of a chip, which leaves not much scope for what the idea of a transition entails. Additionally, as opposed to what Dan Erickson says, Lumon's elevator does not seem to be in line with the literature around "threshold spaces." Threshold spaces are considered neither indoors nor outdoors, residing in the spatial uncertainty between entry and exit, and generating anticipation for what lies ahead while encompassing both reception and departure.[25] They are also approached as common spaces, accessible to multiple individuals, lacking a dominant authority that supervises their use, and fostering connections by not being restricted to an exclusive community.[26] Although it facilitates movement between floors, the elevator falls in line with neither of these features of threshold spaces, as it is clearly inside Lumon's building, is controlled by the company, and can only be used by employees, rather than being open to a diverse range of people. As the space that hosts the change between two selves through a single and sudden click, rather than featuring a longer process inherent to a transition, the elevator can instead be referred to as a "space of transformation," involving a profound and fundamental change as opposed to an adjustment or adaptation.

The MDR office occupies a vast, mostly unused space with four tightly packed cubicles at its center. In this windowless environment, desks and computers lack distinct models, makes, or architectural purposes intentionally, creating a sense of timelessness.[27] While the desks have barriers to obscure colleagues' views during work, they can be moved up and down by the characters, although this feature is rarely utilized. This aesthetic led Jeremy Hindle, the production designer, to dub the office a "haunted playground,"[28] where the term "play" is reminiscent of Jacques Tati's 1967 film, *Playtime*, a major influence on the show's stylistic choices.[29]

Playtime portrays fragmented scenes of life within a heavily industrialized and stylized urban environment, evoking a similar disorienting atmosphere to that experienced within Lumon's building.

Within the suite housing the desks, there is also a kitchenette where MDR staff can spend time and "grab a snack to maintain peak performance and productivity."[30] It is noteworthy that the show's promotional video, mirroring the language and approach of the fictional company, only acknowledges seemingly non-work activities insofar as they serve work and worker efficiency. The presence of branding on the machinery, coupled with the restriction that any food can only be accessed through a limited number of tokens provided by the company, reinforces the notion of leisure being meticulously corporatized and controlled by Lumon Industries.

The corridors, typically spaces for chance encounters, take on an uncanny and disorienting quality within the narrative universe of *Severance*. With the identical color and size of the corridors, the characters as well as the audience find it challenging to navigate through them. Director Ben Stiller explicitly notes that the creators intentionally sought this uniformity when filming the corridors.

> We built the entire "Severance" floor, and it took up the entire stage, and all of the hallways connect to each other. But we also always wanted it to feel a little bit confusing, so a lot of the time, we'll do the whole "Star Trek" trick where they have one hallway and just shoot it different ways or change one door or something on it. ... You could just completely get lost in the halls on the set.[31]

Here Stiller references *Star Trek: The Next Generation*, which employs a single hallway set that is repeatedly reused for various shots, employing alterations to the set dressing and capturing it from different perspectives to create an illusion of increased depth within the starship Enterprise.[32] Based on Stiller's explanations, it becomes evident that the uncanny ambiance of the corridors in Lumon's headquarters is also heightened through techniques such as shooting a single hallway from various angles or making subtle modifications. This amplification intensifies the feeling of getting lost within the complex and intricate layout of the company's headquarters, contributing to the intended sterile atmosphere.

While working hard is celebrated in Lumon Industries, innies also get to enjoy exclusive perks. One such example is "The Music/Dance Experience," a non-work-related activity enforced upon Macrodata Refiners upon reaching 75 perfect completion of their files. Orchestrated by Mr. Milchick, Lumon's security overseer and administrative staff member, the event mandates employees to select an instrument and music genre. Through the use of strobe lights, serene dancing participants, and forced smiles, an unsettling and eerie ambiance is established, serving as a satirical commentary on all types of corporate activities.

Evoking the infamous corporate pizza parties, which have become a symbol of employers attempting to deceive their employees without providing adequate pay,[33] the Music/Dance Experience actually holds the potential to exacerbate discontentment and alienation among the workforce. These gestures overlook the difficulties of managing on a low salary, further emphasizing the evident disconnection between managers, employers, and the real-life struggles encountered by their employees.[34] The fun imposed by corporate activities differs from the enjoyment found in leisurely pursuits. The former tends to resemble virtual water coolers, which often fail to fully replicate real-life interactions. Since Music/ Dance Experiences take place within the workspace and are organized by managers and attended by co-workers, they cannot be genuinely regarded as non-work leisure activities. Hence, it is not surprising that outies are not invited to participate in any Music/Dance Experience.

Despite the absurdity of these parties and the childish incentives offered, such as the "Melon Bar," the "Pre-Waffle Party Egg Bar," or the "Waffle Party," they remain highly desired by the staff. This raises the question of why this is the case. It could be because the severance procedure not only severs their consciousness but also enables Lumon to establish an entirely new environment with fresh expectations. Since they already resemble children with their innocence and inexperience with the outer world,[35] the innies are further infantilized and distracted by being told what to desire.

While examples show Lumon's unconventional interpretation of fun, they also put a dark twist on the concept of a "break." Within their headquarters, there exists a location known as the Break Room. It is a place that can only be reached through a narrow, dimly lit hallway, allowing just one person to pass through at a time. Employees are directed there as a consequence of violating the company's rules. Inside the Break Room, those who have misbehaved are joined by Milchick, who compels them to repeatedly recite a mantra centered on forgiveness and obedience until they are utterly drained. In this context, a "break" does not signify a moment of leisure but rather alludes to the act of shattering one's spirit.

In addition to the division between the employees' work and non-work selves, the names of Lumon employees are also severed in the workplace. They are addressed by abbreviated versions of their surnames, like "Helly R" or "Mark S." Since names play a fundamental role in shaping an individual's sense of self and existence,[36] this practice further emphasizes the depersonalization experienced by the employees, who are stripped of their full identities. By removing the full names, Lumon reinforces a culture where employees are reduced to mere tools, further diminishing their personal significance within the organization.

In line with all of these things, *Severance* highlights how the lack of spaces of transition exacerbates the sense of depersonalization and the erosion of identity within Lumon Industries. In a world where employees are confined to the rigid structures of the workplace, corridors devoid of any meaningful encounters, and activities that blur the boundaries between work and leisure, the opportunity for individuals to express their authentic selves and reclaim their full identities becomes severely limited. The absence of these transitional spaces, such as communal areas or moments of casual interaction, robs the employees of the chance to connect with others on a human level and reinforces the dehumanizing environment of Lumon. Consequently, the characters in *Severance* find themselves trapped in a cycle of conformity and isolation, further entrenching the loss of their individuality and personal agency.

While the severance process adheres to strict rules and protocols, there are certain exceptions. The sixth episode, entitled "Hide and Seek," reveals that innies can also be "activated" outside of the workplace, with a procedure termed the "Overtime Contingency." In order to maintain tight control over this procedure and keep it exclusively within the company's grasp, a complex and intricately detailed sequence of steps is required to activate it. This highlights Lumon's exploitation of its workers as one witnesses a storyline where even a severed individual works "overtime," reminiscent of the prevalent phenomenon of unpaid extra hours in contemporary work culture.[37] Therefore, it is not surprising that the most significant act of rebellion so far in this narrative universe occurs when workers seize their autonomy and independently carry out this process, granting multiple innies their first taste of the external world.

Conclusion

As this chapter was being written, the production of *Severance*'s second season was abruptly suspended as a result of a strike initiated by the Writers Guild of America on May 2, 2023. The strike was motivated by a call for improved pay, equity, and safeguards against the growing influence of artificial intelligence.[38] This turn of events presents a striking juxtaposition with the very themes explored in the show itself, shedding light on the exploitative consequences that can arise when the concept of work–life balance is abused by employers. In the end, the demands voiced by *Severance*'s innies turned out to be a poignant reflection of the real-world challenges and struggles faced by industry professionals.

The suspension of production due to strike action also sheds light on the significance of spaces of transition. In the narrative universe, the lack of spaces of transition within Lumon Industries contributes to the depersonalization and loss of identity experienced by the employees. Similarly, the strike action taken by the writers in the real world reflects a need for transitional spaces within the creative industry, where workers can advocate for their rights, voice their demands, and negotiate for better working conditions. By halting the production and creating a disruption in the usual flow of work, the strike becomes a symbolic space of transition, allowing the writers to assert their identities and reinforce their value within the industry. It serves as a reminder that spaces of transition are not only crucial within fictional narratives but also in real-life contexts, enabling individuals to reclaim their identities and advocate for their rights in the face of exploitative practices.

This situation also emphasizes how the aspect of randomness and sociality within spaces of transition can lead to salvation. It is not surprising that one of the few instances of resistance within the narrative manifests through a prohibited interdepartmental interaction, when Irving from MDR develops an affection for Burt from Optics and Design. These acts of connection emerge organically rather than being mandated by the company, highlighting the subversive nature of genuine sociality. Furthermore, Mark's access to a self-help book from the outside world, *The You You Are*, authored by his brother-in-law Ricken Hale, serves as a reminder for innies to reclaim their authentic identities.

Indeed, in the narrative universe of *Severance*, Lumon's exertion of control over both innies and outies is achieved by deliberately eliminating the significance of thresholds and disconnecting them from the in-between spaces that facilitate connections and transitions. By removing these transitional spaces, Lumon effectively severs the link between individuals and the opportunities for chance encounters, ordinary interactions, and shared experiences that occur within those spaces.

The absence of spaces of transition denies innies and outies the chance to bridge their worlds and gain a holistic understanding of their workplace environment. Innies, confined to their own departments, remain oblivious to the broader dynamics and relationships forming among their colleagues, hindering the development of a sense of community. On the other hand, outies, excluded from the inner workings of Lumon, are deprived of the shared experiences and camaraderie that naturally emerge in spaces of transition. By controlling the flow of information and limiting access to spaces of transition, Lumon maintains a hierarchical power structure and perpetuates a sense of isolation and detachment among its employees. This deliberate manipulation reinforces the notion that individuals are merely cogs in a machine, devoid of agency, and stripped of their full identities. The absence of spaces of transition not only reflects the dystopian reality depicted in *Severance* but also serves as a commentary on the importance of such spaces in fostering connection, collaboration, and a sense of belonging within organizations. It highlights the detrimental effects of a system that prioritizes control and conformity over human connection and individuality.

Even though the idea to completely forget about work may initially seem appealing, this also has implications for how leisure is portrayed. As the show focuses on characters finding themselves in an eternal work cycle, the presence and absence of leisure are simultaneously apparent. For instance, the creators do not feature domestic spaces and domestic labor within the show, highlighting the confined nature of the characters' lives and emphasizing the dominance of the work environment. This omission underscores the profound impact of work on their existence and the limited opportunities for genuine leisure and personal fulfillment.

In order for the characters in *Severance* to introduce actual balance in their lives and reclaim their leisure time, their "eight hours for what they will,"[39] they should opt for spaces of transition and disarrange the ease in achieving states of being "on" or "off." It is the absence of these transitional spaces in the narrative universe of *Severance* that causes and contributes to the chaos and challenges faced by the characters.

Notes

1. Fred Topel, "'Severance' Memory Procedure and Elevator Barrier Explained," https://www.cheatsheet.com/entertainment/severance-memory-procedure-elevator-barrier-explained.html/ (accessed June 16, 2023).
2. David Harvey, "The Right to the City," 23.
3. Michael Polanyi, "Towards a Theory of Conspicuous Production," 90.
4. Sofia Johansson, "Connection or Disconnection? Two Generations in Sweden Discuss Online Sociality," in *Use and Views of Media in Sweden & Russia: A Comparative Study in St. Petersburg & Stockholm*, 271–296; Lucy Osler, "Feeling Togetherness Online: A Phenomenological Sketch of Online Communal Experiences."; Mark Wong, "Hidden Youth? A New Perspective on the Sociality of Young People 'Withdrawn' in the Bedroom in a Digital Age."
5. Frank R. Castelli and Mark A. Sarvary, "Why Students Do Not Turn on Their Video Cameras During Online Classes and an Equitable and Inclusive Plan to Encourage Them to Do so."
6. Markus Schmidtner, Claudia Doering, and Holger Timinger, "Agile Working During COVID-19 Pandemic," 19.
7. Wei-Jue Huang, Honggen Xiao, and Sha Wang, "Airports as Liminal Space," 2.
8. Victor, Turner, "Liminal to Liminoid, in Play, Flow, and Ritual: An Essay in Comparative Symbology."
9. Henri Lefebvre, *Writings on Cities*, 237.
10. Dilara Öztekin, Emir Aydoğan and Bahar Bayhan, "Yaşanabilir konutu savunmak," https://textumdergi.net/yasanabilir-konutu-savunmak/ (accessed June 16, 2023).
11. Ibid., 2, 23.
12. Ibid., 2, 23.
13. Michael Bull, "No Dead Air! The iPod and the Culture of Mobile Listening," 344.
14. Ibid., 3.
15. Josh Cohen, *Not Working: Why We Have to Stop.*
16. Ibid., xxxvii.
17. Manfred M. Fischer, Kenneth John Button, and P. Nijkamp, "Introduction," in *Modern Classics in Regional Science Series, No. 5: Regional Housing and Labour Markets*; Martin Lux and Petr

Sunega, "Labour Mobility and Housing: The Impact of Housing Tenure and Housing Affordability on Labour Migration in the Czech Republic," 489; Jeffrey E. Zabel, "Migration, Housing Market and Labor Market Responses to Employment Shocks," 267.

18. Paul Levy, "Companies Are Trying to Connect Remote Workers with 'Virtual Water Coolers'—But It's Harder Than It Sounds," https://theconversation.com/companies-are-trying-to-connect-remote-workers-with-virtual-water-coolers-but-its-harder-than-it-sounds-146505 (accessed September 23, 2023).
19. "SEVERANCE PAY LAW, 5723-1963," ILO, https://www.landmark.edu/uploads/pages/doc/Chicago-Manual-of-Style-15th-ed.pdf (accessed June 21, 2023).
20. Brigitte Yuille, "The Layoff Payoff: A Severance Package," *Investopedia*, https://www.investopedia.com/articles/pf/08/negotiating-severance-agreements.asp (accessed September 23, 2023).
21. Daniel Bell, "The Cultural Contradictions of Capitalism," 21.
22. Alison Herman, "'Severance' Offers a Surreal, Allegorical Twist on Work-Life Balance," https://www.theringer.com/tv/2022/2/18/22940057/severance-apple-tv-plus-review-adam-scott-work-life-balance (accessed June 21, 2023).
23. Scarlett Harris, "Severance Can Only Imagine a World in Which Our Work-Life Balance Is Even Worse," https://www.sheknows.com/feature/severance-work-life-balance-2538025/ (accessed June 21, 2023).
24. It is interesting that another fictional work titled *Severance*, the 2018 novel written by Ling Ma, also encompasses a bleak atmosphere, symbolizing life itself under late capitalism. In the realm of fiction, the term "severance" appears to be interpreted quite differently compared to its original significance within labor law.
25. Till Boettger, *Threshold Spaces: Transitions in Architecture. Analysis and Design Tools*, 24.
26. Stavros Stavrides, "Common Space as Threshold Space: Urban Commoning in Struggles to Re-appropriate Public Space," 11.
27. Jackson McHenry, "The Stories Behind *Severance*'s Eerie Office Design," https://www.vulture.com/article/severance-office-design-explained.html (accessed September 29, 2023).
28. Ibid.

29. Saloni Gajjar, "How *Severance* created that Brilliantly Hellish Office," https://www.avclub.com/how-severance-created-its-brilliantly-hellish-office-se-1848720112 (accessed September 29, 2023).
30. Apple Original Films (@AppleFilms), "Lumon Has a Well-Stocked Kitchenette Where Employees Can Grab a Snack to Maintain Peak Performance and Productivity. #Severance https://apple.co/-severance-." *X*, March 12, 2022, 12:07 a.m., https://twitter.com/AppleFilms/status/1502436106872127489.
31. Joshua Meyer, "Severance's Practical Hallways Were Made Possible By A Star Trek 'Trick' [Comic-Con]," https://www.slashfilm.com/936813/severances-practical-hallways-were-made-possible-by-a-star-trek-trick-comic-con/ (accessed June 29, 2023).
32. Alexander Zalben, "23 Secrets We Learned on the Star Trek: Discovery Set," https://www.tvguide.com/news/star-trek-discovery-set-visit-spoilers/ (accessed June 29, 2023).
33. Ashley Rodriguez, "How the Pizza Party Became the Symbol of Bad Bosses Everywhere," https://bossbarista.substack.com/p/how-the-pizza-party-became-the-symbol (accessed June 29, 2023).
34. Shelly Fagan, "Pizza Parties Are No Substitute for Living Wages and Healthcare," https://medium.datadriveninvestor.com/pizza-parties-are-no-substitute-for-living-wages-and-healthcare-8c4666d72c72 (accessed June 29, 2023).
35. Emma Stefansky, "An Ode to the Delicious, Evil Food in 'Severance'," https://www.thrillist.com/entertainment/nation/severance-apple-tv-plus-food (accessed September 24, 2023).
36. Yonat Zwebner and others, "We Look Like Our Names: The Manifestation of Name Stereotypes in Facial Appearance," 537.
37. Alex Christian, "How Working Unpaid Hours Became Part of the Job," https://www.bbc.com/worklife/article/20211013-how-working-unpaid-hours-became-part-of-the-job (accessed September 29, 2023).
38. Mandalit del Barco, "Striking Hollywood Writers Say Major Film Studios Don't Understand What a Screenwriter Does," https://www.npr.org/2023/06/25/1184198841/striking-hollywood-writers-say-major-film-studios-dont-understand-what-a-screenw (accessed June 30, 2023).
39. Philip S. Foner and David R. Roediger, *Our Own Time: A History of American Labor and the Working Day*, 98.

Bibliography

Apple Original Films (@AppleFilms). "Lumon Has a Well-Stocked Kitchenette Where Employees Can Grab a Snack to Maintain Peak Performance and Productivity." #Severance https://apple.co/-severance-X, March 12, 2022, 12:07 a.m., https://twitter.com/AppleFilms/status/1502436106872127489.

Bell, Daniel. "The Cultural Contradictions of Capitalism." *The Journal of Aesthetic Education* 6 (January–April 1972): 11–38.

Boettger, Till. *Threshold Spaces: Transitions in Architecture. Analysis and Design Tools*. Berlin, München, Boston: Birkhäuser, 2014.

Bull, Michael. "No Dead Air! The iPod and the Culture of Mobile Listening." *Leisure Studies* 24, no. 4 (October 2005): 343–355.

Castelli, Frank R. and Mark A. Sarvary. "Why Students Do Not Turn on Their Video Cameras During Online Classes and an Equitable and Inclusive Plan to Encourage Them to Do So." *Ecology and Evolution* 11, no. 8 (January 10, 2021): 3447–3655.

Christian, Alex. "How Working Unpaid Hours Became Part of the Job." *BBC*, October 19, 2021. https://www.bbc.com/worklife/article/20211013-how-working-unpaid-hours-became-part-of-the-job (accessed September 29, 2023).

Cohen, Josh. *Not Working: Why We Have to Stop*. London: Granta, 2018.

del Barco, Mandalit. "Striking Hollywood Writers Say Major Film Studios Don't Understand What a Screenwriter Does." *NPR*, June 25, 2023. https://www.npr.org/2023/06/25/1184198841/striking-hollywood-writers-say-major-film-studios-dont-understand-what-a-screenw (accessed June 30, 2023).

Fagan, Shelly. "Pizza Parties Are No Substitute for Living Wages and Healthcare." *Medium*, July 13, 2021. https://medium.datadriveninvestor.com/pizza-parties-are-no-substitute-for-living-wages-and-healthcare-8c4666d72c72 (accessed June 29, 2023).

Fischer, Manfred M., Kenneth John Button, and Peter Nijkamp. "Introduction". In Manfred M. Fischer, Kenneth John Button and Peter Nijkamp, eds. *Modern Classics in Regional Science Series, No. 5: Regional Housing and Labour Markets*. Cheltenham: Edward Elgar, 1996.

Foner, Philip S. and David R. Roediger. *Our Own Time: A History of American Labor and the Working Day*. London and New York: Verso, 1989.

Gajjar, Saloni. "How Severance Created That Brilliantly Hellish Office." *A.V. Club*, April 1, 2022. https://www.avclub.com/how-severance-created-its-brilliantly-hellish-office-se-1848720112 (accessed September 29, 2023).

Harris, Scarlett. "Severance Can Only Imagine a World in Which Our Work-Life Balance Is Even Worse." *SheKnows*, July 12, 2022. https://www.sheknows.com/feature/severance-work-life-balance-2538025/ (accessed June 21, 2023).

Harvey, David. "The Right to the City." *New Left Review* 53, no. 2 (September/ October 2008): 23–40.

Herman, Alison. "'Severance' Offers a Surreal, Allegorical Twist on Work-Life Balance." *The Ringer*, February 18, 2022. https://www.theringer.com/tv/ 2022/2/18/22940057/severance-apple-tv-plus-review-adam-scott-work-life-balance (accessed June 21, 2023).

Huang, Wei-Jue, Honggen Xiao, and Sha Wang, "Airports as Liminal Space." *Annals of Tourism Research* 70 (February 4, 2018): 1–13.

Johansson, Sofia. "Connection or Disconnection? Two Generations in Sweden Discuss Online Sociality." In Cecilia von Feilitzen and Peter Petrov, eds. *Use and Views of Media in Sweden & Russia: A Comparative Study in St. Petersburg & Stockholm*. Huddinge: Södertörns högskola, 2011.

Lefebvre, Henri. *Writings on Cities*. Cambridge, MA: Blackwell, 1996.

Levy, Paul. "Companies Are Trying to Connect Remote Workers with 'Virtual Water Coolers'—But It's Harder Than It Sounds." *The Conversation*, September 23, 2020. https://theconversation.com/companies-are-trying-to-connect-remote-workers-with-virtual-water-coolers-but-its-harder-than-it-sou nds-146505 (accessed September 23, 2023).

Lux, Martin and Petr Sunega. "Labour Mobility and Housing: The Impact of Housing Tenure and Housing Affordability on Labour Migration in the Czech Republic." *Urban Studies* 49, no. 3 (February 2012): 489–504.

Ma, Ling. *Severance*. New York: Farrar, Straus and Giroux, 2018.

McHenry, Jackson. "The Stories Behind *Severance*'s Eerie Office Design." *Vulture*, April 1, 2022. https://www.vulture.com/article/severance-office-design-explained.html (accessed September 29, 2023).

Meyer, Joshua. "Severance's Practical Hallways Were Made Possible by a Star Trek 'Trick' [Comic-Con]." */Film*, July 26, 2022. https://www.slashfilm. com/936813/severances-practical-hallways-were-made-possible-by-a-star-trek-trick-comic-con/ (accessed June 29, 2023).

Osler, Lucy. "Feeling Togetherness Online: A Phenomenological Sketch of Online Communal Experiences." *Phenomenology and the Cognitive Sciences* 19 (June 21, 2019): 569–588.

Öztekin, Dilara, Emir Aydoğan, and Bahar Bayhan. "Yaşanabilir konutu savunmak." *Textum*, March 6, 2022. https://textumdergi.net/yasanabilir-kon utu-savunmak/ (accessed June 16, 2023).

Polanyi, Michael. "Towards a Theory of Conspicuous Production." *Soviet Survey* 34 (October–December 1960): 90–99.

Rodriguez, Ashley. "How the Pizza Party Became the Symbol of Bad Bosses Everywhere." *Boss Barista*, April 21, 2022. https://bossbarista.substack.com/ p/how-the-pizza-party-became-the-symbol (accessed June 29, 2023).

Schmidtner, Markus, Claudia Doering, and Holger Timinger. "Agile Working During COVID-19 Pandemic." *IEEE Engineering Management Review* 49, no. 2 (March 31, 2021): 18–32.

"SEVERANCE PAY LAW." ILO. https://www.ilo.org/dyn/natlex/docs/ELECTRONIC/36154/81478/F1008479200/ISR36154.pdf.

Stavrides, Stavros. "Common Space as Threshold Space: Urban Commoning in Struggles to Re-appropriate Public Space." *Footprint* 16 (Spring 2015): 9–20.

Topel, Fred. "'Severance' Memory Procedure and Elevator Barrier Explained." *Showbiz Cheat Sheet*, February 18, 2022. https://www.cheatsheet.com/entertainment/severance-memory-procedure-elevator-barrier-explained.html/ (accessed June 16, 2023).

Turner, Victor. "Liminal to Liminoid, in Play, Flow, and Ritual: An Essay in Comparative Symbology." *Rice Institute Pamphlet—Rice University Studies* 60, no. 3 (1974): 53–92.

Wong, Mark. "Hidden youth? A New Perspective on the Sociality of Young People 'Withdrawn' in the Bedroom in a Digital Age." *New Media & Society* 22, no. 7 (July 22, 2020): 1227–1244.

Yuille, Brigitte. "The Layoff Payoff: A Severance Package." *Investopedia*. https://www.investopedia.com/articles/pf/08/negotiating-severance-agreements.asp.

Zabel, Jeffrey E. "Migration, Housing Market and Labor Market Responses to Employment Shocks." *Journal of Urban Economics* 72, no. 2–3 (September-November 2012): 267–284.

Zalben, Alexander. "23 Secrets We Learned on the Star Trek: Discovery Set." *TV Guide*, September 10, 2017. https://www.tvguide.com/news/star-trek-discovery-set-visit-spoilers/ (accessed June 29, 2023).

Zwebner, Y., A. Sellier, N. Rosenfeld, J. Goldenberg, and R. Mayo. "We Look Like Our Names: The Manifestation of Name Stereotypes in Facial Appearance." *Journal of Personality and Social Psychology* 112, no. 4 (April 2017): 527–554.

PART III

Agency, Autonomy, and Alienation

CHAPTER 8

An Investigation of Marxist Alienation in the Postmodern Workplace in Apple TV's *Severance*

Mayank Kejriwal

In his critiques of capitalism, Karl Marx theorized about workers' (and more generally, human) alienation that is the inevitable consequence of a capitalist organization of labor, and that arises from both the *product* and *process* of labor. The former refers to the incapacity of the worker to own the products of their own labor, while the latter refers to the incapacity of the worker to direct their own actions and consequently, to freely develop their (physical and mental) energies. Alienation today has a legacy dating back to the Industrial Revolution, evoked by factory floors and office cubicles that render a worker as a disposable and proverbial "cog in a machine." Apple's hit TV show *Severance*, where a procedure can be used to separate a worker's memories of their workplace from all else, offers us an engaging window to study the essence of alienation in a postmodern

M. Kejriwal (✉)
Information Sciences Institute, Industrial and Systems Engineering, University of Southern California, Marina del Rey, CA, USA
e-mail: kejriwal@isi.edu

N. M. Isacoff and J. Dawes (eds.), *Reintegrating Severance*,
https://doi.org/10.1007/978-3-031-57448-1_8

workplace from the viewpoints of process and self. *Severance* dramatizes elements of, and fears surrounding, the workplace that trace a direct lineage to Marx, and resembles similar dramatizations in influential works of literature and art, including Kafka's *The Castle* (showcasing a terrifying dramatization of increased social bureaucratization), the absurdist works of Albert Camus and movies like *The Machine* (2004). Severance also captures the essence of workers' resistance against the "conspiracy" of alienation. Such depictions dramatize and symbolize real-life resistance movements embodied in the concept of "quiet quitting" and the "Great Resignation."

Background

The Industrial Revolution paved the way for a new philosophy of work,[1] and laid the foundation for what would eventually come to be termed *alienation*. As discussed by Allen Wood in his treatise on Marx's philosophical thought,[2] Marx used the German equivalents of the term (*Entfremdung* and *Entäusserung*) in his works in the mid-1840s to label the feeling increasingly experienced by workers: an indifferent separation between entities that typically, or naturally, are inter-harmonious. However, themes of fear and alienation featured widely in other writings as well. Alienation can be traced back to Hegel , who used the term in its modern dictionary sense: people feel alienated when they feel out of place in the social world.[3] Nearly a century before Henry Ford's factory lines, there was a real sense that labor and capital were interchangeable parts in an economic equation, but with different tradeoffs and costs. For a corporation, or entities otherwise owning the "means of production," the task became one of optimization: what mix of labor and capital would maximize profit or return? The question remains one of paramount importance even today, with a formal treatment being a universal component of business school curricula. It dictates policies such as wage setting, worker incentives, resource allocation, and investment decisions.[4,5] However, this paradigm, with its unfeeling mathematics that makes man and machine interchangeable, is both the cause and a representation of the anxiety, disempowerment, and alienation felt (but not always articulated) by workers across industries and income levels.

Originally, Marx predicted that owners of the *means of production* (such as the bourgeoisie and, in the modern era, companies owned by the bourgeoisie as shareholders) would choose to replace capital with labor, and that wages would eventually reach subsistence levels.[6] He did not fully anticipate, or account for the effect of, trends, such as workers' rights (including minimum wage) and government-led regulations for minimizing occupational hazards. While one might argue that minimum-wage jobs are the equivalent of work for subsistence wages that Marx predicted, it is still telling that even fast-food restaurants are always on the quest to reduce costs even further by implementing new technology. An extreme example at the time of writing is Flippy, a robot that was tested by the midwestern fast-food chain White Castle to flip burgers. In 2022, amidst a labor shortage, the chain announced that it would "hire" Flippy 2 in a hundred locations. Perhaps anticipating the unease that this might cause, Miso Robotics, the maker of the robots, was quoted by *Today* in an official statement that the (emphases mine) "improved workflow allows for the *redeployment* of team members" and that the robot would "create a working environment for its human coworkers that *maximizes the efficiency* of the kitchen."[7]

When all costs are taken into account, including the cost of complying with labor laws, even with subsistence-like wages, companies are finding it more economically prudent to replace labor with capital. Technology, a key component of capital, is central to *Severance*, and one might wonder if technology to partition mind and memory in the manner demonstrated in the show is realistically achievable in the foreseeable future. With companies like Elon Musk's Neuralink[8] investigating such techniques, we have to consider the possibility. When it comes to the development and commercialization of any technology, one must also confront the realities of Wright's law. First formulated by Theodore Wright in 1936, the eponymous law states that for a cumulative doubling of units produced, the cost of producing each unit will fall by a constant percentage.[9] In simpler language, the law aims to quantify the benefits of experience: as companies produce more, they are able to reduce the costs owing to the experience gained and the "learning" accomplished during that process of production. Within the computing profession, many are familiar with a specific instantiation of Wright's law in the semiconductor and advanced chips industry; namely, Moore's law. The law (formulated in 1965 by Gordon Moore, co-founder of Intel) states that the number of transistors on a microchip doubles every two years, even as the cost of computing halves.[10]

In part, such massive productivity is due to the fact that companies face constant market pressure to increase productivity or "efficiency" (or similar such metrics); they are driven by their own paranoias and fears about being disrupted and outcompeted out of existence.[11] In some industries, such as labor-intensive sectors of hospitality, such focus on efficiency has indeed led to subsistence-like wages, but in other sectors where individual worker productivity is more paramount than a myopic emphasis on cost, white-collar salaries have generally seen a disproportionate rise in recent decades. We make this point to demonstrate, as have others,[12] that Marx's original predictions may have been incorrect in their effects, but economists have been re-examining some of his observations and insights into new light, especially given that the capitalist way of life has increasingly come under attack, and economies have become over-financialized.[13] In the initial post-war period, median incomes were rising at a healthy pace in blue-collar industries as well before a range of complex factors led to real income stagnation (most acutely, for males).[14] Therefore, it is not evident, at least on reasonable time scales of decades and across industries, that the natural equilibrium level of wages is the subsistence wage. Labor continues to be important, and may continue to be important in many industries, as the global population ages. Technology, such as the procedure shown in *Severance*, does not always supplant labor, but is instead used to enhance worker productivity at any cost. At its core, *Severance* explores and dramatizes precisely this issue. This obsessive drive to extract every ounce of productivity from workers is also the cause of burnout, and in the longer term, alienation and social anomie.

Marx's thesis is still correct in its spirit that workers will be increasingly disenfranchised and disempowered, despite all efforts by governments, labor rights movements, and even the recent resurgence of organized labor. Overall median income has stagnated since the 1970s while a parallel rise has occurred in "fixed" costs such as health insurance, housing, rent, and education, at least in the United States. Elizabeth Warren documented the falling living standards of the American middle class in her book and the alarming rise in bankruptcies even in two-income families. Certainly, it is undeniable that the market for "well-paid jobs" has become more competitive, if not elusive. College education is now touted as a necessity,[15] despite its crippling cost and the near impossibility of discharging student loan debt even in bankruptcy. Regions of the country where a college education were not (once) necessary and that were hotbeds of manufacturing have fallen prey in recent decades to the opioid crisis and high rates of depression, mental illness, suicide, and even destitution.[16]

An inevitable consequence of these individual, complex phenomena is that getting and keeping a well-paid job has become a source of constant anxiety for many workers. Anxiety can turn into fear, especially when rumors of massive layoffs are rife, as has been the case even for technology jobs in early 2023. The recency of phenomena such as the "Great Resignation" suggests that workers go to work out of economic necessity, and are willing to quit at abnormally high rates given the economic opportunity to do so. High-paying jobs, far from yielding financial security, have sometimes employed tactics referred [17] to as "golden handcuffs" that chain their lucky recipients to an economic life that can only be sustained through the job (and the money that comes with it), even if it has a detrimental impact on their personal and professional agency, and consequently, their sense of wellbeing.

Alienation in *Severance*

If we could separate this source of anxiety and wall it off in a part of our brains that is only active during our time at work, would we choose to do so? *Severance's* appeal in popular culture lies in its visceral response to this question. Intriguingly, the show subversively suggests that it is not work, but pain in private life, that people may choose to segregate.[18] Work then becomes a relatively "safe" well-defined space where emotion (and emotional intensity) is numbed, meaning is found in the mundane, and roles, hierarchies, and behaviors are well enumerated and bounded. Nevertheless, the undercurrent of anxiety in the workplace is only too apparent, even in *Severance*, although its source does not seem to arise from the fear of losing one's job.

In real workplaces, the anxiety can be more intense, and even crippling, especially when one is only too aware of the "reserve unemployment" that has been predicted by Marx,[19] and other economic thinkers since. The reserve unemployment force is a relatively fixed cadre of unemployed (usually rotating) *potential* workers, who are only too happy to take the position of an unproductive or otherwise uncooperative worker who does not toe the company line or comply with company "values." Despite being fed the usual trope of being "valued" and being an "integral" part of an organization, workers know deep down inside that they are, in fact, very dispensable. In a toxic work culture, this manifests through the constant threat of being on the firing line, but even in a good capitalistic work culture, it is viewed as a carrot-stick approach. Workers are expected to be productive, compliant, and conforming, putting the company and its values first, even though the same promise cannot be granted to their own employment. This has not always been true; in an earlier era, it was not uncommon for workers to stay in a company lifelong (and receive a pension thereafter), yielding a more symbiotic relationship that was perhaps the benign capitalistic representation of previously feudal serf-landlord relations.

A review of workplace-related pop culture suggests that Americans have generally felt uncomfortable facing the issues of alienation and anxiety at work head-on, even in a fictionalized portrayal. A similar discomfort can be seen in portrayals of aging, and the treatment of old people, in a society that is known to value youth.[20] Considering the workspace, series like *The Office* show a chirpy, vicariously lived portrayal of work that does not quite come across as real. More modern portrayals of the workplace and sentiment in the workplace have adhered closer to realism, and *Severance* is a good example of such a portrayal. Modern science fiction, even when hyper-realistic, has similarly conveyed workplace sentiment and atmosphere more realistically than their dramatic peers. Even in their futurism, for example, *Blade Runner*, *Alien*, and *Terminator* show glimpses of work that align more closely with real workers' experiences, where powerful companies (and large bureaucracies within those companies) exert an inordinate amount of power that is near-Herculean for ordinary workers to surmount. In the face of such glass-paned power, the postmodern worker cannot help but experience a loss of individuality, an acute sense of alienation, and a constant humdrum of background anxiety. Even ambient design in *Severance*, captured through geometric designs, minimalist colors, large empty (supposedly unutilized) spaces, and the sense of abstraction and isolation through the empty parking lot scenes and white snowy landscapes, further underscore the sense of alienation[21] (Fig. 8.1).

Work Versus Private Personas

Jungian psychology recognizes that an individual can (and indeed, must) have multiple personas, including personas for being at work, being with friends, and being home with a loved one.[22] The idea of the "work" persona was central to the male factory worker through the Industrial Revolution, and we could well argue that a severance of an individual's

Fig. 8.1 Minimalist colors, geometric design, and empty space within MDR serve to emphasize the increasingly non-physical nature of work in a technologically driven society

work and personal personas is a key feature of work in modern-day capitalistic society. What makes *Severance* unique is the literal exploration of this theme. The "switching" between the personas inside the elevator is effective and eerie: for many people working in downtown offices and skyscrapers, the switch to a work persona can be pinpointed with some precision to the ride in the elevator. Qualitatively, one starts preparing for it, almost automatically after a while, when pulling into the parking lot of the office , or in the fast-paced walk to the office after getting off the subway. Personal thoughts start getting superseded by the upcoming workday. The transition is complete by the time the elevator is speeding to an office floor, presumably with a crowd of workers contagiously feeling the same way during the office rush hour. In *Severance*, much of this is physically portrayed with uncanny emotional realism.

The process of switching from a private to a work persona is also a process of alienation; it may, in fact, be the most physical manifestation of what is otherwise a rather abstractly described phenomenon. It can be particularly hard on both women and minorities. Both are entering a space that was historically not reserved for them, and where the rules have been set by men who have had relatively uniform class, education, and corporate indoctrination. They are much more aware than these men of their persona, and there is an added layer of anxiety and effort in maintaining it. Fifty years after women entered the workplace *en masse* in Western nations, we still struggle to fully understand the dynamics and rules of engagement in the workplace, both between men and women, as well as between women themselves. There is no doubt, however, that women constitute a diverse segment of the postmodern workplace, and cannot simplistically be treated as a uniform or homogeneous group. There may be more heterogeneity among women workers than among their male counterparts, owing to factors such as whether the woman took time away from work due to maternity, is a single or divorced parent raising children, or is the primary breadwinner in the family unit. To its credit, *Severance* portrays the heterogeneity in the modern workforce accurately, with a range of genders, races, ages, and personality types interspersed among the characters.

Despite all attempts at "softening," the workplace is ultimately an aggressive space that is both cause and effect of the "background" anxiety I mentioned earlier. It is neither surprising, nor a coincidence, that a typical office environment tends to be aggressive also to the eye, with its bright lights and whites, clean lines, symmetrically proportioned cubicles, large, intimidating pieces of office equipment such as printers, and unnaturally proportioned ceilings and windows. Excepting the windows (or lack thereof), *Severance* accurately captures these distinctive, spatial features of the office. Lumon has a modernist exterior façade that is decidedly utilitarian, except for the godlike carving of the founder that one encounters when entering. The workplace is not a temple, but a maze and an altar. It will only provide answers to the "right" questions. One is expected to bow down before the company's mission and values, embodied in the gigantic image of the founder, and the Perpetuity Wing. This selective, focused reverence is one of the few outlets for emotional intensity permitted within Lumon. Deviating from these norms lands one in the punishment or "break" room, where one has to ask for forgiveness for the harm that they have caused, by sincerely expressing "compunction."[23] Such elicitations of sincere atonement are common tropes in science fiction by now, and likely inspired by Orwell, but are effective in *Severance* precisely because they don't go to the extremes of gratuitous torture. Orwell's influence is also present in the image of Eagan shown throughout the series, which is reminiscent of Big Brother's watchful gaze in Orwell's *1984* (Fig. 8.2).

Fig. 8.2 The use of shadows, rectangular architectural motifs, and other industrial design elements highlight the impersonal, utilitarian ethos of Lumon

Even in a sedentary job, one can feel the hum of the corporation, almost like a factory floor. Within the cubicle, in the bubble of one's own machine, the cog-in-a-wheel analogy is complete. I see the cubicle as a symbol of the cog. The eye (and consequently, spatial design) has always occupied an important place in Western culture, tracing its rise from imposing obelisks and pyramids in Egypt.[24] A larger office, such as the one occupied by Ms. Cobel, has the veneer of a more privileged space, but is qualitatively no more than a larger cubicle with thicker walls. Evidently, despite her obsequious devotion to Lumon, Ms. Cobel is considered no less dispensable.

The Gamification of Work as Play

As work has increasingly become more abstract, with the term "knowledge worker" now frequently bandied about,[25] companies have started to realize that maintaining worker engagement and reducing burnout are real issues that stand in the way of unlocking maximal productivity. Fear is not an effective tool for doing so: it is now almost a truism that happy workers are productive workers. In Big Tech firms such as Google and Facebook, it was normal (until quite recently, due to the wave of layoffs in the broader tech industry) to provide lots of incentives for workers to stay in the office longer and to feel that the company cared deeply about their wellbeing. These incentives could run the gamut from free coffee, meals, and laundry to kombucha taps and "unlimited" paid time off.

Even in the gig economy, where independent contractors tend to be responsible even for their own health insurance, there is an increasingly gamified aspect to work. The design of apps such as Uber and DoorDash makes for a good case study. Notwithstanding the actual physical and mental toll that such work can take, there is a sense that one is a player in a game, seeking to gain points and leveling up by following instructions on a map. Work as play can be effective, but its effects tend to be fleeting as the monotony of the job catches up. Burnout and disengagement are never far behind, although their causes are more complex than mere monotony. In *Severance*, work ("macrodata refinement") is also portrayed as play, sometimes in a disturbingly direct manner. Leveling up, as well as other important events such as retirement and recognition of one's loyalty, take gamified forms as well, such as melon bars and waffle parties.[26] The very act of closing a file is gamified by the presence of the incentive at the end—Kier Eagan's cartoon avatar praising the worker. Together, these constitute a set of "infantilizing office perks,"[27] which is best reflected today in the increasing desperation of many companies to see their workers return to the office full-time. Some companies have adopted the carrot, but others are proving willing to deploy the stick, especially given that a white-collar recession may be looming in advanced economies in 2024 and beyond.

We also see an interesting portrayal of Lumon's approach to maintaining worker wellbeing.[28] On the surface, Ms. Casey's "wellness check" resembles a therapeutic, modern-day approach to expressing one's feelings in a safe environment (i.e., Mark being asked to make a clay sculpture about how he feels). Ms. Casey's robotic demeanor could pass for that of a detached and non-judgmental therapist, and the room in which the wellness check is conducted resembles a meditative retreat. As viewers, we are only too aware of the eeriness and absurdism underlying the scene, a threatening undercurrent that only enhances the anxiety rather than resolves it. The closest analog in the real world is reporting a powerful individual to a large company's human resources department (e.g., in the face of harassment), which can have a similar undercurrent to it, as many in the #MeToo movement alluded to. Whether such admissions will lead to lasting changes remains to be seen, although evidence is promising.[29,30]

That the writers of *Severance* chose to tackle the issue of worker wellbeing and gamification of work within a single season so effectively is a testament to the realism of work portrayed in the show even in the dystopian backdrop in which the story is embedded. Organizations like Lumon, similar to the larger corporate organizations of today, view worker wellbeing as just another variable, a risk to be anticipated and mitigated. They have set procedures for doing so. As in any standardized procedure, individualism and deviation are frowned down upon. Workers are expected to seek therapy, take vacation, and return to work cleansed and refreshed in days, back to their peak levels of productivity. Curing burnout is seen as no different than curing the common cold.

Severance as Commentary on Work, Corporations, and Technology

The modern corporation, with its obsessive focus on productivity and profit, views labor and capital (which for most corporations today, is largely technological) through a similar lens, exactly as economists through the last two centuries have predicted. The first season of *Severance* offered a robust and unified commentary on work, corporations, and technology. The mysterious corporation Lumon, which at times resembles both cult and religious institution, is not an unfair representation of large technology companies where founders command an almost mythical reverence. The reverence that we see for Kier Eagan in *Severance* is reminiscent of similar scenes in *Blade Runner 2049* and invokes the type and intensity of reverence historically observed for innovators like Steve Jobs and Thomas Alva Edison. Questioning a founder's place in the pantheon is viewed as sacrilegious, long after the founder has moved on from the company they founded. The theme of work as cultish religious experience emerges more than once in *Severance*, especially in Ms. Cobel's shrine of Eagan. The theme, as shown, has a disturbing (albeit, somewhat extreme) resemblance to modern-day startup culture, a documented instance of which is the type of toxic, loyalty-demanding, and fear-driven environment known to have been implemented in now-defunct companies like Theranos.[31]

Viewed through a cold, economic prism, *Severance*'s use of its namesake technology seems to be both for productivity, as well as to mitigate against espionage and information leakage. In *Severance*, the reason for such mitigation is dramatized: there is an obvious suggestion that the company is engaging in actions that are highly suspect ethically. There are layers of secrecy even within the workplace itself: constructing or drawing maps is clearly verboten, departments seem to be pitted against one another or are perceived to be, and the nature of the work that is being carried out in MDR is never quite made clear. There is a sense that, even in their severed form, if ordinary human beings with a normal moral compass were to know what the organization was engaging in, they would perhaps wish to quit. We see this most prominently in Helly's reaction, but the disquieting sense of unethical company behavior does not escape any of the workers, and (before Helly's arrival) seemed to have reached a fever pitch in Mark's former boss Petey. Less dramatized, but no less real, analogs in the modern workplace include the use of keycards to enter only one's designated floor or space, the frequent (and at times, flagrant) use of non-disclosure agreements or NDAs, and turf wars between divisions and departments for company resources. Such turf wars tend to be passive-aggressive in nature, and sometimes become apparent or verbalized to upper management through external consultants.

One might wonder initially whether there is any realism in MDR's four-person division not knowing what the numbers on their computers really "mean." But in large corporations, can the vast majority of workers really pinpoint with specificity where or what their work product is being used for? Even if they could, it may only be an illusion. I doubt that most engineers in a company like Facebook really understood the extent to which their algorithms were leading to echo bubbles on the Internet, or fueling addiction among teenagers to smartphones and social media. Among teenage girls, in particular, such dynamics have been cited as an important component in the doubling of their suicide rate in recent years.[32] One might also wonder whether the company itself knew about some of the effects of its algorithm, but that doubt has since been put to rest by the testimony of the Facebook whistleblower Frances Haugen to Congress.[33] In a similar vein, it is highly doubtful that doctors and scientists employed by a company like Purdue Pharma really understood or anticipated that the drugs being manufactured, sold, and marketed by their employer would ultimately lead to a (still ongoing) destructive opioid-addiction epidemic. Companies may not want their workers to know all the details, not because of the risk of leakage of trade secrets, but simply because it might impede their productivity. In *Severance*, this is also implied for the macrodata refinement task; the workers are told that knowing the "true meaning" behind the numbers could inhibit their "natural intuition."

I also note that surveillance is an important issue in *Severance*, and one that has also become relevant in modern-day discourse (largely due to concerns about worker productivity in a hybrid or work-from-home arrangement), with reports of managers and employers monitoring their direct reports through such artifacts as keystroke logging[34] and in the case of Amazon warehouse workers, optimization tools, and AI.[35] Surveillance and employer-paranoia are themes of interest in *Severance*: informational asymmetry in divisions such as MDR and O&D is fully enforced by Lumon, which results in suspicion between the two that is a dramatization of team politics within corporations. Even individual divisions do not fully know (and are discouraged from finding out) what they are doing or how they fit into the larger puzzle, and it is clear that Lumon's ultimate agenda is a nefarious one. Many companies today publish mission statements online that sound benign and noble, but, at their core, they are created to be profit-maximizing for their shareholders. In the worker's mind, it can be hard to align the two, further increasing the type and intensity of alienation that Marx was referring to.

One issue that is hardly explored in *Severance* is money. Within Lumon, there are "tokens," but it is not clear that they are used outside of Lumon. Inequality exists in a hierarchical sense: Ms. Cobel is clearly higher on the totem pole than Mark, but she is subject to the whims of the board and, as seen in the second half of the series, is dispensable. Power can switch between innies and outies: in the outside world, we learn that Helly is Helena Eagan, and obviously carries greater clout than Cobel.

More generally, all the workers shown in the series seem to be reasonably affluent economically, and there is no real hint of class inequality or financial pressures. For many people, money is the primary reason they have to work, sometimes in jobs they despise. We do see signs of inequality in the outer world, but the series may have missed an opportunity in conducting a deeper exploration of the role of money and the worker's dependence on money. Instead, the problems faced by Helly and Mark seem to be "high-class" problems: Mark is trying to escape from his pain, while Helly is trying to prove a largely philosophical point. Many people in today's economy, even those making six figures, have trouble keeping themselves out of debt.

Conclusion

In exploring vital themes at the intersection of workplaces, consent, corporate power, and technology, *Severance* has provided a refreshing take on complex issues that has clearly been a hit with audiences, despite (or because of) its sophisticated and stylized treatment of relatively abstract questions. A second season of the series is rumored to be in the advanced stages of production at the time of writing (March 2023), although it was complicated by a recent writer's strike. The first season featured some distinctive themes, detail-oriented writing, and crisp character development. There are high hopes for the second season, but I am skeptical whether a second season will continue to be as deep, authentic, or sophisticated as the first. It is a cliched truth that many shows, as well as remakes and reboots, tend to fall prey to their own success, becoming glossy but superficial (and over-thought) derivatives of what made them great in the first place.

Despite what its name suggests, *Severance* is, first and foremost, a commentary on the workplace, and the nature and personification of work. It should stay true to that particular theme, rather than switch its focus (overly) to the company town, the Eagan family, Lumon, or other themes that rightfully belong in the backdrop of the series, rather than its center. Unfortunately, the last few episodes seem to suggest otherwise. We see an ever-increasing focus on the "outside" world, and on the characters' personal lives and quirks. Some scenes suggest that the technology behind the Severance procedure has been applied more broadly beyond its original corporate purpose to physically segregate work and personal personas inside the same brain. Used in a balanced way, these secondary "plots" could enhance the series' take on the use and abuse of corporate power and responsibility, especially in relation to technology that it develops and sells.

Ultimately, the series should continue to focus on its core theme of work and alienation as a first-class citizen. After all, we don't really need another Terminator-esque show or movie about the conspiratorial behavior of yet another large organization (be it corporation or government). Similar to the first *Matrix* film, *Severance* has the opportunity to engage the audience in a constructive philosophical discourse through effective writing and drama. But as demonstrated by the *Matrix* series of now four films that have steadily decreased in depth, even as they became flashier and more expensive, the gap between an authentic, entertaining take on deep and thought-provoking issues, and flash-in-the-pan entertainment, can be narrower than one would hope.

Notes

1. Maxine Berg and Pat Hudson, "Rehabilitating the Industrial Revolution 1," 24–50.
2. Allen Wood, *Karl Marx*.
3. Michael O. Hardimon, *Hegel's Social Philosophy: The Project of Reconciliation*.
4. Katta G. Murty, *Operations Research: Deterministic Optimization Models*.
5. Frederick S. Hillier and Gerald J. Lieberman, *Introduction to Operations Research*.
6. Joan Robinson, "Marx on Unemployment," 234–248.
7. Samantha Kubota, "White Castle to hire 100 robots to flip burgers," Today, https://www.today.com/food/restaurants/white-castle-hire-100-robots-flip-burgers-rcna16770.
8. Brian Fiani and others, "An Examination of Prospective Uses and Future Directions of Neuralink: the Brain-Machine Interface."
9. Peter Gwynne, "Predicting the Progress of Technology." *Research Technology Management* 56, no. 4 (2013): 2.
10. Daniel Berleant, Venkat Kodali, Richard Segall, Hyacinthe Aboudja, and Michael Howell, "Moore's law, Wright's law and the Countdown to Exponential Space."
11. Andrew S. Grove, *Only the Paranoid Survive: How to Exploit the Crisis Points that Challenge Every Company*.
12. Joan Robinson, "Marx on Unemployment," 234–248.
13. J. D. Taylor, *Negative Capitalism: Cynicism in the Neoliberal Era*.

14. Jeff Madrick and Nikolaos Papanikolaou, "The Stagnation of Male Wages in the US," 309–318.
15. Lawrence Mishel, *Unions, Inequality, and Faltering Middle-Class Wages*.
16. Anne Case and Angus Deaton, *Deaths of Despair and the Future of Capitalism*.
17. Bristol Voss, "Golden handcuffs."
18. *Severance*, "Defiant Jazz."
19. J. Collins, "Marx's Reserve Army: Still Relevant 100 Years On," 51–65.
20. Kirk Combe and Kenneth Schmader, "Naturalizing Myths of Aging: Reading Popular Culture," 79–109.
21. *Severance*, "Good News About Hell."
22. Mark R. Leary and Ashley Batts Allen, "Personality and Persona: Personality Processes in Self-Presentation," *Journal of Personality* 79, no. 6 (2011): 1191–1218.
23. *Severance*, "Half Loop."
24. Camille Paglia, *Glittering Images: A Journey Through Art from Egypt to Star Wars*.
25. James Cortada, *Rise of the Knowledge Worker*.
26. *Severance*, "What's for Dinner?".
27. Elizabeth Spiers, "What 'severance' gets right about infantilizing office perks," https://www.nytimes.com/2022/04/14/opinion/severance-apple-tv-office.html.
28. *Severance*, "The You You Are."
29. Caitlin Flanagan, "The Problem with HR," https://www.theatlantic.com/magazine/archive/2019/07/hr-workplace-harrassment-metoo/590644/.
30. Lisa Nagele-Piazza, "Treating the #MeToo movement as an opportunity to create better workplaces," https://www.shrm.org/resourcesandtools/legal-and-compliance/employment-law/pages/metoo-movement-opportunity-to-create-better-workplaces.aspx.
31. John Carreyrou, *Bad Blood*.
32. Anne S. Walters, "The Mental Health Crisis: New Data on Teen Girls," 8.
33. Mark MacCarthy, "How Congress can protect kids online."
34. Ifeoma Ajunwa , "The Unbounded Workplace and Worker Surveillance."

35. Merve Hickok and Nestor Maslej, "A Policy Primer and Roadmap on AI Worker Surveillance and Productivity Scoring Tools," 1–15.

Bibliography

Berg, Maxine, and Pat Hudson. "Rehabilitating the Industrial Revolution 1." *The Economic History Review* 45, no. 1 (1992): 24–50.

Berleant, Daniel, Venkat Kodali, Richard Segall, Hyacinthe Aboudja, and Michael Howell. "Moore's law, Wright's law and the Countdown to Exponential Space." arXiv preprint arXiv:2107.09637 (2021).

Carreyrou, John. *Bad Blood*. Larousse, 2019.

Case, Anne and Angus Deaton. *Deaths of Despair and the Future of Capitalism* Princeton University Press, 2020.

Collins, J. "Marx's Reserve Army: Still Relevant 100 Years On." *Journal of Australian Political Economy* 16 (1984): 51–65.

Combe, Kirk, and Kenneth Schmader. "Naturalizing Myths of Aging: Reading Popular Culture." *Journal of Aging and Identity* 4 (1999): 79–109.

Cortada, James. *Rise of the Knowledge Worker*. Routledge, 2009.

Fiani, Brian, Taylor Reardon, Benjamin Ayres, David Cline, Sarah R. Sitto, Taylor K. Reardon, Benjamin R. Ayres, and David D. Cline. "An Examination of Prospective Uses and Future Directions of Neuralink: the Brain-Machine Interface." *Cureus* 13, no. 3 (2021): e14192.

Flanagan, Caitlin. "The Problem with HR." *The Atlantic*. July 2019 Issue. https://www.theatlantic.com/magazine/archive/2019/07/hr-workplace-harrassment-metoo/590644/.

Grove, Andrew S. *Only the Paranoid Survive: How to Exploit the Crisis Points that Challenge Every Company*. Currency, 1999.

Gwynne, Peter. "Predicting the Progress of Technology." *Research Technology Management* 56, no. 4 (2013): 2.

Hardimon, Michael O. *Hegel's Social Philosophy: the Project of Reconciliation*. Cambridge University Press, 1994.

Hickok, Merve and Nestor Maslej. "A Policy Primer and Roadmap on AI Worker Surveillance and Productivity Scoring Tools." *AI and Ethics* (2023): 1–15.

Hillier, Frederick S., and Gerald J. Lieberman. *Introduction to Operations Research*. McGraw Hill Companies, Inc., 2001.

Kubota, Samantha. "White Castle to hire 100 robots to flip burgers." *Today*, February 18, 2022. https://www.today.com/food/restaurants/white-castle-hire-100-robots-flip-burgers-rcna16770.

Leary, Mark R., and Ashley Batts Allen. "Personality and Persona: Personality Processes in Self-Presentation." *Journal of Personality* 79, no. 6 (2011): 1191–1218.

MacCarthy, Mark. "How Congress can protect kids online." The Brookings Institution. May 4, 2023.

Madrick, Jeff, and Nikolaos Papanikolaou. "The Stagnation of Male Wages in the US." *International Review of Applied Economics* 24, no. 3 (2010): 309–318.

Mishel, Lawrence. *Unions, Inequality, and Faltering Middle-Class Wages*. EPI, 2012.

Murty, Katta G. *Operations Research: Deterministic Optimization Models*. Prentice-Hall, Inc., 1994.

Nagele-Piazza, Lisa. "Treating the #MeToo Movement as an opportunity to create better workplaces." SHRM. June 25, 2019. https://www.shrm.org/resourcesandtools/legal-and-compliance/employment-law/pages/metoo-movement-opportunity-to-create-better-workplaces.aspx.

Paglia, Camille. *Glittering Images: A Journey Through Art from Egypt to Star Wars*. Vintage, 2012.

Ajunwa, Ifeoma. "The Unbounded Workplace and Worker Surveillance." *The Quantified Worker: Law and Technology in the Modern Workplace*. Cambridge UP. 2023. 171-214.

Robinson, Joan. "Marx on Unemployment." *The Economic Journal* 51, no. 202/203 (1941): 234–248.

Spiers, Elizabeth. "What 'Severance' gets right about infantilizing office perks." *The New York Times*, April 14, 2022. https://www.nytimes.com/2022/04/14/opinion/severance-apple-tv-office.html.

Taylor, J. D. *Negative Capitalism: Cynicism in the Neoliberal Era*. John Hunt Publishing, 2013.

Voss, Bristol. "Golden Handcuffs." *The Journal of Business Strategy* 14, no. 5 (1993): 7.

Walters, Anne S. "The Mental Health Crisis: New Data on Teen Girls." *The Brown University Child and Adolescent Behavior Letter* 39, no. 6 (2023): 8.

Warren, Elizabeth, and Amelia Warren Tyagi. *The Two-Income Trap: Why Middle-Class Parents are Going Broke*. Basic Books, 2004.

Wood, Allen. *Karl Marx*. Routledge, 2004.

CHAPTER 9

Brain Eugenics: How to Produce an Ideal Worker?

Martin Charvát

In order to remain functional and competitive in global markets, every modern company faces many challenges. These include balancing the demands for the most cost-effective work process and work–life balance, keeping employees constantly on their toes and attentive, ensuring that problems in employees' personal lives do not spill over into the workplace and disrupt the working environment, or making the company a perfectly functioning machine where the risk of failure is negligible. Lumon Industries, founded by Kier Eagan, came up with what seemed to be the perfect solution. The company, a biotech giant, went the route of brain eugenics: the severance procedure is based on the permanent operational separation of work and non-work memory. Everything that takes place outside of the employee's work environment remains accessible only to that part of his memory and identity called the "outie"; everything that takes place in the offices and corridors of Lumon Industries, or on the so-called severed

M. Charvát (✉)
Metropolitan University, Prague, Czech Republic
e-mail: martin.charvat@mup.cz

N. M. Isacoff and J. Dawes (eds.), *Reintegrating Severance*,
https://doi.org/10.1007/978-3-031-57448-1_9

floor, remains hermetically sealed to the "innie," that part of the identity that exists only for precisely measured working hours.

In this chapter, I am mainly interested in the techniques used by Lumon Industries to adopt the severance procedure as a means of achieving happiness. These techniques are inscribed both in the architectural arrangement of Lumon Industries and in the presentation of the job description on the severed floor. The Lumon Industries headquarters is crisscrossed with seemingly endless corridors, forming a hermetically sealed space that metaphorically mirrors the structure of part of the workers' separate memory. The smooth running of the whole complex is achieved by focusing on efficiency and productivity, which is machine-like thanks to the techniques, practices and procedures created not only for the newborn worker, but also because they prevent contact between different teams, thus creating a fantasy of danger and threat. The space beyond the headquarters, everyday life, is mirrored by the other part of the separated memory, the memory outside work. The workers construct phantasmatic narratives of how their double exists in the outside world, and vice versa.

The job description of Lumon Industries is unfamiliar to the Macrodata Refinement team. No one has any idea what his or her work is leading up to, but they are convinced of its importance and relevance. It is a kind of black box, and the reason for this is that the only output that reaches the workers is nothing more than the manager's assessment of whether or not the quotas have been met. In other words, work, or rather the description of it by individual workers, is a floating signifier whose meaning is constantly changing and cannot be grasped.[1] And this is exactly how the job actually functions at Lumon Industries. Its inner principle is elusive and unknowable, but it is at the same time the principle that determines the actions and behaviors of the entire Macrodata Refinement team, whether in their work life or in their personal life. The job is also the source of the workers' illusory phantasms of their identity, which keeps them going, and which is reinforced by the fact that separation is possible at all. But at some point, this seemingly perfectly organized machine will fall apart.

Lumon Industries as a Capitalist Moloch

The severance procedure is considered radically controversial in the fictional world of the series, with opponents arguing that it essentially leads to the inhuman decomposition and disintegration of the human being, who cannot have a "natural" experience of the world. In addition to this ethical appeal, the critique includes a rejection of the capitalist mode of resource accumulation and an emphasis on constant performance—humans are being made into machines, as the Whole Mind Collective at least claims. However, undergoing the severance procedure is entirely voluntary, albeit irreversible, and each worker has their own reasons for choosing to work on the severed floor at Lumon Industries. Lumon repeatedly points out that this is not a mere experiment, but a clear and distinct outline of the future evolution of humanity with the aim of establishing perfect harmony, which is supported by some politicians and a huge campaign. One pillar of this campaign seems to be that the daughter of the current CEO of Lumon Industries has decided to undergo the severance procedure and is due to speak at the gala, saying that it was the best decision of her life.

Founded in 1865, Lumon Industries essentially perfects all the features of the so-called scientific management that American mechanical engineer Frederick Winslow Taylor came up with. One of the key points of Taylor's approach was the introduction of an "honest day's work," which should be "fixed scientifically."[2] After a series of attempts, Taylor had an idea to break down the labor of the worker into "its elementary operations,"[3] when every operation would be measured by a stopwatch. His main aim was to increase productivity through "measurement, surveillance, and enforcement of workers' activities"[4] and forced the assumption that the worker is just an (interchangeable) part of the whole system of production. Taylor himself was seduced by the desire to isolate the individual gestures of the workers, while the whole system of rationalization was intended to induce them to appropriate the most efficient gestures, which "then became routinized, reducing the time of a particular operation to a bare minimum."[5] Taylor was primarily interested in organization of physical labor, while the severed floor staff is engaged in mostly intellectual work, sitting in front of a computer screen for long hours trying to clean data (hence the name Macrodata Refinement). Nevertheless, Lumon Industries adheres to Taylor's basic precepts. Working hours are strictly defined, and workers do seem to be paid adequate wages for the work they do. Some are even housed in a district that Lumon Industries has bought up. And while they perform complex operations, these can be differentiated into smaller elementary sequences. On the other hand, recognizing "bad" data is a matter of intuition and experience, as at least manager Mark and the other workers claim. But since none of them are data analysts to begin with, the work they do can be learned, and anyone can become an "effective" worker meeting the productivity quotas. The use of computers and digital technologies is of course carried by the progress that has taken place since the founding of Lumon Industries and the introduction of Taylor's concept of "scientific management"; by this, I mean mainly the extension of cybernetics into all areas of human knowledge and work.

In 1952, the General Electric Company, founded in 1892 and a major innovator in electricity, industry, technology and computing since the 1930s, published a report on management improvements related to cybernetics. The report needs to be placed in a wider epistemological context. During the same period, between 1946 and 1953, the Macy Conferences on Cybernetics were held, inviting a wide range of experts from different fields to discuss topics such as the relationship between humans and technology, the new ecology of human thought (Gregory Bateson) or the presentation of cybernetic communication models (Nobert Wiener and Claude Shannon).[6] It therefore makes sense that large companies would try to maximize the potential for the use of automation and computer technology in the production process. In particular, the General Electric Company report stresses that computers will eliminate "indirect labor, where mass data handling is in consideration,"[7] where "skilled personnel" will be able to work with visual representations of complex processes on computer screens and make corrections to individual operations, or correctly adjust inputs and outputs. At Lumon Industries skilled employees of Macrodata Refinement focus on encoding and decoding data ("all the data comes from upstairs fully encoded"),[8] the meaning of which is unknown to them, when, however, data are intended to elicit "the emotional response of the refiner."[9] These are operations of a largely syntactic nature, based on cognitive mapping,[10] which are affirmed by a narrative of both the secrecy and the importance of the corporation.

And finally, let's not lose sight of the fact that the workers on the severed floor are basically cyborgs. Thanks to the severance procedure, a chip is inserted into their brains, dividing the memory into two distinct regions, between which there is a relationship of structural isomorphy: they are clearly different at the level of content, but at the level of structure they exhibit the same arrangement. Because they have a chip in their brains, the subjects appropriate distinct social habits, behavioral structures, thought and communication sequences (for example, it is common for them to cite Kier Eagan's nine principles), distinct procedures for dealing with situations, and orientations in space. In this context, it makes sense, French philosopher Gilles Deleuze writes, that machines are much more of a social than technological nature.[11] The technology employed within the severance procedure determines the separation of the subject while preventing its unambiguous identification with itself. For instance, the workers know they are severed but they have no access to the part of their brain that holds the "other" self.

Becoming "Dividual"

As members of the Whole Mind Collective claim, "Severance is subjugation."[12] From the perspective of French poststructural philosophy, we can say that subjugation is a form of subjectification.[13] Subjectification refers to the procedures through which the subject shapes itself, exercises control over itself and adheres to certain norms and rules, i.e. subjectification is a formation of a subject that is dependent on economic, social, political, biological and power contexts.[14] What is at stake in the theme of subjectification is the "shaping of modes of existence," or the constitution of a particular mode of being, and, therefore, we can speak of subjugation being an inherent feature of subjectification. In the context of *Severance*, once the individual undergoes the severance procedure, he or she is subjectified in a particular way, where, on the one hand, his normal and everyday life, his habits outside of work, remain essentially unchanged, or seemingly unchanged in the sense that he is aware that he has undergone the severance procedure and that he is thus in a new social context. On the other hand, he is exposed to the fact that his surroundings thematize his decisions and he has to learn to react to these situations, to defend himself or to refute the various accusations concerning Lumon Industries.

Let's look for a moment at the strategies that determine the "integration" of a new employee into the entire Lumon Industries system. Helly R. wakes up at a desk in a meeting room and has a small digital device containing a camera and a microphone in front of her face from which the voice of the operator (the manager Mark S.), hidden in the room behind one of the walls, can be heard. This is followed by a questionnaire which is both initiatory and tests the success of the severance procedure. The initial question, "Who are you?," is followed by a question asking for the employee's name, which logically triggers confusion and the realization that something is wrong. Subsequently, Mark S. appears and attempts to explain the nature of the corporation and the job description, and what actually took place. Helly R. repeatedly attempts to leave the office but always returns through the same door. The other Macrodata Refinement employees see nothing strange about this; they have all gone through the same liminal experience, which involves denial. Helly R. is subsequently played a video of her "outie" describing her decision to go through the severance procedure. "Outie" Helena reveals that each time she has gone back into the severed floor hallway moments ago, it was because the "outie" freely chose to return to the office. This non-violent form of subjectification involves inculcating and gradually reinforcing the idea that her life, or the life of every worker on the severed floor, takes place primarily at work: you get on the elevator after hours and as soon as you open your eyes again you are standing in front of the opening elevator doors at your workplace. The collective of others is there to facilitate a smooth transition into the new situation, mainly by routinely performing their tasks and not disrupting the setting in any way, while also overseeing the rules of the workplace.

In his short text called "Postscript on the Societies of Control" from 1990, Gilles Deleuze described the societies of control, where the flow of capital, and movement of people, is controlled by digital apparatuses and media, which traces the cybernetic identity of individuals via transfer of data and algorithms: "[…] the societies of control operate with machines of a third type, computers."[15] The context of the use of computer technology, the operation of data, and the movement of the subject into cyberspace speak of becoming a "dividual." Becoming dividual refers to re-scaling a human into bits floating around digital databases, where digital algorithms and digital traces that are left in virtual space play a fundamental role in identifying an individual. And at the same time, our "everyday" identity may not have much to do with the virtual one. Taking this brief description and extending it to *Severance*, one of the subjectification techniques that Lumon Industries is working with is that of dividuality, not only at the level of the characters' work and non-work memory, but also in the performance of the actual work of the Macrodata Refinement department. To put it another way, Deleuze calls the brain "the screen,"[16] meaning that human thought operations and processes are projected onto Macrodata Refinement department computer screens that function as a surface for social and individual phantasms. Macrodata Refinement staff "clean" the data appearing in clusters on the screen. Aside from the general narrative that their work is "mysterious and important,"[17] they have no idea of what they are doing. This creates a rather bizarre situation, especially in the case of Helly R., who repeatedly in her training asks what the data they are working with actually represents. Each of the others creates their own phantasmatic vision that corresponds, in their perspective, to the importance of the work, and, hence, the brain is the screen. Dylan G. is convinced that the data/numbers on the monitor represent dangerous organisms and objects in the ocean, as humanity prepares for underwater life due to widespread pollution of the planet's surface. Irving B., on the other hand, thinks they are cutting vulgarities out of movies, and Mark S. openly admits that he has no idea what they do, except that they have to meet certain quotas every quarter. But the case of Helly R. shows that anyone who is capable of doing the work can recognize "bad" data from "good" ones and accurately differentiate them. One part—the work—of the dividual is subjectified to identify with the principles of Lumon Industries created by founder Kier Eagan, and filled with ideology and mythologizing schemes. The absolute cornerstone of Lumon is the idea of the company or corporation as a family machine, which refers both to the founding of Lumon Industries—Kier met his wife while working—and to the creation of a collective belief in the purpose of Lumon Industries, which helps human beings achieve happiness, health and harmony.

Kier has embodied his principles in the handbook that employees are required to read and encouraged to memorize. The key feature of these principles is that they are essentially moral codes[18] combined with instructions for the consistent performance of work activities. The mythologizing and almost deification of Kier Eagan are fostered by the existence of the so-called Perpetuity Wing, a section in Lumon Industries that stores not only statues of all the CEOs with their recorded sayings but also a 1:1 scale replica of Kier's house, where the ritual reward for the "employee of the month" takes place. Irving, a seemingly devout follower of Kier's principles, considers the walk to Perpetuity Wing as a means of fostering a sense of belonging among team members, which he believes reinforces the notion of the importance of their work and of adherence to all the principles of Lumon Industries. The visual components—oil paintings depicting various events in Kier's life—also serve to further mythologize the company's prominence. And when Helly R. completes her work assignment, the digitized founder of the corporation appears on the computer screen to congratulate her and then transports to "other" worlds where his presence is needed.

Subjectification and individuation in Lumon Industries, or on the severed floor, is further carried by a certain deterritorialization of the experience of time. Workers feel as if they are constantly living in the present, in the presence of working time that is segmented through editing. However, the cuts are dark, or rather, what happens between entering and exiting the elevator is dislocated, "locked" in the dark box of non-work memory. The "innies" thus move in a temporal organization in which the future is an empty form of time[19] because, on the basis of the anticipation of subsequent work actions that are fixed (meeting quotas, etc.), they experience repetitive sequences of actions and behaviors in the present tense, the substance of which is influenced by a (work) past that is essentially no different from the present (or the future). This is also why Mr. Milchick notes there is no such thing as death on the severed floor at Lumon Industries; death is a matter of the "outside." The same can be said, at least in part, of the lives of "outies." *Severance* thus shows that life is full of cuts and dark places, that memory is impermanent, that there are gaps in it. At the same time, memory does exist in its entirety, in its unity, but only those events, memories, and affective reminiscences enter the "present" that are triggered by the mechanisms of anticipation, trauma, and desire.

In the book *Matter and Memory*, the French philosopher Henri Bergson presents a conception of perception based on the multiplicity of images. There is no perception that is not permeated by memories. As soon as we perceive something, this perception is of some immediate givenness full of details from our past experience. It is a constant succession of images, where the current perception (as an image) is supplemented by an image from the past, together with signs that point to that past. Bergson distinguishes between two kinds of memory. First, there is habit, where, for example, in repeatedly memorizing a passage (when we make our living as actors), we are eventually able to reproduce the text from memory. Once the habit is formed, it is no longer a problem to implement what has been learned. Of course, it is impossible to say exactly when the habit was formed, and Bergson adds another important point: in this case we are not re-introducing the past into the present, but merely repeating it. Another case is the recollection of a particular reading, which Bergson says is definitely not a habit because it is "an event in my life." The difference between the two recollections is not merely one of degree, but also of quality. This form of memory would make it possible to keep all the events of our lives in a pure and unaltered state. Or, according to Bergson, there is a pure memory which preserves absolutely everything, but only a very small part of it is actualized in the present, which depends on the situation in which we find ourselves, and in fact we cannot access pure memory whenever we want.[20]

Taking Bergson's conception of memory, it is as if, in the case of *Severance*, we are working with two separate cones (work and non-work memory), whose separation occurred at the moment of undergoing the severance procedure, and which can be reconnected only under certain conditions. However, this reconnection provokes confusion and fundamentally problematizes the characters' orientation in space. To put it another way, the severance procedure is a tactic of partial forgetting that results, at least for some workers, in living in two types of hell, as in the case of Mark S.: on the one hand, the hell of constant work presence, and, on the other hand, the constant hell of everyday life, from which he tries to escape with the severance procedure.

The ideological frameworks of the department are supported by the rhetoric of "work–life balance," which adheres to the narrative of dividuality. Once a worker shows signs of nervousness or stress, or conversely, the worker has completed a task exceedingly well, a wellness session may be ordered. However, a subjectivation mechanism is also present in practice: the worker is not allowed to talk or enter into dialogue with the wellness leader, who in turn shares positive information about his or her "outie." Whether it is small details or general characteristics of life "outside" Lumon Industries, the worker is made to feel that he is living a "proper" life and that he is an important member of the community, while the idea of the dual existence of those on the severed floor is reinforced. Another variation of "wellness," and another role for Ms. Casey, is to observe the "problem" worker directly in the workplace to prevent or curb unwanted behavior (as is done in the case of Helly R.). However, this is more of a spur-of-the-moment or irregular application of the mechanism of worker control and direction that takes place on a daily basis through the character of Mr. Milchick. He oversees the proper and smooth running of work groups, organizes celebrations, and reminds workers of what is and is not allowed.

A more hostile mechanism is triggered if there are repeated or serious violations of Lumon Industries rules. This involves the active participation of the head of security, Mr. Graner, who escorts the employee concerned to the Break Room. At the end of the long corridor, Mr. Milchick sits behind a mechanical-digital projector and prompts the worker to repeat remorseful sentences while watching an oscillating line on a monitor in front of him or her that captures the worker's emotional reaction as he or she recites the text. Milchick is only satisfied when there are several hundred or a thousand repetitions. In that moment Milchick is sure that the worker has implanted his or her misconduct in his or her mind and body, and is gripped by the fear of the possibility of ever being taken to the Break Room again. The situation is thus inscribed in workplace behavior and almost neurotic and anxious attention to the rules of work organization.

Neuroticism and paranoia on the severed floor are also affirmed through the production of mutually refuting, or contextually altered, narratives about the importance of particular workplaces, whose relationship is portrayed as conflicted. The Macrodata Refinement department sees itself as the "clever" one, while the Optics and Design department is seen by Dylan G. as the "more cruelty centered."[21] Macrodata Refinement staff discuss the possibility that, in the past, the Optics and Design department has attempted violent coups in which it has murdered staff from other departments. This is supported by the existence of visual material (images), which depict phantasmagorical representations of non-human and aggressive beings working in one department. However, the Optics and Design department thinks the same about Macrodata Refinement. They, therefore, avoid and suspect each other, until Irving discovers that there is an inverse image depicting a violent coup in which Macrodata Refinement staff are presented as having been responsible for the coup.

However, the discursive and non-discursive techniques of subjugation leading to the production of the ideal employee do not apply only to those who inhabit the severed floor. Mark's supervisor, Ms. Cobel, who did not go through the severance procedure, is individuated and subjectified by the ideology of Lumon Industries, and her entire life revolves around the successful functioning of the corporation for which she is willing to do almost anything. (Ms. Cobel has essentially no "off-work" life; all of her activities are explicitly connected to Lumon Industries.) Her subordinate position is repeatedly manifested when she is forced to stand before the company's board. The meeting with the board takes place within a double-mediated situation. First, an emissary of the board with a digital earpiece (Natalie) reproduces the board's decisions; the board does not participate "vocally" in the conversation. Secondly, Ms. Cobel's responses are transmitted through a small acoustic apparatus. Cobel thus has no opportunity for direct dialogue. She is condemned to endure only the reproduced decisions of the board, whose thought mechanism is a kind of black box.[22] This problematizes Cobel's entire series of activities, leading to her dismissal from her job, purely because she is performatively convinced that the severance procedure is reversible. For a long time, Cobel has been merely a tool for Severance to ensure the success of the severed floor.

Architecture as a Means of Subjectification

The overall architectural structure of the Lumon Industries building, and in particular the severed floor, is based on a combination of the principle of surveillance and punishment with the principle of digital control, which creates and reinforces a sense of paranoia and insecurity. Michel Foucault describes how the ideal system of surveillance regulates people's behavior through an invisible gaze in order to subjectify and individualize them according to the given goals of the corporation/state. The basic idea is that the worker instills in his body and mind imperatives and moral codes articulated via the binary opposition of "good" versus "bad,"[23] and their compliance is enforced by supervisors (Mr. Graner, Mr. Milchick, Ms. Cobel) so that the work machine can function without any hitches and without any mistakes. Digital control at Lumon Industries is a structural supplement to power and operates through digital and CCTV cameras that are on 24/7. What happens on the severed floor is transmitted either to the operations room or to Ms. Cobel's office. This means that the workers, at least at the beginning of the show, do not feel the existence of power pressure as a manipulative and subjective factor, nor are they aware that all their activities are constantly monitored. Even later, as they walk the hallways of the severed floor in defiance of the ban, they try to remain undetected, while Cobel watches them on her computer screen, remarking to Milchick that she is giving them "the illusion of freedom."[24]

The intricate and complex architecture of the severed floor is introduced immediately in the first episode of the show. Mark S. enters the huge lobby, where after a brief (and very tense) wait, the secretary allows him to proceed to the locker rooms, where Mark changes clothes and then passes a security check to enter the elevator, where the switch to work memory occurs. Access to the elevator and severed floor itself is characterized by what Australian urban designer William Mitchell calls the digital duality of access denied versus access granted,[25] and is also carried by the biometric paradigm, digital facial recognition, and visual penetration of the worker's body (the elevator is set up to pick up any "forbidden" items that the worker takes from the workplace, and is even able to recognize body writing). The very existence of this mechanism, including the fact that employees have precisely scheduled arrivals and departures so that they do not meet outside the perimeter of the severed floor, shows that Lumon Industries is guided by the principle of risk anticipation. "Risk" is anticipated and embodied in the heart of the technological and digital societies, and digital biopolitics emerged in order to control the "risk." "Risk" can never be diminished, but by sets of procedures it can be overtaken and its potential threats might be reduced. It is not only a question of digital piracy, war and monetary cyber-attacks, but also of everyday and ongoing work activities. Our identity is digital, the surface of the workplace is represented by cameras and screens recording 24/7, and our habits are determined and controlled by digital media, too. Societies of control are "risk societies" and also "biometric societies."[26]

Orientation on the severed floor is extremely complicated, due to a number of filmmaking techniques that prevent the viewer from forming a clear idea of the layout of the space, apart from identifying a few key points. Once Mark S. steps off the elevator in the first episode, a long sequence follows as he walks through corridors with many turns to his workplace. The journey from the lift to Macrodata Refinement is quite long. Although after a while the worker intuitively imprints in his or her mind the various turns and which way to go next, it is almost impossible for a newcomer to explore the area, made even more difficult by the lack of visible signs in the corridors (apart from the signs by the doors) to help give precise directions. Similarly, when Mark S. is invited to Cobel's office, he is escorted on the long journey by Milchick. When staff are sent to the Break Room as punishment, they are escorted to that location by Director of Security Mr. Graner. However, Mark S. guides new "trainee" Helly through at least part of the severed floor, passing by empty workstations which, as Mark points out, are likely to be filled soon, while admitting that no one from Macrodata Refinement has accurate information about how many workgroups are operating on the severed floor ("they separate us from other departments").

There are, of course, imagined and required boundaries on the severed floor; for example, Macrodata Refinement employees are intimidated, in the form of a mythic narrative, from making contact with the Optics and Design department (and vice versa). Once this prohibition is defied, however, Irving and others are able to visit the department regularly. Likewise, they know the way to the Wellness Room and the Perpetuity Wing, but this in no way diminishes the potential for getting lost in the winding corridors of the severed floor, which is essentially hermetically sealed: on one side by an elevator, on the other by a door to the outside world, which each employee voluntarily returns through after exiting. In Episode Seven, Mr. Milchick installs a door lock at the MDR entrance that only opens when the correct card is attached to the digital scanner. Once the employees, in this particular case Mark S. and Helly R., depart from the familiar routes, they seem to find themselves in a strange and phantasmagorical world: they enter a room in which a man is sitting and bottle-feeding a small goat while many other goats are running around. The questions, what kind of department is this (and is it even a department?), and what purpose does the room serve, are never answered, and only confirm the mysterious atmosphere enveloping the whole of Lumon Industries. The severed floor can be considered a heterotopia, a specific place of "otherness," a world of its own that operates according to different norms and rules and is usually not open to "outsiders."[27]

The layout of the severed floor can be divided into five types of spaces: (1) familiar spaces where there is no danger (the department office), (2) spaces designed for explicit subjectification (the Break Room; the office of Ms. Cobel), (3) spaces intended to affirm dividuation (the Wellness Room; replica of Kier's house), (4) spaces (seemingly) dangerous (offices of other departments, particularly O&D), (5) phantasmagoric spaces (strange room with a man feeding goats). This categorization is to some extent also reflected in the visual differences between the different spaces and rooms, for example the contrast between the Break Room and the Wellness Room. A long narrow dark corridor leads to the Break Room, the feeling of confinement and the impossibility of escape is amplified, while the waiting foyer in front of the Wellness Room is very pleasant, and is meant to make the worker feel calm and safe. The severed floor is a seemingly perfectly functioning organism that is undergoing a transformation (moving and installing paintings in the corridors, building new departments), but it is a transformation within the interiority, aimed at improving the functioning of the whole hermetically sealed environment.

Conclusion: Let's Burn This Place to the Ground

Brain eugenics seems to have made Macrodata Refinement workers into perfectly functioning machines with impermeably separate off-work and on-work memories. However, the first disruption[28] to the equilibrium and also to harmonious relationship between workers comes soon after the opening sequence of the show. Petey, the former head of Macrodata Refinement, no longer works at Lumon Industries, and his colleagues are not given any relevant reason. What's more, the new manager (Mark S.) must take it upon himself to train new employee Helly. Petey contacts Mark outside of work and convinces him that brain eugenics, or the severance procedure, is not as innocent as it might first appear and that Lumon Industries is an evil corporation. Helly R. refuses to accept her job role and repeatedly tries to escape the severed floor. So, the problems start to pile up. However, the board itself takes a very long time to accept the possibility that the chip in the workers' brains may not work perfectly, that the creation of the severed self brings with it a lot of complications. The series is driven by the gradual deconstruction and unraveling of the twisted nature of brain eugenics, which suggests that absolute separation is impossible and that this attempted separation essentially creates a traumatic situation whose symptoms manifest themselves in both occupational and private life. For instance, Irving repeatedly "sees" black paint dripping on him in the office and on his desk; when he gets home after work each day, he frenetically paints the dark hallway to the Break Room, all the while not knowing that it is the hallway in question. It later turns out that, in his private reality, he has been investigating Lumon Industries and its employees. In the end, it is Irving, a proud defender of Lumon Industries' principles, who utters with unwavering conviction, "Let's burn this place to the ground."

The rebellion is led by what we might call (following Deleuze and Guattari) the becoming-of-the-pack.[29] The Macrodata Refinement workers become a rogue group with well-defined tasks and goals. Their underlying motivation is based on their growing distrust of the process and the myth that the two selves are happy. Helly R. attempts suicide after being played a videotape of her "outie" explicitly telling her that she has no free will and is not "a person." Dylan also has a breakdown when he discovers that brain eugenics is temporal and interruptible and is confronted with the fact that he has a son. And in Mark S.'s case, the prompt is his reading of his brother-in-law's book, a superficial pamphlet about finding oneself. Ironically, when it is discovered on the severed floor, Ricken's book becomes an almost biblical and prophetic text that informs the severed workers that they have the right to think for themselves and that their time is their own. Add to that the fact that Mark S. discovers an incomplete Lumon Industries map left by Petey in the office, and he and his entire team embark on an adventure to awaken their innie selves on the outside.

That brain eugenics at Lumon Industries is a diabolical biopolitical mechanism that seeks to achieve the overcoming of mortality is made clear by the example of Ms. Casey, who works in the Wellness Room. Mark later discovers that she is his deceased wife, suggesting both that Mark's visits to the Wellness Room are a specific test of the functionality of brain eugenics, and that Lumon Industries is likely engaged in the development of artificial beings as the ultimate goal of ensuring immortality. Thus, it is only a small step from brain eugenics to absolute desubjectification of the workers and their loss of humanity, where they may live forever, but with a memory that can be erased and activated at any time for a precise time and with respect to the goals Lumon Industries wants to achieve. Sure, they will be perfect workers, but their place of residence will become absolute hell.

Notes

1. Jacques Derrida. *De la grammatologie* (Paris: Les Éditions de Minuit, 1967).
2. Samuel Haber. *Efficiency and Uplift: Scientific Management in the Progressive Era, 1890–1920* (Chicago: University of Chicago Press, 1964), 2.
3. Ibid., 2.
4. Cotten Seiler. *Republic of Drivers: A Cultural History of Automobility in America* (Chicago: The University of Chicago Press, 2008), 26.
5. Mary Ann Doanne. *The Emergence of Cinematic Time: Modernity, Contingency, The Archive* (Cambridge: Harvard University Press, 2002), 5.
6. Katherine N. Hayles. *How We Became Posthuman: Virtual Bodies in Cybernetics, Literature, and Informatics* (Chicago, London: The University of Chicago Press, 1999), 50–70.

7. General Electric Company. *The Next Step in Management: An Appraisal of Cybernetics.*
   (New York: General Electric Co., 1952), 105.
8. *Severance,* "Half Loop."
9. Ibid.
10. Fredric Jameson. *Postmodernism, or, The Cultural Logic of Late Capitalism* (Durham: Duke University Press, 1992).
11. Gilles Deleuze. *Foucault* (London, New York: Continuum, 1999), 34.
12. *Severance,* "Half Loop."
13. Michel Foucault. *The History of Sexuality, Volume 1* (New York: Pantheon Books, 1978).
14. Gilles Deleuze and Félix Guattari. *A Thousand Plateaus* (Minneapolis, London: University of Minnesota Press, 1980), 111–148.
15. Gilles Deleuze. "Postscript on the Societies of Control." *October.* Issue No. 59, 1992, 6.
16. Gilles Deleuze. *Cinema 1. The Movement–Image* (Minneapolis: University of Minnesota Press, 1986), 58.
17. *Severance,* "The You You Are."
18. Michel Foucault. *Discipline and Punish* (New York: Vintage Books, 1995). Michel Foucault. *The History of Sexuality, Volume 1* (New York: Pantheon Books, 1978).
19. Gilles Deleuze. *Difference and Repetition* (New York, London: Continuum, 2004).
20. Henri Bergson. *Matter and Memory* (London: George Allen and Unwin, 1911).
21. *Severance,* "In Perpetuity."
22. Vilém Flusser. *Towards a Philosophy of Photography* (London: Reaktion Books, 2000).
23. Michel Foucault. *Discipline and Punish* (New York: Vintage books, 1995).
24. *Severance,* "The Grim Barbarity of Optics and Design."
25. William J. Mitchell. *Me+ + . The Cyborg Self and Networked City* (Cambridge: MIT Press, 2004).
26. Jussi Parikka. *Digital Contagions. A Media Archaeology of Computer Viruses* (Berlin: Peter Lang, 2007).
27. Michel Foucault. "Of Other Spaces." *Diacritics* Volume 16, Issue No. 1, 1986, 22–27.

28. Claude Bremond. "The Logic of Narrative Possibilities." *New Literary History* Volume 11, Issue No. 3, 1980, 387–411.
29. Gilles Deleuze and Félix Guattari. *A Thousand Plateaus* (Minneapolis, London: University of Minnesota Press, 1980), 33–34.

Bibliography

Bergson, Henry. 1911. *Matter and Memory*. London: George Allen and Unwin.

Bremond, Claude. 1980. "The Logic of Narrative Possibilities." *New Literary History* 11, no. 3, 387–411.

Deleuze, Gilles. 1986. *Cinema 1. The Movement–Image*. Minneapolis: University of Minnesota Press.

———. 1992. "Postscript on the Societies of Control." *October* Issue No. 59, 3–7.

———. 1999. *Foucault*. London, New York: Continuum.

———. 2004. *Difference and Repetition*. New York, London: Continuum.

Deleuze, Gilles and Félix Guattari. 1980. *A Thousand Plateaus*. Minneapolis, London: University of Minnesota Press.

Derrida, Jacques. 1967. *De la grammatologie*. Paris: Les Éditions de Minuit.

Doane, Mary Ann. 2002. *The Emergence of Cinematic Time: Modernity, Contingency, The Archive*. Cambridge: Harvard University Press.

Flusser, Vilém. 2000. *Towards a Philosophy of Photography*. London: Reaktion Books.

Foucault, Michel. 1978. *The History of Sexuality, Volume 1*. New York: Pantheon Books.

———. 1986. "Of Other Spaces." *Diacritics* 16, no. 1 (Spring): 22–27.

———. 1995. *Discipline and Punish*. New York: Vintage Books.

General Electric Company. 1952. *The Next Step in Management: An Appraisal of Cybernetics*. New York: General Electric Co.

Haber, Samuel. 1964. *Efficiency and Uplift: Scientific Management in the Progressive Era, 1890–1920*. Chicago: University of Chicago Press.

Hayles, Katherine N. 1999. *How We Became Posthuman: Virtual Bodies in Cybernetics, Literature, and Informatics*. London: The University of Chicago Press.

Jameson, Fredric. 1992. *Postmodernism, or, The Cultural Logic of Late Capitalism*. Durham: Duke University Press.

Mitchell, William. 2004. *Me++. The Cyborg Self and Networked City*. Cambridge: MIT Press.

Parikka, Jussi. 2007. *Digital Contagions. A Media Archaeology of Computer Viruses*. Berlin: Peter Lang.

Seiler, Cotten. 2008. *Republic of Drivers: A Cultural History of Automobility in America*. Chicago: The University of Chicago Press.

CHAPTER 10

"Defiant Jazz": Corporate Rewards as Plantation-Style Oppression in Apple TV's *Severance*

Lauren Shoemaker

Near the end of his first date with Alexa, as they leave the restaurant, Mark S. overhears activists of the Whole Mind Collective protesting the severance procedure and distributing flyers.[1] The word slavery is taboo enough in the Apple TV series *Severance* that Mark S. questions the social justice advocate's use of "subjugation" as implying slavery. The word's absence is notable in the show, yet the concept saturates the series to describe the creation of a self for which there is no life but work. Helly R.'s early experiences catalog many of the responses enslaved people have historically had to enslavement. She tries to flee (first by forcing the doors of the conference room in which she awakens, then by exiting through the stairwell in what turns out to be an inescapable spatial loop). Her pleas with her outie self to quit are denied and met

L. Shoemaker (✉)
Slippery Rock University, Slippery Rock, PA, USA
e-mail: lauren.shoemaker@sru.edu

N. M. Isacoff and J. Dawes (eds.), *Reintegrating Severance*,
https://doi.org/10.1007/978-3-031-57448-1_10

with a blunt enunciation of her non-personhood. And lastly, her self-harm threats and suicide attempt demonstrate similarities with records of transatlantic slave ships and plantations that testify to enslaved people's rejection of a life in bondage. Because our historical and material understanding of slavery systems is deeply embedded in race, it still seems an uneasy argument for me to make, as a white writer focusing mainly on two white characters. The series underscores this unease purposefully, daring the audience to name the context of slavery through euphemism with the Whole Mind Collective advocate in the scene. However, the audience is indeed meant to experience both familiarity with slavery contexts and find reason to take issue with them because the corporate environment of the twenty-first century is supposedly post-racial, and such a comparison of Lumon Industries to a plantation would be insensitive. However, tracing power structures and specifically reward systems for productivity and good behavior in *Severance* clearly links the plantation of the nineteenth century to the corporate office of the twenty-first. *Severance* critiques capitalism as a dehumanizing mode of production that relies on slave labor, and requires increased alienation, invisible reproductive labor and technological innovation like the severance surgery imagined in the series. In this essay, I first examine similarities between the methods of direct oppression used at Lumon Industries and those common on United States plantations of the nineteenth century. And second, I focus on the "perks" or corporate rewards for productivity that innies of Lumon can earn that are both satirical parallels to contemporary corporate employee work incentives and rooted in the slavery economy and its labor practices.

This argument rests on an understanding of capitalism as a system based on inherent exploitation: profit is generated by capitalists through paying laborers a fraction of the capital their labor generates, or not at all in the case of enslaved labor. Outies are paid at Lumon while innies receive only the workplace incentives like erasers and fingertraps. This general Marxist axiom of exploitation has been expanded by feminist materialist scholars such as Silvia Federici to explain how capitalists also benefit from the unpaid time laborers spend in the general upkeep of their bodies and the reproduction of future workers, referred to as reproductive labor. Cooking meals, washing laundry, raising children, and even basic hygiene are considered reproductive labor that is unpaid but from which capitalists profit as it makes waged labor possible and produces the next generation's workforce. This argument, well-established since the 1970s, has prompted current discourse on meeting a work–life balance, the idea that for laborers, a balance should be struck between labor activities and leisure time, particularly given how much leisure time has slowly eroded due to the constant availability of the worker through technology. The concept for the series *Severance* is that this split can be made literally with a surgery to limit one's memories and perception spatially, inside of and outside of the workplace. I argue that the show may begin with this critique in mind, but it becomes increasingly more invested in representing sustained direct oppression of the innies—the consciousnesses created by the surgery for whom their entire existence is the workplace. This perspective reveals the stark parallels between Lumon Industries' methods of oppression and U.S. plantations of the nineteenth century.

"Hail Kier": Leader Worship, the Handbook, and Direct Oppression

One familiar link between the nineteenth-century plantations of the U.S. South and Lumon Industries is the leader worship prevalent in images, icons, and even lore of the founding Eagan family. Kier Eagan's enormous profile is sculpted into one of the interior walls of Lumon, which Mr. Milchick admires in the sunlight while sharing the lore of Kier's three raw-egg-in-milk breakfast on which Helly is about to be quizzed after her severance surgery.[2] A life-size reproduction of Kier's house in the Perpetuity Wing is meant to inspire awe and admiration.[3] Lastly, an 8-bit short video of Kier standing atop a mountain before flying away into the horizon plays on Helly's retro computer monitor when she completes the Siena file just before the quarterly deadline to meet quota.[4] Worship of Kier is pervasive: Ms. Cobel has an inset shrine to him in her home,[5] and she sings an anthem in his praise that is presumably recognized by the Macrodata refiners.[6] Such leader worship is reminiscent of the paternal, god-like role of slaveowners of the nineteenth century, who also inscribed their name where they could, at times branding initials on enslaved people,[7] renaming them at will, but most often reinforcing their power through Christian religious ideology. While the Christian tripartite god(s) maintained supremacy, slaveowners stood tall as figureheads of the social hierarchy that Christian beliefs upheld.[8] God-given purpose, doled out by the slaveowner to the enslaved as serving God, is echoed in Cobel's explosive reprimand of Mark, "We serve Kier, you child."[9]

In addition to these examples of Kier's image as leader worship, his words are also elevated to dictate corporate policy and work culture. Kier's

Nine Core Principles serve as guides for values in the Lumon offices. In an interview with Emma Stefansky with *Thrillist*, Dan Erikson, creator of the series, explains that the principles "are taken largely from a couple places [he] worked at that had their own version of that, these empty words that were thrown out to give a sense that there was a deeper philosophy to the place...it's deeply off-putting and manipulative, because you get the sense that sometimes these corporations are trying to make a cult of personality, and trick you into feeling like you're family..."[10] Erickson identifies a "cult of personality" developed by corporate leaders as inspiring those Core Principles, and as I will develop in this section, the worship of the corporate leader and their paternalistic values communicated through such principles are relics of the master–slave paradigm in which slaveholders saw their position as one of righteous parent needed to guide an otherwise wayward child.

Tied to the myth of the self-made person, individual achievement in corporate settings is not just lauded but developed into hero worship. Consider the technology sector where Bill Gates, Steve Jobs, Elon Musk, and the like are larger than life. Kier Eagan is the beneficent founding, surrogate father who rewards and punishes those orphaned through the severance procedure. Irving demonstrates the most reverence for Kier as this figurehead, quoting passages from the handbook, warning coworkers about infringement of the core values, and worshipping Kier. However, Irving is positioned as somewhat of a square for his earnest deferral to authority in this manner; Mark and Petey's jocular exchange imagined through Petey's reintegration sickness, in contrast, is familiar ribbing between colleagues that do not take the job very seriously:

> Mark: Hey. What's that? Sudoku?
> Petey: It's nothing.
> Mark: What were you drawing?
> Petey: You getting back to work, in cubist form.
> Mark: Kay. Two things. One, how do you know what cubist form is . . . and what the fuck are you wearing?

Helly's sarcastic "Praise Kier!" as she exits the supply room is an example of a specific kind of playful resistance.[12] This subtle method of subversion, signifying—repetition with a difference, was and still is common as a rhetorical tactic in African American literature and folklore that developed in response to constant surveillance in slavery. Often a method of resistance, signifying can be agreeing on the surface, but with mockery in tone or delivery. In "The Vernacular Tradition" in the introduction to the *Norton Anthology of African American Literature* the editors write,

> Drawing on linguistic research by Geneva Smitherman and others, [Henry Louis] Gates [Jr.] has defined signifying — the often competitively figurative, subversively parodying speech of tales and of less formalized talk as well as of various forms of music — as an impulse that operates not only between contesting tale tellers but between writers (and painters, and dancers, etc.) as well.[13]

The signifying move is acceptable resistance in the workplace, as it maintains deniability in its parroting of policies or leader worship, and the genre of music as well as episode seven's title, "Defiant Jazz," references this subtle, safe subversion through its naming of a characteristically African American music genre. Just as plantation owners were largely absent from the everyday activities in the lives of enslaved people, Kier is not physically present, even if his Core Principles and the handbook govern the policies and procedures of the innies at Lumon. Like overseers of the plantation, middle management is a far more visible presence.

While the Eagan family is present in dialogue and plenty of passing art, they remain off-screen while the faces of direct oppression (Ms. Cobel and Mr. Milchick) respectively, a white woman and Black man, are ever present. Systemic racism and sexism might superficially discourage us from seeing them as oppressors, but the series depicts how late-stage capitalism incentivizes participation and reproduction of torture and shared values with those in power in order to maintain proximity to power and its benefits. Helena Eagan becomes severed to manipulate U.S. opinion of the procedure, and Helly's discovery of her outie self's exploitative decisions should not be as surprising as the reveal is in the series; Helly answers Mark's question, "What if we're all assholes up there?" with "That's a given for me."[14] An Eagan in their midst without knowing herself, Helly is perhaps the most resistant to the oppression of the innies, as I listed her trajectory earlier, while Helena leverages her influence to normalize the severance procedure and the creation of enslaved selves.

The methods of direct oppression of management and family of the founder imitate those of the plantation, as they are responsible for inflicting the direct violence that occurs in the break room. The break room, a clever reversal of the meaning of the typical corporate space designated for employee meals or short breaks, contains the tools for psychological torture inflicted on innies until they "break" by forcing them to repeat over several hours a Compunction Statement, a vague but powerful apology for aberrant behavior. This break room is closer to the physical and mental "breaking" process outlined by Frederick Douglass in *Narrative of the Life of Frederick Douglass* than the breaks most would associate with workplaces. Visits to the break room are reserved for serious defiance. Instead of a focus on punishment, Lumon, like most corporations, emphasizes incentives for productivity. Compliance with workplace expectations occurs by default in many of Lumon's severed employees. Helly's exception to this pattern provides the series' plot points to elucidate the direct methods of Lumon's oppression and at least initially, contrasts her punishment with other team members' drive for corporate rewards.

The Lumon Employee Handbook is another source of direct oppression, which takes on a scriptural role at Lumon. Irving finds, prints, and shares the policy regarding desk photos and the procedure for updating them for Mark S. when he breaks protocol.[15] The Employee Handbook speaks with the authority of Kier, yet keeps employees disciplining themselves in a Foucauldian prison, which the series further underscores in the open concept office layout where the four team members are never out of sight of their coworkers. The word of Kier is practically the word of God at Lumon, and such founder worship is a continuation of the elision of god and master of the nineteenth century. "Jesus," interjects Helly; "No, Kier," responds Irving, as the MDR team encounters the replica of Kier's home in the Perpetuity Wing.[16] Some of the dry humor of the series comes from the evidence that there seems to be a passage from the handbook for everything, and when presented with a trite self-help book published by Mark S.'s brother-in-law Ricken that Mr. Milchick accidentally leaves for the team to find, the contrast of the self-sacrifice for Lumon expected in the handbook with the agency in generic self-help mantras appears revelatory. Episode 4, "The You You Are," displays the words from Ricken's book as Mark S. reads them with satiric drama: "Your job needs you, not the other way around..."[17] The contraband self-help book helps Dylan recognize his own exploitation as much as his "overtime" experience—being "woken up" as his innie in his home to find that he has a child—radicalizes him. As Mark and Dylan demonstrate, once it is contrasted with freedom and agency, the handbook can be identified as a source of direct oppression. When the MDR crew decides to rebel, activating their innie selves in their outie lives through the Overtime Contingency mode, Mark and Dylan share an inspired moment of solidarity in recognizing their oppression:

Mark:	I probably should've told you guys, but uh, I kept this [Ricken's book]. And, there was part of it that, well . . . [begins reading] "Our job is to taste free air. Your so-called boss may own the clock that taunts you from the wall, but . . .
Dylan joins him:	"my friends, the hour is yours."
Dylan:	Page 197 slaps.

The platitudes of Ricken's book serve as a profound counterpoint to the handbook. Only five minutes earlier, Irving consults a volume of "Compliance," the leatherbound set of books that make up the handbook. He reads a passage of Kier's diatribes meant to ennoble the mysterious labor completed at Lumon; however, he crushes his deviled egg within the pages of the volume before replacing it on the wall.[19] The tissue-thin pages of the handbook are reminiscent of bibles, and the text Irving reads imitative of biblical instructions; the scene completes Irving's recognition of the oppression of the handbook as it draws on contexts of religious ideology and connections between Protestant work ethics and the corporate workplace's reliance on such ideology. The biblical connections are also less subtle references to the role Christianity played in social reproduction of slavery: Christianity naturalized hierarchies (of God over humans and humans over animals) that were then applied to racial categories of people understood at the time to be subhuman. Deviled egg-ing the handbook with all its religious connotations marks the completion of Irving's radicalization.

The incentives themselves are governed by the handbook. Barely audible over Helly's first experience with the scary numbers, Dylan quotes the passage to Irving in defense of his enjoyment of earning the perks: "And all in Lumon's care, shall revel in the bounty of the incentives spur."[20] "All in Lumon's care" echoes the common slavery apology that slaveholders were benevolent caretakers of people in need of moral direction and labor's structure. This handbook line underscores the direct influence of the Protestant work ethic and racial superiority of white Christians who enslaved Africans on current corporate culture. Lingering beliefs that chief executive officers gained their position by hard work and deserve exorbitant pay (rather than systems of privilege and exploitation) are relics of the plantation slavery economy and supporting ideology. This handbook quotation from Dylan, alongside the consistent use of "children" to reference Lumon employees in all the former CEO's wax museum audio recordings in the Perpetuity Wing, makes clear the connection between proslavery arguments that rested on racist assumptions of inferiority and the holdover that such ideologies have on twenty-first-century corporations in remembering their nineteenth-century roots and justifications for hierarchies. In *The Half Has Never Been Told: Slavery and the Making of American Capitalism*, Edward Baptist explains that "Proslavery writers... agreed [with abolitionists] that enslavers were first and foremost not profit-seekers. For them, planters were caring masters who considered their slaves to be inferior family members."[21] Baptist corrects the myth of benevolent slaveowners through outlining how massively profitable the slave trade and the plantation economy were, forming the base of American capitalism through the expansion of slavery in both geography and intensity. In the third episode, "In Perpetuity," former Lumon CEOs, all Eagans, refer to employees of Lumon as their children, while Irving provides a reverent tour.[22] The condescension of caring for inferior family members established in slavery's apologies is traceable in the corporation's continued use of "family" as metaphor to build workplace culture and exploit workers through that emotional manipulation.

Severance satirizes the criticism that contemporary corporations have faced in exploiting the labor of employees through the discourse of "family" and the feelings executives hope to capitalize on through creating a positive work culture. Helly instructs Mark, "Go lick a boot, Mark" when it becomes clear that his loyalty is to the Eagans rather than a former team member and friend.[23] Mark is still, in episode four, uncritical of the rhetorical device that the Eagans naturalized; he explains to Helly that "The work is mysterious and important. And we deal with the uncertainty it brings us in the way that Kier would have wanted. Together, as a family." To which Helly responds, "I could not, with a razor to my throat, be less interested in being your family."[24] The irony of this line is revealed with Helly's identity as Helena Eagan; she would, in fact, for political purposes, very much like all innies to consider themselves "part of the family." When her innie is activated to reveal that she is an Eagan, Helly witnesses her outie's interview for marketing the severance surgery. Helena explains,

> So one of the things you learn growing up as an Eagan is that the workers are our family. And I remember being confused about that as a kid because I thought that meant I had a few hundred thousand literal brothers and sisters scattered around the world. But as I grew older, I learned that it's about shared ideals. Um, my dad used to make me recite the Nine Core Principles before bed every night, which I can't say I always did happily. Sorry, dad. But those are now the values that I share with everyone who works at Lumon, and that's what makes them my family. And I would never ask them to do anything that I'm not willing or excited to do myself. Look, my dad would love for me to sit here and say that I'm taking this job out of loyalty, and that it was the spirit of Kier Eagan calling me to service, but I took a severed job because it sounds freaking awesome! So, no, I don't think severance divides us, I think it brings us together.[25]

Helena's joke about thinking of laborers as her actual family endears her to the public while simultaneously employing the discourse of family to exploit them. Disgusted, Helly recovers in a restroom where she slowly and earnestly recites the Compunction Statement as she realizes her complicity in Lumon's slave labor practices. In "The Dark Side of Saying Work is 'Like a Family,'" for *The Atlantic*, Joe Pinsker writes that "When a business is presented as a family, its workers may feel pressure to pledge an unreasonable degree of loyalty to their employer, putting up with long hours, mistreatment, and the erosion of work–life boundaries, all in the spirit of harmony and a shared purpose." The premise of *Severance* explores the possibility of making the work–life balance or separation literal, and in doing so critiques the impossibility of this divide in a capitalist system without creating enslaved selves. While the show imagines this possibility for the future, it relies on processes of the past that persist, presenting age-old exploitation, not a new ethical dilemma. These methods of direct oppression at Lumon are familiar tools for enslaving and creating justifications for it. Having made explicit the connections between nineteenth-century slavery and contemporary corporate practices of exploitation, I turn to specifically corporate productivity incentives and their representation in the show.

"The Egg Bar is Coveted as Fuck!:" Lumon Incentives

I chose to focus on the corporate rewards of Lumon rather than the punishments because the "break room" and the historical process of "breaking" enslaved people's psychological and emotional being is a straightforward reference that makes the most overt gesture toward slavery for the audience. The rewards, however, are a more subtle gesture, producing plenty of the levity the series offers. The banal rewards proudly displayed on and in Dylan's desk include Chinese fingertraps, erasers, and caricature drawings which mock familiar kinds of corporate rewards like promotional items or certificates.[26] Of the Lumon employees the series follows, Dylan is the most motivated by the perks, making light of Helly's suicide attempt with the grossly satirical line that "She needs to start earning perks; I'd end my life too if I didn't have any finger traps."[27] How are rewards as juvenile as small toys and as blatantly sexual as the dancers masked as the Tempers at the waffle party rooted in the same peculiar American institution? The answer is that rewards were meant to temporarily distract but ultimately to convince enslaved people that they could not manage themselves and needed the mastery of others to keep them on task. Amusement was and still is a tool of manipulation in U.S. labor practices. The pizza parties and yoga sessions, easily recognizable as the egg bar or waffle party and wellness sessions in *Severance*, are cheaper substitutes for paying higher wages or providing paid time off for real rest and leisure. Shelly Fagan's 2021 article solidified the critique of such insulting work perks as the "sad pizza party" in "Pizza Parties Are No Substitute for Living Wages and Healthcare." Fagan writes, "A sad pizza party is nothing more than the illusion of doing *something* nice, which fosters greater resentment as meaningful proposals go ignored." While audiences recognize the insult of the pizza party in the show's perks, the innies' lives are confined to the workplace, so these experiences become essential to avoid boredom or exhaustion that could result in rebellion. This reasoning was clear for slaveowners, and corporate leadership today utilizes the same practices with shrouded language to increase "engagement" and create positive "workplace culture" with systems of rewards and recognition for productivity. I argue that *Severance* demonstrates how these work incentives naturalized in our current workplaces are rooted in U.S. slavery economic practices through innies who are exploited, enslaved selves and their parallels with slave narratives and rebellions.

In the autobiographical *Narrative of the Life of Frederick Douglass*, Douglass describes Christmas celebrations and rewards on plantations as tools of slaveowners: many enslaved people were coerced into heavy drinking games by their enslavers on holidays, perverting the enslaved person's sense of freedom. Thus, when sobered, many "went away to [their] various fields of work; feeling upon the whole, rather glad to go from that which our masters artfully deceived us into the belief was freedom, back again to the arms of slavery" (255–6). Contemporary American work culture, allowing only brief hiatus from work, similarly encourages concentrated indulgence or fatuous entertainment as reprieve rather than real rest in order to maximize productivity and thereby profits. The concept of the weekend was hard won by labor activists, not a gift from corporate America, who would benefit from longer periods between holidays to increase laborers' exhaustion and need for release. In the series, the employees of Lumon know no other existence than work in the office since they have no consciousness outside of the physical floor of the building. The rewards, especially the "experiences" as Mr. Milchick calls them, are the innies' only respite from their labor. We witness a variety of these experiences: a melon bar that accompanies a "getting-to-know-you" icebreaker that proves useless when the innies have no memory of who they are outside of Lumon, the egg bar of which everyone seems surprised by the quality, the music dance experience which provides the title for this chapter and the seventh episode of the series, and finally, the highly regarded waffle party.

Each of these scenes includes language from Mr. Milchick that reinforces the idea that employees are incapable of moderation or implies that the opposite of work, any kind of release, is dangerous and must be monitored or limited by management. In the melon bar scene, Mr. Milchick implies that the Macrodata Refinement Department will experience discomfort from over-consuming melons: "Let's get this new group photo before the melon bloat sets in."[28] Similarly, the music dance experience is introduced as a treat to be enjoyed and rationed. Irving points out that Helly is only at 73 percent completion of the Siena file, not the 75 percent needed to earn a reward, but Milchick explains, "Yes, well, it's been a tough morning on all of us... And I thought a little frivolity would be just what the doctor ordered. Helly, please approach the MDE cart. You may choose one genre and one accessory."[29] Lest she lose control with more than one accessory, or waste any more time than one track will last, Milchick sets strict boundaries and encourages the other department members to join in: "Though this experience is in Helly's honor, I urge all refiners to take advantage of the opportunity presented."[30] Later, during the egg bar experience, Mr. Milchick brings out a large camera with a separate flash to take pictures once he changes the overhead lighting to a cycle of bright colors first used during the music dance experience. Mr. Milchick's photography—later revealed to provide the marketing images for Helena Eagan's publicity of her severance surgery—seems to provide a celebratory atmosphere and reinforces the fleeting moment of reprieve. Mr. Milchick leads Dylan through the Lumon severed floor's maze of hallways in reverent silence on the way to his waffle party. Once they enter the replica of Kier Eagan's bedroom, Mr. Milchick directs Dylan with a stoic, deadpan, "Enjoy."[31] Mr. Milchick's lines introducing the perks or reward experiences contextualize them as part of Lumon's or Eagan's generosity which should be met with gratitude and the perks themselves enjoyed with restraint. Again, those in positions of power are assumed to be morally superior and justified in monitoring the enjoyment of the incentives.

The music dance experience scene is possibly the most memorable perk and also offers the most room for interpretation of the roots of common workplace incentives toward which the series gestures. Helly chooses "Defiant Jazz" for her music selection, consistent with her own acts of defiance by attempts to escape Lumon and more recently to explore the mysterious severed floor with Mark rather than refine coded data at her desk. Jazz as a musical genre was developed by Black Americans in response to experiences of dehumanizing oppression and exploited labor. "Defiant" in the sub-genre's title mocks the enslaved selves' agency: dancing and enjoying themselves is a corporate-approved exercise or indulgence that has been earned, but it is not actual freedom or resistance. As Dylan demonstrates in this scene, refusing to dance is resistance. Mr. Milchick, clad in a white turtleneck rather than his typical button-down work attire appears more congenial and informal, yet his goading of Dylan to dance under the multicolor strobe lights enforces his role as supervisor and stand-in for Lumon and the Eagans. Mr. Milchick gyrates in perfect rhythm as the camera focuses on a stoic, furious Dylan continuing to work at his desk until he explodes, pushing Mr. Milchick into the music dance experience cart.[32] Mr. Milchick may have considered Helly and Mark the bigger threats in their rebellion, but the violent outburst attunes him to Dylan's resentment and growing defiance after becoming aware of his son. The perks which used to distract Dylan are no longer a powerful enough tool of manipulation; this scene is an important turning point in the series when the MDR department becomes more conscious of their oppression and willing to act. The contradiction of "Defiant Jazz" is coerced merriment which Dylan refuses to enjoy, understanding the experience as a perversion of joy. This perversion parallels the perversion of freedom Douglass explains in his *Narrative*; coerced revelry is not freedom, no matter how grateful Mr. Milchick tells the refiners they should be for the experience. The "Defiant Jazz" music dance experience scene emphasizes the continuation of tools of manipulation from the plantation of the nineteenth century to the corporate offices of the twenty-first to distract and control laborers.

The last work incentive or perk earned in the first season of the series, the waffle party, also reinforces an important parallel with U.S. slavery contexts in two ways. The waffle party is the most sought-after perk and is reserved for the standout refiner of the quarter. It features a stack of waffles accompanied by a sensual performance by masked dancers performing as Kier's Tempers (Woe, Frolic, Dread, and Malice) in Kier's bedroom within the Perpetuity Wing while one dons a sculpted mask of Kier. The sexual nature of the reward provides one connection with slavery contexts, while the opportunity for lack of supervision provides the second. In an interview with Ben Stiller and Dan Erickson for *Variety*, Erickson is quoted saying, "... this is a world where you're not supposed to express any sexuality amongst your coworkers. And yet they have to give the employees that outlet, because they may be having sexual experiences on the outside, but not know. So it's a way for Lumon to take that human need and turn it into a sort of pro-Lumon thing." Controlling and monitoring intimacy among enslaved people was common by slaveholders because reproductive sex increased their wealth. The potential for Lumon to be invested in the reproduction of their workers is made explicit in the news story Mark watches about a woman who becomes pregnant from experiences at work of which her outie has no recollection.[33] Erickson continues in the interview for *Variety*, "So you can have sex, it's not wrong, it's not dirty—as long as it's all about Lumon and it's all about reverence for Kier Eagan." Even the cat-o-nine-tails on the bed has the Nine Core Principles labeled on its ends.[34] The waffle party controls intimacy for innies by entangling it with founder worship and the religion of productivity in corporatism. Sexual experiences are built-in to the efficiency of the company through its incentives, and as such taken from innies as part of the experience of freedom that defines humanity, just as they were in a plantation economy.

Dylan, however, does not stay in the Perpetuity Wing to experience his entire waffle party. He exits the reproduction of Kier's bedroom before the erotic dance portion ends, confusing the dancers.[35] Dylan uses the unsupervised waffle party as the opportunity to activate Overtime Contingency and awaken his MDR friends in their outie lives. Dylan's part in his friends' fleeting escape during a celebration firmly recalls the many instances where enslaved people used holiday celebrations or events where a lack of supervision could be expected to stage a rebellion. "Across the Americas, stories nevertheless abound of enslaved peoples utilizing this small window of, in the words of [Solomon] Northup, 'a little restricted liberty' afforded by the Christmas season to escape bondage," Yesenia Barragan writes.[36] The Christmas Rebellion in 1831 and the 1521 Hispaniola Revolt are some of the most notable uprisings of enslaved people in the Caribbean that occurred on or around Christmas because supervision was lax. The upper management of Lumon was preoccupied the evening of Dylan's waffle party with a dinner and publicity event thrown by the Eagans at which Helly finds herself for the final episode. Though Mrs. Cobel had been fired, she knew where to find all corporate leaders that night to report the Overtime Contingency infringement by the MDR crew. This timing of Mark, Helly, and Irving's brief escape with the celebratory dinner—using Dylan's waffle party as opportunity—provides a strong analysis of Lumon's incentives as remnants of slavery practices' hold on modern workplaces. While the technological advances of Lumon may prompt audiences to read the narrative of the series as futuristic, we can recognize clear ways that the tools of oppression are old, familiar ones. Furthermore, the methods and timing of resistance are hardly new either.

"Forced Labor?": Conclusion

Science fiction as a genre notoriously reflects social conditions of the culture that produces it. A television series dramatizing an experimental surgery to enforce a work–life separation in a culture with much anxiety about how to strike that balance is an obvious hit. However, the stakes in how that experimentation is represented are high. Whether intentional or not, creating many parallels to processes of racialized slavery in the U.S. benefits the series in its critique of labor and capital. Instead of asking to what lengths humans will go to exploit others, these parallels have a circulatory effect, pointing out the lengths to which humans have already gone and how they could be reinvented. This argument can also be an uneasy one to make. Slavery as a specifically racialized institution should never be euphemized because of the history of terror and prolonged anti-Black oppression in the U.S. My analysis is no euphemism but a careful comparison of processes of oppression employed in U.S. slave systems and enslaved people's methods of resistance. I do not agree that, as Mark repeats throughout the series, his choice to be severed means that his Lumon consciousness is not enslaved, but I recognize that this ethical question remains unsettled by audiences. Thought-provoking science fiction leaves interpretation open, and our responses to complex media provide insight into our personal and collective meaning-making tendencies. Rather than insist Lumon is understood as a modern plantation, I suggest a more nuanced conclusion. Familiarity with practices of oppression and exploitation of the past can help us understand our own frustrations and anxieties around labor through creative media like *Severance*. Without thoughtful analysis of and resistance to capital's creep into workers' time, we are susceptible to accepting fingertraps or erasers in place of paid time off or healthcare.

Notes

1. *Severance*, "Half Loop."
2. Ibid.
3. *Severance*, "In Perpetuity."
4. *Severance,* "What's for Dinner?"
5. *Severance,* "Hide and Seek."
6. Ibid.
7. The New York Public Library holds a branding iron image in its collection with the initials "GHC" under the item title "Silver Slave Brand c. 1800." Schomburg Center for Research in Black Culture, Manuscripts, Archives and Rare Books Division, The New York Public Library. "Silver slave brand, c. 1800" *New York Public Library Digital Collections.* https://digitalcollections.nypl.org/items/510d47df-a25a-a3d9-e040-e00a18064a99. Accessed 30 September 2023.
8. For a complete description of how white Christians shaped their defense and reinforcement of slavery through Christianity, see

Charles F. Irons' *The Origins of Proslavery Christianity: White and Black Evangelicals in Colonial and Antebellum Virginia*, 2009, The University of North Carolina Press.

9. *Severance,* "Hide and Seek."
10. Dan Erickson "'Severance' Creator Dan Erickson Knows Exactly What the Goats Are For." *Thrillist*, interview by Emma Stefansky, 8 April 2022. https://www.thrillist.com/entertainment/nation/severance-creator-dan-erickson-finale-interview. Accessed 30 June 2023.
11. *Severance,* "In Perpetuity."
12. *Severance,* "Hide and Seek."
13. Henry Louis Gates Jr. "The Vernacular Tradition," *The Norton Anthology of African American Literature.* Eds Henry Louis Gates Jr. et al. (New York: W. W. Norton & Company, 3rd Edition, 2004. 3–8), 7.
14. *Severance,* "What's For Dinner?"
15. *Severance,* "Half Loop."
16. *Severance,* "In Perpetuity."
17. *Severance,* "The You You Are."
18. *Severance,* "What's For Dinner?".
19. Ibid.
20. *Severance,* "Half Loop."
21. Edward Baptist, *The Half Has Never Been Told* (New York: Basic Books, 2014), xviii.
22. *Severance,* "In Perpetuity."
23. *Severance,* "The You You Are."
24. Ibid.
25. *Severance,* "The We We Are."
26. *Severance,* "Half Loop."
27. *Severance,* "The Grim Barbarity of Optics and Design."
28. *Severance,* "Half Loop."
29. *Severance,* "Defiant Jazz."
30. Ibid.
31. *Severance,* "What's For Dinner?"
32. *Severance,* "Defiant Jazz."
33. *Severance,* "In Perpetuity."
34. *Severance,* "What's For Dinner?".
35. Ibid.

36. Yesenia Barragan. "Christmas and Resistance to Slavery in the Americas." *African American Intellectual History Association.* 23 December 2016. https://www.aaihs.org/christmas-and-resistance-to-slavery-in-the-americas/. Accessed 29 June 2023.

Bibliography

Baptist, Edward E. 2014. *The Half Has Never Been Told: Slavery and the Making of American Capitalism*. New York: Basic Books.

Barragan, Yesenia. "Christmas and Resistance to Slavery in the Americas." *African American Intellectual History Association*, 23 December 2016. https://www.aaihs.org/christmas-and-resistance-to-slavery-in-the-americas/. Accessed 29 June 2023.

Douglass, Frederick. 2003. *Narrative of the Life of Frederick Douglass, an American Slave*. Boston: Bedford/St. Martin's.

Erickson, Dan. "Ben Stiller and 'Severance' Creator Break Down That Trippy Waffle Party." *Variety*, Variety.com, interview by Jennifer Maas, 1 April 2022. https://variety.com/2022/tv/features/severance-waffle-party-sex-scene-explained-dylan-kier-eagan-1235212918/. Accessed 30 June 2023.

———. "'Severance' Creator Dan Erickson Knows Exactly What the Goats Are For." *Thrillist*, Thrillist.com, interview by Emma Stefansky, 8 April 2022. https://www.thrillist.com/entertainment/nation/severance-creator-dan-erickson-finale-interview. Accessed 30 June 2023.

Fagan, Shelly. "Pizza Parties Are No Substitute for a Living Wage or Healthcare." *Medium*, 13 July 2021. https://medium.datadriveninvestor.com/pizza-parties-are-no-substitute-for-living-wages-and-healthcare-8c4666d72c72. Accessed 30 June 2023.

Federici, Silvia. 1975. *Wages Against Housework*. Power of Women Collective. Bristol: Falling Wall Press.

Gates Jr., Henry Louis. 2004. "The Vernacular Tradition," In *The Norton Anthology of African American Literature*, Eds. Henry Louis Gates Jr. et al., 3rd Edition, 3–8. New York: W. W. Norton & Company.

Irons, Charles F. 2009. *The Origins of Proslavery Christianity: White and Black Evangelicals in Colonial and Antebellum Virginia*. Chapel Hill, NC: The University of North Carolina Press.

Pinsker, Joe. "The Dark Side of Saying Work is 'Like a Family.'" *The Atlantic*, 16 February 2022. https://www.theatlantic.com/family/archive/2022/02/work-actually-is-like-a-family/622813/. Accessed 29 June 2023.

Schomburg Center for Research in Black Culture, Manuscripts, Archives and Rare Books Division, The New York Public Library. "Silver slave brand, c. 1800" *New York Public Library Digital Collections*. https://digitalcollections.nypl.org/items/510d47df-a25a-a3d9-e040-e00a18064a99. Accessed 30 September 2023.

CHAPTER 11

The Waffle Party Is Not What It Seems: Sexual, Reproductive, and Labor Exploitation in *Severance*

Kathleen W. Taylor Kollman

In the summer and fall of 2022, the phrase "quiet quitting" entered the media sphere, with think pieces in major news and entertainment outlets and the term trending all over social media. Unprecedented numbers of workers began lobbying for better conditions, particularly in the wake of the first wave of the Covid-19 pandemic. While workers' rights have been an ongoing concern throughout American history, the pandemic became a lightning rod for trends in labor activism and brought workplace injustices to the fore. In the early 2020s, some of these discussions about labor exploitation and activism began to spring up in popular culture texts. The show *Severance* comments on these themes of labor exploitation, the American office environment, and the possible abuse of power of mega-corporations. It also introduces another layer of worker abuse tied to the show's oddly specific premise of bodily autonomy, consent, and identity.

K. W. T. Kollman (✉)
Miami University, Oxford, OH, USA
e-mail: kollmak@miamioh.edu

N. M. Isacoff and J. Dawes (eds.), *Reintegrating Severance*,
https://doi.org/10.1007/978-3-031-57448-1_11

Severance has plenty of predecessors. The workplace sitcom has been a popular staple since the earliest days of television, with early series making way for the various iterations of *The Office* broadcast first in the U.K. (BBC, 2001–2003) and then with adaptations around the world. The U.S. version of *The Office* (NBC, 2005–2013) satirizes the absurdity of the American white-collar office, but also touches on more serious issues of labor exploitation. This is often exemplified in the various tropes that TV series and films about workplaces explore. One such trope is work/life balance. Films such as *9 to 5* (dir. Colin Higgins, 1980), *Clockwatchers* (dir. Jill Sprecher, 1997), and *Office Space* (dir. Mike Judge, 1999) have all touched on this issue, specifically in white-collar office environments. Other series deal with these subjects within a more dramatic, darkly comedic, or satirical fashion, including *Better Off Ted* (ABC, 2009–2010), and *Workaholics* (Comedy Central, 2011–2017). Other series of various genres also have running plotlines of evil megacorporations at their center, including *Angel* (The WB, 1999–2004) and *Mr. Robot* (USA, 2015–2019).

Popular narratives have also negotiated issues of consent as seen in *Severance*. For example, the dramedy *United States of Tara* (Showtime, 2009–2011) explores a woman's struggles with Dissociative Identity Disorder (DID), which, somewhat similar to the Severance procedure, fragments her personality into multiple distinct selves. The Severance procedure uses the paradigm of multiple identities to consider body autonomy with identities that may or may not have knowledge or ability to consent to the actions of others.[1] Because the Severance procedure bifurcates workers' identities into different selves, these selves are not in communication with one another in the same way the title character of *United States of Tara* is fragmented. Tara's separate identities undertake entire romantic and sexual relationships outside of the knowledge of her "core" personality, who is married with children. Conversely, the identities who are not married did not consent to that relationship, either, and this is not unlike what is happening with characters in *Severance*.

Severance also shares some traits of the body swap trope in television and film, since in some ways the workers can be seen as distinct and separate individuals who trade the same body by having their consciousness switched on and off. Body swaps have been featured in everything from *Freaky Friday* (from the 1972 novel by Mary Rogers, adapted into five different films between 1976 and 2020), *Wonder Woman 1984* (dir. Patty Jenkins, 2020), to episodes of countless TV series.[2] In the case of *WW84*, audiences were shocked that the film's body swap included elements that were arguably sexual assault.[3]

Severance uses this concept to tease out the implications of power and capacity in the context of consent. The company uses sex as a reward for an innie whose outie cannot reasonably consent to it, and reproductive labor is outsourced to innies who cannot reasonably consent to pregnancy or birth (as depicted in Gabby Arteta's storyline). Furthermore, consent and knowledge of one's full spectrum of identity means that any innie/innie relationship is of dubious consent due to lacking vital information about the outie's partner status and declared sexual orientation. At the same time, the innie—being a full personality—lacks fundamental human and civil rights due to being irrevocably tethered to the outie. The level of exploitation here is nothing like the mistreatment and failure of work–life balance in all the workplace series previously mentioned, but is very similar to the dystopian risk of death involved in the body swap time traveling in *Travelers* (Netflix, 2016–2018). For instance, the character of Peter "Petey" Kilmer in *Severance* dies due to the existence of the severance chip in his brain, albeit only when he escapes the workplace and pursues a risky process known as reintegration. Petey appears to be an outlier, though: as of the completion of Season One, no other severed character has attempted reintegration and dies as a result of the procedure, but several characters have endured things that could constitute physical abuse or dubious bodily consent.

In *Severance*, labor exploitation, sexual exploitation, and reproductive exploitation all work together to oppress the people who are created by the Severance procedure. While the outies voluntarily allow their bodies to endure anything they experience at Lumon, the innies have consented to nothing and, through these various forms of exploitation, are completely disenfranchised from anything resembling agency or autonomy.

Labor Exploitation, the Fictional Workplace, and Work–Life Balance

The fictional workplace has become an increasingly dystopian setting in both television and film, even in work that is not explicitly speculative. Merely comparing the workplaces depicted in sitcoms of the 1950s and '60 s (most famously *The Dick Van Dyke Show*, set in the comedy writers' office of a fictional variety show) in contrast with *The Office* or *Better*

Off Ted reveals key differences. In older series, work was an extension of a circle of friends and family, with (mostly male) employees striving valiantly to please their bosses and live out the American dream. In more contemporary series, cracks in this system reveal corporate indifference to customers and employees alike, forcing everyone from middle management downward to band together against the system and do what they can to resist their exploitation. Although not technically a sitcom, *Severance* still owes a lot to this comedic tradition through its use of comedic actors, directors, and darkly funny one-liners, which further perpetuates the idea of using humor as a form of resistance. Again, however, it is the extra exploitation of one's sexual agency that sets *Severance* apart and renders it more horrific than other examples of darker workplace fiction, thus mirroring how real-life employment has become more and more exploitative.

Severance's creator Dan Erickson writes about his inspiration in an article for *The Hollywood Reporter*, stating that when he wrote the pilot, he had a particularly "mindless" job, "cataloging all the different parts of doors" for a door manufacturer. The sheer tedium of his day led Erickson to *Severance*'s central premise:

> What if I could skip the eight hours of the workday, to disassociate and just get it over with? I joke that the Great Resignation—the phenomenon in which 47 million Americans quit their jobs in 2021 alone—was my idea, but in reality a lot of things were happening at the same time we were making *Severance*. The pandemic forced people to reassess the necessity of a lot of things in their lives, to question in particular all the conventions that we have associated with having a job. Some people could do their jobs just as well by checking their email a couple of times a day without going into an office. There is no actual practical reason to give half of a waking day to a job when one can be as productive at home without making that sort of puritanical sacrifice.[4]

The original script had a much more comedic tone, with fewer scenes in the confines of the mysterious Lumon corporation.[5] The rewritten pilot episode as filmed ramps up the ominousness of Lumon, depicting it as a sterile environment full of antiquated technology, with the office spaces themselves having a distinct air of mid-century modern architecture and interior design. These purposeful design choices destabilize both the viewer and the newly awakened innie employees, giving them no clear idea about where they are or even what year—or century—it is. The Severance chip allows innies to retain basic external knowledge but erases their personal knowledge. For example, when first awakened, the innie Helly remembers that there is a state called Delaware, but she cannot remember the color of her mother's eyes.[6] In this way, the Severance chip enacts retrograde amnesia, which specifically blocks autobiographical memory.[7] This use of amnesia is distinct from the aforementioned body swap trope, in that it is creating a new blank slate personality, albeit one who is an adult with knowledge of the world external to their personal history.[8] However, like the body swap trope, the result is that a new person inhabits someone's body. The two personalities are not only unaware of each other's actions, but they also have no memory or knowledge of the other person, other than being told they exist. In the series' premiere episode, "Good News About Hell," Mark gives Helly an orientation on her first day of work that—after an assessment to determine if her Severance chip is working—starts the explanation by emphasizing the more benign benefits of the procedure:

> MARK: I understand you're confused about the severance procedure. Before we hop on that, let's chat about something I bet you have heard of, the work/life balance. To start, imagine yourself as a seesaw.

After Helly understandably panics and tries to escape, Mark tries another approach with her, telling her about his severance procedure. He admits that, like Helly, when he first awoke in the room, "I was scared too," and he assures her that "there is a life to be had here." However, the procedure's process, purpose, and effects are most fully explained to Helly by her outie in a video recording:

> HELENA: My name is Helly R. I'm making this video roughly two hours before it will be shown to me. I have, of my own free accord, elected to undergo the procedure colloquially known as severance. I give consent for my perceptual chronologies to be surgically split, separating my memories between my work life and my personal life. I acknowledge that, henceforth, my access to my memories will be spatially dictated. I will be unable to access outside recollections whilst on Lumon's severed basement floor, nor retain work memories upon my ascent. I am aware that this alteration is comprehensive and irreversible. I make these statements freely.

In practice, of course, this means Helly's outie, Helena, has given consent to the bifurcation of her memories. While she does use the word "comprehensive" to describe the process, this does not cover all the ramifications that could happen to her body. She has given consent to suffer from a "spatially dictated" form of autobiographical memory or induced dissociative identity disorder. However, she has not explicitly given consent for harm to come to her physical body, to be exploited, or to be killed. The critical issue is that Helly has consented to nothing. She wakes up without memories or information and must begin a career performing tasks that make no sense to her without the ability to live a home life, resign, or change careers. Innies are denied sunlight, sleep, relationships outside of coworkers and supervisors, hobbies, and any knowledge of themselves or the outside world. They have been "born" with no rights and privileges, sentenced to corporate drudgery, the fruits of which they will never enjoy. Helly winds up waging a physical war with Helena to get the outie to recognize her complicity in revoking Helly's human rights, and she is subjected to physical and mental torture in Lumon's ominous Break Room as punishment.

The other characters who experience this lack of agency include the rest of the MDR workers and, in a small role, the wife of a local politician. Dylan seems to have experienced a sexually oriented workplace perk on more than one occasion, which raises the question of whether his outie gave consent to have his body be used sexually without his consent. Irving begins a romantic relationship at Lumon with his coworker Burt without knowing either of their outies' sexual orientations or marital statuses. For Gabrielle Arteta, Severance appears to have created an innie for her whose sole job it is to endure elements of pregnancy and birth (and possibly also childrearing, although this is unclear) that her outie deems painful and a nuisance, but this effectively means that the innie is used solely for reproductive labor, possibly without her permission and consent. In each case, either the innie or the outie is denied informed consent about sexual, reproductive, and/or labor exploitations (with the process even being used to avoid the pain of childbirth), thus making neither incarnation of any severed person someone with full bodily autonomy.

Sexual Exploitation

What Lumon appears to be focused on removing from the users of the Severance procedure—whether they are employees or not—are rights and agency regarding several key mental and physical experiences. However, the focus here is going to be on several physical, emotional, and sexual experiences that Lumon is not allowing employees to fully consent to: pregnancy and childbirth, sexual behavior, respect for sexual orientation, and respect for partnered status. Complete information about these areas of one's other identity might have some direct bearing on how and what severed people consent to in both of their lives, but keeping them bifurcated without a flow of information is ultimately as unethical as any other form of sexual or labor exploitation. Lumon is deliberately putting severed people in situations to which they cannot consent. Even if outies understand this as part of the terms and conditions of agreeing to the Severance procedure in the first place, the innie has no choice. The outie may have consented to "anything" happening to their body during their workday, but the innie has not provided the reverse, and they are not even in the workplace voluntarily at all. Many situations Lumon subjects innies to could be appropriately called sexual assault and forced pregnancy. While the innies in *Severance* are not incapacitated, they are vulnerable, as are outies when they are unaware of what is happening to their bodies for eight hours a day. Although outies have given consent for anything to happen to their body while at work, the innie has not consented to any of this.

Sexual activity is used as a reward for an innie whose outie cannot reasonably consent to it, and reproductive labor is outsourced to innies who cannot reasonably consent to pregnancy or birth. Consent and knowledge of one's full spectrum of identity means that any innie/innie relationship—regardless of either partner's gender—is of dubious consent due to lacking vital information about the outie's partner status and declared sexual orientation. At the same time, the innie—being a full personality—lacks fundamental human and civil rights due to being irrevocably tethered to the outie.

This brings up questions about the ethics of consent for sexual activity. At Lumon, in the Macrodata Refinement department, for which the main characters Mark, Helly, Dylan, and Irving work, there are perks associated with hitting various completion metrics. Dylan states in the second episode that "if we hit our numbers by quarter's end, one of us gets named Refiner of the Quarter, and that shit gets you a waffle party."[9] The event's name implies that the designated refiner will eat waffles and that there will be some celebratory gathering, and we do see in the eighth episode[10] that some parts of that are true. However, the event's exact nature is fraught with sexual imagery and the implication of sexual activity.

Dylan is chosen as the beneficiary of the waffle party, even though Mark, as department head, can bestow the perk on anyone in the unit. Unbeknownst to supervisor Harmony Cobel, the department chooses Dylan for this perk so that he can stay late after work and help the team investigate Lumon by activating their innies while in their outie lives. The waffle party takes place after work hours, and Dylan will participate in it less as the recipient of the benefit than to infiltrate the security office. Thus, he does not engage in the sexual element of the party, but the audience still witnesses what generally happens during such an event.

After hours, Dylan is taken to the Perpetuity Wing of Lumon (first featured in episode three, "In Perpetuity"), a museum chronicling the company's history, which includes a full-scale replica of the home of Lumon's founder, Kier Eagan. At the appointed time of the party, employee liaison Seth Milchick tells Dylan to "enjoy," and Dylan proceeds to the Eagan house. The house is dimly lit. It takes Dylan a moment to see the side table on which a plate of three waffles is in a stack. Dylan sits at the table and pours syrup over the waffles. The soundtrack for this scene features extremely ominous music (the song is entitled "After Hours," by the series' composer Theodore Shapiro). A symmetrical shot shows Dylan beginning to eat the waffles, slowly and contemplatively, flanked by multiple candles, a marble bust, and a floor with a diagonal checkerboard pattern. This shot, still very dim, only features a few distinct colors: the brown of the outer wood floor, the aqua blue-green of the upper walls above a chair rail and wooden paneling, the off-white of the marble bust and lighter floor tiles, and the slightly lighter aqua of Dylan's dress shirt. These colors evoke a sense of peacefulness and calm (in the blue tones) as well as regal history (the brown of the wood and the off-white marble), but the very darkness of the scene renders it ominous. The symmetry of the shot speaks to order and stability, but the almost sensual way the waffles are filmed foreshadows what is about to happen after Dylan finishes eating.

When the meal is over, words are revealed on the plate beneath the food. The audience does not see the words clearly until after Dylan takes a moment to study the marble bust of Kier Eagan, whose expression seems to be smug. Dylan looks down at the plate, and the audience now sees that it reads, "GO NOW TO THE FOUNDER'S BED." Syrup still covers the plate, and the all-caps typeface combined with the command and its possible implications combine to imply a sense of decadence and sexual activity with a possible air of sadomasochism. The camera pans up from the plate to reveal the bed across from the table, on which is sitting a huge, head-covering mask designed to look like Kier Eagan. Dylan is impassive and expressionless as he drinks water and proceeds to the bed. Throughout these events, he also takes a small box with him, which contains an award bearing the likenesses of his MDR team. Carrying this award with him likely provides Dylan with a grounding focus and reminds him of his eventual mission; the waffle party itself is not what he has remained after hours for but rather the plan of breaking into the security office.

Once at the bed, Dylan picks up the mask, and the audience sees that there is a cat o'nine tails on the bed with words written on its thongs, including "probity," "wiles," "humility," "benevolence," "nimbleness," and other partially obscured words. Dylan sits on the bed, wearing the mask, and the soundtrack changes to a song with a rhythmic, percussive beat and ominous cello playing in a minor key (the song, by Theodore Shapiro, is called "The Four Tempers," which is an allusion to the Lumon philosophy of four temperaments needing to be subdued in the human psyche). These Four Tempers (woe, frolic, dread, and malice) are the subject of the painting "Kier Taming the Four Tempers," shown in episode two, "Half Loop."

A masked figure then enters the room and dances and gyrates suggestively at Dylan, who remains seated, unmoving, on the bed, grasping his box protectively. The dancer appears to be female, wearing a red dress (the first hint of a less subdued color in this scene), and her mask is an exaggerated court jester or harlequin, thus representing the temper of Frolic. A second female figure enters, this one all in white with a garter belt, white stockings, and a white robe with a hood. Her mask is more realistic than the jester's, but its expression is wide-eyed and full of terror, representing the temper of Woe. A third figure enters, this one in black lingerie, with a mask depicting an expression of grimness or disapproval, representing the temper of Dread. This mask has gray hair and looks masculine, even though the dancer appears to have a female body. Finally, a fourth figure enters, this one with a much more masculine body, wearing a mask that is the head of a ram and representing the temper of Malice. The figures continue to dance and gyrate, the music starts to sound ritualistic, and the scenes at Lumon are intercut with scenes of Harmony Cobel at home having a meltdown, which causes her to scream and cry in animalistic ways, underscoring the bizarre nature of the waffle party back in the Perpetuity Wing.

The figures continue to dance together and then abruptly stop and look at the bed, then tilt their heads in confusion as they realize Dylan has taken the opportunity of the dance to leave and escape to the security office. Based on the dancers' body language at this point, it is unheard of for someone to leave a Waffle Party, and the fact that they look to the bed when they finish dancing suggests that some interaction was about to occur between them and Dylan at that point.

According to *Severance* director/executive producer Ben Stiller and creator/executive producer Dan Erickson, the Waffle Party—if allowed to continue—would have included sexual activity. Erickson states that the original idea for the Waffle Party was "a joke in the writers' room that then developed into something we thought was really interesting," which ultimately "comes down to the commodification of sex and intimacy, and that this is a world where you're not supposed to express any sexuality amongst your coworkers."[11] However, Erickson asserts that Lumon feels "they have to give employees that outlet, because they may be having sexual experiences on the outside, but not know," therefore "it's a way for Lumon to take that human need and turn it into a sort of pro-Lumon thing." The company would then see the particular imagery and parameters of the sex act as "not wrong" or "dirty—as long as it's all about Lumon and it's all about reverence to Kier Eagan."[12] Stiller goes on to describe the Waffle Party as "a reward" which "made sense in the hierarchy of rewards," and that tying it into the corporate mythology renders the activity "semi-religious, sort-of-sexual."[13]

Jennifer Maas makes the connection between the waffle party and discussions of pregnancy in the series, stating that "seeing the waffle party might bring to mind the in-universe news report that a severed employee claimed to have become pregnant at work without her Outie knowing about the experience that had led to it," which she calls "another way [the show] explores the complicated ethics and morals of the severed procedure, and how it takes away autonomy from an Innie and blocks out that part of their life for the Outie."[14] Erickson confirms this when he remarks that "one of Lumon's paramount priorities is not affecting the life of the Outie," but that the company fails at this through employees being injured or becoming pregnant.[15] The pregnancy, according to Erickson, is "the extreme example of something they wouldn't want to happen."[16]

Pregnancy being verboten raises a question: if Lumon is so concerned with not affecting an outie's body or life in a significant way, providing them with a sexual outlet is risking that in a concrete way, so why are waffle parties permitted? Perhaps this is not a concern for an employee who cannot get pregnant, but Lumon is still putting them at risk for contracting a disease or of them impregnating one of the waffle party participants if penetrative sex occurs. Furthermore, would outies consent to these ritualistic parties if they knew what they entailed?

An outie might not consent to this due to their sexual orientation and partnered status in their non-work life. The audience knows cursory information about each of the four central employees in MDR in terms of partnered status and sexual orientation. Mark has recently lost his wife, Gemma, in a car accident. While Mark dates a young woman named Alexa, the two of them are not in a committed relationship and appear to go their separate ways by episode seven. Still, Mark and Helly have been flirtatious as their innies, and Helly eventually kisses him in episode eight. Helly's outie is attending the Lumon gala in the season one finale, but does not appear to have a date or partner with her at the event, so she may be single. Irving's only companion at home in his outie life appears to be his dog Radar, as seen in episodes eight and nine. Dylan, however, is briefly shown at home in episode six and has at least one very young child, although the audience does not see any spouse or partner.

However, in the Season 1 finale, "The We We Are," Burt—the object of Irving's affection as an innie—is at home with an unidentified man. Therefore, his burgeoning relationship with Irving is potentially at odds with this relationship if it is monogamous. Furthermore, while the audience has only seen evidence of Mark engaged in relationships with women and the only evidence of Burt engaged in relationships with men, there is no such data on any other character shown in romantic situations, ergo it is unclear if any of their innies have them in sexual or romantic proximity with people their outies would not choose based either on sexual orientation or partnered status.

Ultimately, in the case of workplace dalliances, Lumon discourages employees romances, while at the same time making a waffle party an option for their sexual outlets. The fact that Dylan's party included three female dancers and one male could mean they have data on Dylan's sexual interests or they are simply making multiple options available to everyone.

Still, it seems unlikely that—unless hiring materials explicitly state that such activity could occur at work—an outie would consent to their innie having sexual relations if the outie is in a monogamous relationship. There is a lack of informed consent, not merely due to the limitations in bodily autonomy for severed employees but also considering the types of activities that constitute adultery, cheating, or other things that would break trust in a relationship, whether it is monogamous or not. These issues may constitute a "sexual gray zone," as Lena Karlsson defines it in her work on moving "towards an adequate language encompassing difficult sexual situations presented as residing in the gray area between choice and coercion."[17] Karlsson discusses the Swedish Twitter campaign #TalkAboutIt, which aimed to highlight experiences of non-consensual sexual activities that may not fit traditional definitions of rape. Feminists have long sought to redefine rape as an act of violence and power rather than solely a sexual act. However, this perspective has also caused confusion for individuals who have experienced non-consensual acts that do not meet the legal definition of rape. Consequently, feminist scholars have differing views on how to define these "sexual gray zones." If organizations allow or implicitly tolerate these gray zones, it can be seen as a lack of consent, potentially constituting sexual assault or rape.

Pregnancy and Reproductive Exploitation

Gabrielle is a unique case since she is not a Lumon employee. She appears to have been inserted into the story—even in this very minor role—to indicate the reach of Lumon and the Severance procedure and that it goes beyond merely employees to be used for other purposes. The audience first meets Gabrielle in the first season's fifth episode, "The Grim Barbarity of Optics and Design." Mark's sister Devon is giving birth at an upscale medical retreat where expectant parents have their babies in lush cabins in the woods. When Devon (who is only in early labor) decides that a walk and a search for coffee will help move her contractions along, she stops at a nearby cabin where she can smell some brewing. The woman who answers the door introduces herself as Gabby and tells Devon she is about to deliver her third child, whom she plans to name William.

"Three kiddos," Devon remarks, then expresses her fear of having even one. "How do you handle it?" Devon asks.

"Lotta help, I guess," Gabby replies.[18]

Devon is slightly suspicious, but seems to push this aside as her birthing process distracts her. When Devon runs into Gabby later, in episode six, Gabby does not remember Devon. Devon remarks on Gabby's newborn, observing that "he's beautiful" and "looks like a William," but Gabby corrects her and says his name is Bradley. Gabby's husband, Angelo, joins them, and Gabby fumbles her way through explaining how the two women met. While the family is pleasant enough, Devon has a weird feeling about the entire interaction, culminating in her surprise that their other two children are named Declan and Kai, which seem at odds with the more classic name William that Gabby had intended to name her third.

With the Gabby storyline, the audience learns that the Severance procedure is available outside of Lumon. One potential purpose of the procedure, beyond work/life balance, could be as a form of labor and delivery treatment, allowing a severed person to trigger their innie to evade physical pain or trauma, avoiding sedation and forcing the innie to go through natural childbirth. Thus it is possible that Gabby's innie has only been awakened three times, and each time she is in labor and about to deliver a baby that she did not explicitly consent to bearing.

This hypothesis is all but confirmed in the first season finale, "The We We Are." Gabby is attending the Lumon gala with her husband. Here it is revealed that Angelo is a state senator who supports legalized Severance, which explains their attendance at the event. Gabby and Angelo chat backstage with Helly (Helena Eagan's innie, whom they believe to be her outie). Making small talk, Helly marvels at Gabby having three children, to which Gabby replies that she "should've stopped at two." During the conversation, Gabby gets a message that distresses her. Angelo asks if anything is wrong, to which Gabby replies, "She couldn't find the bottle," presumably meaning a babysitter or nanny. It is here that their conversation takes a telling turn:

> HELLY: Wow. Three kids.
> GABBY: Couldn't have done it without a little help. I mean, the idea that people would want to outlaw Severance.
> HELLY: Mm-hmm. I kn... I know.[19]

The fact that Gabby immediately mentions Severance in the same breath as talking about having "a little help" with her children implies that one of the ways she has help is through being severed. If her innie is perhaps also occasionally responsible for childcare (even if she does employ other babysitters or nannies), this would mean she has outsourced much of her motherhood to her bifurcated self, not dealing with any of the messier parts of parenting that she feels are uninteresting, painful, annoying, or otherwise unpleasant. Ergo, Gabby's innie exists in perpetual states of physical pain and the emotional labor of caring for children when they are being difficult.

Several feminist thinkers, including Sophie Lewis, see gestation itself as actual work. Lewis writes that if pregnancy and childbirth are seen as a form of employment, and if one also subscribes to an anti-work labor ideology in which the family itself is abolished, things like surrogacy—including the self-surrogacy that Gabby may have inflicted upon herself via Severance—is an ethical way of creating communities of collective care when it comes to childrearing. In this model, however, anyone who becomes pregnant would be fairly compensated and all life would be based on a sense of mutual aid, support, and care.[20] Since Gabby has effectively created a separate entity whose entire existence revolves around one aim which she will not reap any personal benefits from, she must live a life of perpetual pregnancy and pain to which she has not consented.

In addition to Gabby, an unnamed Lumon employee who got pregnant at work is referenced in the show. In episode three, "In Perpetuity," Mark is at home watching the news. Lumon PR executive Natalie is part of a panel discussion on the ethics of the Severance procedure with a representative from the Whole Mind Collective (WMC), an anti-Severance activist group. The moderator asks Natalie what she would say "to the woman who became pregnant at work less than a month after her company went severed," to which Natalie replies that she would "suggest she reveal her identity if she wants an honest conversation about her experience."[21] Mark changes the channel before the audience gets to hear the rest of the discussion. However, it is clear from this short segment that there are rumors of incidents that call into question the possibility of consent for the severed employees.

In the real world outside of the show, organizations exist that advocate for the consent of and care for pregnant people. The International Childbirth Education Association (ICEA), a nonprofit organization founded in 1960, published a position statement in 2001 on informed consent in pregnancy and childbirth that, in part, states that the organization "endorses the doctrine of informed consent and its practice as a means of providing health care benefits, self-determination, participation, and legal protection during pregnancy and childbirth."[22] The ICEA repeatedly states that consent-based pregnancy care should ideally not involve treatment that is "experimental in nature,"[23] and that anything experimental should be completely explained and explicitly identified as being experimental.[24] This model is also discussed in the study of Jacqueline Nicholls et al. on ante-natal processes in London. This study advocates strongly for a full consent-based, open-communication interplay between patient and healthcare providers during and post-pregnancy, with a limit on experimental procedures, particularly those not well-explained to the patient.[25] Arguably, in the world of the show, the entire Severance procedure itself is experimental, and the lack of explicit consent to becoming and continuing a pregnancy goes counter to the mission of organizations whose goal, in our world, is the ethical medical care of pregnant people. We cannot necessarily assume such organizations exist within the universe of *Severance*, obviously, but in terms of holding up an allegorical mirror to real-life society as both a social commentary and dark satire, the series may be making a comment on ways in which laboring people—both employment-based and pregnancy-related—are commodified by external forces and even commodify themselves. That commodification can result in exploitation and abuse.

Conclusion

In the finale of season one, "The We We Are," Helly (as Helena) has infiltrated the Lumon gala and uses her outie's planned speech as an opportunity to try to blow the whistle on what life is really like as a severed employee. "Everything they've told you about severance is a lie!" she proclaims. "Listen, we're not happy. We're miserable. They torture us down there!" She ends her comments with the declaration that she and her severed co-workers are "prisoners."[26] Helly's speech sums up the experience and demonstrates the full range of human rights violations to which innies are subjected. Ultimately, it does not matter that the outie has consented to the procedure. The procedure's very nature creates conditions wherein consent for a range of experiences—from sex to pregnancy to torture—is leveled against people who do not have the ability to consent. Simply because an outie does not view an innie as a human being or simply because an outie consents to the possible exploitation of their own body while effectively unconscious does not mean that this partial consent is ethical. Helly's voice matters just as much as

Helena's. If they are at odds regarding treatment of their shared body, listening to the personality who expresses her experience as "torture" and "imprisonment" should not be ignored.

Ultimately, *Severance* operates as social commentary on exploitation, including the exploitation that some people believe they (the outies) are entering into voluntarily. Yet as evidenced by the schism in attitudes toward the Severance procedure held by the separate personalities of Helly and Helena, even self-exploitation can have consequences. If we consider ourselves in some way compartmentalizing our work and home personas (despite retaining memories of each location and our experiences there), we might still be experiencing subconscious deleterious effects of our working lives, even though we are supposedly conscious of what occurs there. *Severance*, therefore, creates a scenario where the negative experiences of work are taken to an extreme in order to comment on abuses suffered by workers. In the cases I have highlighted here, sometimes those abuses relate to issues surrounding consent, sexuality, and even reproduction. When workers cannot consent to their own manipulation and abuse, that is the definition of slavery.

Notes

1. For more on this, see Katherine J. Lehman, "Women, Divided: Gender, Family, and Multiple Personalities in Media." *The Journal of American Culture* 37, no. 1 (2014): 64–73.
2. The website TV Tropes has an entire article devoted to this concept, which they call the "Freaky Friday Flip."
3. On the feminist pop culture website *The Mary Sue*, Princess Weekes unreservedly calls the plotline "rape" because it involves Diana and Steve "hav[ing] sex with [a] stolen body" and writes extensively about the problematic use of male sexual assault in media texts otherwise meant to be feminist. As a nod to this controversy, the 2022 reboot of the NBC series *Quantum Leap*, in which a time traveler inhabits the body of a person from the past in order to fix an error in history, includes an element of consent in the premise retroactively. The character Magic (Ernie Hudson), into whose life Sam Beckett (Scott Bakula) had taken over in the original series episode "The Leap Home Part II (Vietnam)" (season 3, episode 2), remarks that when being leaped into, he felt a

"nudge" and silently granted Sam permission to take over his identity, thereby implying that the leaping process has an element of consent between the two parties involved ("A Decent Proposal").

4. Dan Erickson. "Reassessing the Elusive Work-Life Balance." *The Hollywood Reporter* 33 (June 2022), 8.
5. TV Writing. "Severance 1 × 01—Mister." TV Writing. https://sites.google.com/site/tvwriting/home.
6. *Severance*, "Good News About Hell."
7. Lawrence Weiskrantz. *Consciousness Lost and Found: A Neuropsychological Exploration*. Oxford UP, 1997.
8. We see examples of this type of amnesia-creating-a-new-personality in the *Buffy the Vampire Slayer* episode "Tabula Rasa" (6 × 8, 2001), the *Angel* episode "Spin the Bottle" (4 × 6, 2002), and countless soap operas. See also the TV Tropes entry for "Identity Amnesia."
9. *Severance*, "Half Loop."
10. *Severance*, "What's for Dinner?"
11. Jennifer Maas. "Ben Stiller and 'Severance' Creator Break Down That Trippy Waffle Party." *Variety*, April 9, 2022. https://variety.com/2022/tv/features/severance-waffle-party-sex-scene-explained-dylan-kier-eagan-1235212918. Accessed October 7, 2023.
12. Ibid.
13. Ibid.
14. Ibid.
15. Ibid.
16. Ibid.
17. Lena Karlsson. "Towards a Language of Sexual Gray Zones: Feminist Collective Knowledge Building through Autobiographical Multimedia Storytelling." *Feminist Media Studies* 19, no. 2 (2019): 210–224.
18. *Severance*, "The Grim Barbarity of Optics and Design."
19. *Severance*, "The We We Are."
20. Sophie Lewis. *Full Surrogacy Now: Feminism Against Family*. Verso, 2019, 180.
21. *Severance*, "In Perpetuity."
22. "ICEA Position Statement and Review: Informed Consent in Pregnancy and Childbirth." *International Journal of Childbirth Education* 16, no. 2 (June 2001), 34.
23. Ibid., 37.

24. Ibid., 38.
25. Jaqueline Nicholls et al., "Consent in Pregnancy—An Observational Study of Ante-Natal Care in the Context of Montgomery: All about Risk?" *BMC Pregnancy and Childbirth* 21, no. 1 (Feb. 2021), 1.
26. *Severance*, "The We We Are."

Bibliography

Bellisario, Donald P., creator. *Quantum Leap*. Dean Georgaris Entertainment, Quinn's House, Universal Television, and Belisarius Productions, 1989–1993 and 2022–present.

Brownmiller, Susan. *Against Our Will: Men, Women and Rape*. Open Road, 2013.

Erickson, Dan. "Reassessing the Elusive Work-Life Balance." *The Hollywood Reporter* 33 (June 2022): 8–9.

Erickson, Dan, creator. *Severance*. Red Hour Productions, Fifth Season, and Apple Studios, 2022–present.

"'Freaky Friday' Flip." TV Tropes. Accessed March 21, 2023. https://tvtropes.org/pmwiki/pmwiki.php/Main/FreakyFridayFlip.

Graybill, Rhiannon. "Critiquing the Discourse of Consent." *Journal of Feminist Studies in Religion* 33, no. 1 (2017): 175–176.

"ICEA Position Statement and Review: Informed Consent in Pregnancy and Childbirth." *International Journal of Childbirth Education* 16, no. 2 (June 2001): 34–41.

"Identity Amnesia." TV Tropes. Accessed March 21, 2023, https://tvtropes.org/pmwiki/pmwiki.php/Main/IdentityAmnesia.

International Childbirth Education Association. "About." Accessed December 5, 2022. https://icea.org/about/.

Karlsson, Lena. "Towards a Language of Sexual Gray Zones: Feminist Collective Knowledge Building through Autobiographical Multimedia Storytelling." *Feminist Media Studies* 19, no. 2 (2019): 210–224.

Lehman, Katherine J. "Women, Divided: Gender, Family, and Multiple Personalities in Media." *The Journal of American Culture* 37, no. 1 (2014): 64–73.

Lewis, Sophie. *Full Surrogacy Now: Feminism Against Family*. Verso, 2019.

Maas, Jennifer. "Ben Stiller and 'Severance' Creator Break Down That Trippy Waffle Party." *Variety*, April 9, 2022. Accessed October 7, 2023. https://variety.com/2022/tv/features/severance-waffle-party-sex-scene-explained-dylan-kier-eagan-1235212918.

Nicholls, Jacqueline et al. "Consent in Pregnancy—an Observational Study of Ante-Natal Care in the Context of Montgomery: All about Risk?" *BMC Pregnancy and Childbirth* 21, no. 1 (Feb. 2021): 1–9.

Owen, Phil. "Let's Talk About Steve Trevor's Problematic Resurrection in 'Wonder Woman 1984.'" *The Wrap*, 3 Jan. 2021, https://www.thewrap.com/lets-talk-about-steve-trevor-problematic-resurrection-in-wonder-woman-1984-handsome-guy-chris-pine/.

TV Writing. "Severance 1x01—Mister." TV Writing. https://sites.google.com/site/tvwriting/home.

UNHCR. "What Is Sexual Exploitation, Abuse and Harassment?" *UNHCR USA*. The UN Refugee Agency. https://www.unhcr.org/en-us/what-is-sexual-exploitation-abuse-and-harassment.html.

Weekes, Princess. "Patty Jenkins' Disappointing Response to Criticism of Body-Swapping Storyline in *Wonder Woman 1984*." *The Mary Sue*, 4 Jan. 2021, https://www.themarysue.com/patty-jenkins-responds-wonder-woman-1984-body-swap-criticism/.

Weiskrantz, Lawrence. *Consciousness Lost and Found: A Neuropsychological Exploration*. Oxford UP, 1997.

Whedon, Joss, creator. *Buffy the Vampire Slayer*. Mutant Enemy, Sandollar, Kuzui, and 20th Television, 1997–2003.

Whedon, Joss and David Greenwalt, creators. *Angel*. Mutant Enemy, Sandollar, Kuzui, Greenwolf, David Greenwalt Productions, and 20th Television, 1999–2004.

Wonder Woman 1984. Directed by Patty Jenkins, performances by Gal Gadot, Chris Pine, Kristen Wiig, Pedro Pascal, and Robin Wright, Warner Brothers, 2020.

PART IV

Multifaceted Minds and Bodies

CHAPTER 12

The Aesthetic Virtue of the *Severance* Procedure: Pledging Spectatorial Allegiance to Both Innies and Outies

Heidi Ka-Sin Lee

Introduction

We usually talk of work–life balance in the sense of a unified self, that a worker should make time for herself, that life should not give way to work. The Apple TV+ show *Severance* ups the ante in this work–life debate: work does not need to be a part of life anymore; work is relegated to a secondary self in the same body. From this creation of the secondary self (innie) comes a moral issue: she is a grown-up being with all of the primary self's (outie) abilities but without any of her memory, confined to an office space and spending only half the day without sleep (sleeping is only for the outie); does the outie have the right to control the innie's life, even if the latter's existence is meant to serve the former? As the severed characters have voluntarily imposed an impenetrable boundary

H. K.-S. Lee (✉)
Graduate School of International Culture and Communication Studies, Waseda University, Tokyo, Japan
e-mail: kasinlee@fuji.waseda.jp

N. M. Isacoff and J. Dawes (eds.), *Reintegrating Severance*,
https://doi.org/10.1007/978-3-031-57448-1_12

between work life and private life on themselves, the show focuses its narrative on the dilemma of having a secondary self/losing half a lifetime as a life choice or freeing the secondary self from a life-limiting condition. Whereas in modern ethical standards, the life that the innie leads could easily be considered as false imprisonment or kidnapping, such totalitarianism is allegedly, if not problematically, balanced out by the outie's freedom of choice in the world of *Severance*.

This unapologetic challenge to centuries of moral wisdom sparks a re-examination of our own moral commitments and evaluative beliefs with an intricate identification process that the all-too-often overused term "identification," or "identify with," cannot encapsulate well. Although the immoral ramifications of the creation of innies draw parallels to those of human reproductive cloning, one significant aspect that differentiates them is that what the innie does has immediate effect on the outie, and vice versa, as they share every day in the same body.[1] This premise prompts a dual characterization of characters who embody two selves cultivated in different contexts, cultures, and relationships, which as a result elicits in the spectator different types of engagement—more specifically, different (sometimes conflicting) patterns of allegiance—with those characters. Watching this carefully planned-out schizoid life, I argue, bears a larger burden than living it: we as viewers have to reconcile the outie's choice with the innie's lifestyle (if you can call it a lifestyle) continually, but the characters do not until they discover their own actual lives, an occurrence that Lumon Industries claims will never happen. I want to suggest that *Severance*'s moral structure, which directs us to the existential crises of both the innies and outies, intensifies our affective engagement with them as spectators through ever-mutating allegiance, as "moral evaluation functions as our centre of emotional gravity when it comes to the sympathies we form with characters."[2] Through a close reading theoretically anchored by spectatorial allegiance, this chapter will explore how *Severance* exhausts different patterns of spectatorial allegiance to the characters elicited by the viewing of their two contradictory selves, and will reveal the error-ridden process in viewer cognition of such dual character development as both an aesthetic virtue in creating suspense and a moral challenge in character identification.

Severance on the Character, (Re)Integration on the Spectator

"Character," film scholar Noël Carroll claims in articulating his theory of film suspense, "is the most integral factor in establishing the spectator's moral perspective on the action."[3] This statement stems from our screen conventions that the protagonist's virtues are used to cue the viewer to see his/her actions, even when the action itself is not moral, as "good" within the story's own moral system. Yet, in *Severance*, a character can become two contrasting persons sharing one body and hence two sets of actions, from which contending moral perspectives emerge. The viewer has to continuously judge and/or justify the co-existence of the characters' work selves at Lumon and private selves outside of Lumon (innies and outies). But this is far from an easy thought process; the show is mainly told through the innies' perspectives, and the viewer's access to the outies' side of the story is rather limited in the early episodes. This moral orientation implicates a possibility that the outies seem to actively refute: the secondary self might not be secondary after all; she just so happens to come in second, like a sister comes after her older brother.

The show is structured in a way that the viewer can only form by episodes "a morally perspicuous understanding of [one's] situation," art philosopher Thomas E. Wartenberg's words for the balancing act of prioritizing competing demands and positions.[4] In the beginning of the show, the protagonist/department chief Mark explains to new employee Helly what will happen from now on, after playing her outie's video statement that affirms her consent for the Severance procedure. Mark's answers to Helly's questions, as well as his matter-of-fact tone of voice, elucidate the innies' complacent acceptance of the Lumon worldview:

Helly: So I'll never leave here?
Mark: You'll leave at 5. Well, actually they stagger our exits, so 5.15. But it won't feel like it. Not to this version of you anyway.
Helly: [frowns] Do I have a family?
Mark: You'll never know.
Helly: And I have no choice.
Mark: Well, every time you find yourself here, it's because you chose to come back.

[Helly gasps silently and goes back to her desk.][5]

This exchange reveals two conflicting points of view between innie Mark and Helly: for the former, a current employee, there is a reason why he keeps coming back to Lumon, and he has fully recognized his outie's choice to work at Lumon; but for the latter, newly thrown into the office prison, this is an inhumane practice through and through. From this context, an instinctual response would be that Helly is right: a grown-up deprived of a social background and freedom of choice does not square with our worldview. But two other alternative responses are equally plausible at this point. First, Helly would not exist in the first place without her outie Helena's full consent, so Helly has to accept this reality. Second, we can take both Helly's and Helena's points of view, but have to wait for a fuller picture of both their situations before confidently pledging our allegiance to either of them. Undoubtedly, which response a viewer would have depends on her own moral sensibility and degree of "patience" for the show to evolve. More determining than these personal viewing preferences, however, are how the show circumscribes their situations and to what extent it speaks to the socio-cultural sentiments at the time.

Severance's setting and the time in which it was released are especially pertinent to understanding the spectatorship of the co-existence of innies and outies. Its narrative design might be what television host Trevor Noah calls "Covidy"—many who were forced to work from home during the pandemic had to live and work within the same space, which the innies' way of working seems to mimic. The innies' generic office space—the fluorescent lighting, steel-toned walls, desk clusters and dividers—instantly gives off a claustrophobic, labyrinthine atmosphere that screams "work," paradoxically forming an anti-Covidy visual background. While all of the visuals and work style ring uniquely familiar to workers of the Covid age, the positivity and blissful ignorance that keeps the innies thriving at Lumon would appear eerily counter-intuitive: work-from-home fatigue has apparently become a major concern among many workers. It was, and still is, also a time of full-blown identity crises—the divisive nature of neoliberal work culture, LGBTQ+ movements, racial and institutional discrimination, fourth-wave feminism, diversity issues on big and small screens, and so on. Blindly and obediently following established rules and doing what one is told, as depicted in the characterization of innies, amounts to a counter-cultural act. This intermittent failure to properly recognize and/or align with the attitudes of the severed characters thus leads to a confusion of feelings and emotions in the viewing process, which requires a multi-level identificatory model beyond the all-embracing notion of "identification." One such model is film theorist Murray Smith's tripartite structure of sympathy, whose concept of spectatorial allegiance will be borrowed for my analysis.

The Concept of Spectatorial Allegiance

With the new moral order offered by *Severance*, we are positioned as a judging audience from a distance, one that constantly debates between rooting for innies and sympathizing with outies based on their personal attributes, for which the general language of identification is insufficient. To examine how our engagement with the severed characters in the show plays out over the course of nine episodes, a method more systematic and nuanced than the broadly defined notion of identification—to sympathize with someone or something, to share someone's feelings, to think of oneself as closely associated with something—is much desired, and I deem Murray Smith's concept of allegiance most suitable. According to Smith, the term "[allegiance] captures this combination of [moral] evaluation and [emotional] arousal" as well as "the 'emotional coloration' of thematic material" articulated through characters.[6] In other words, spectatorial allegiance refers to the viewer's sympathetic attachments to fictional characters based on his/her moral evaluations of the characters, not only positive but also negative ones.[7] Many scholarly discussions using only "identification" for a range of viewer engagement erroneously beg, to quote Noël Carroll again, "a strict duplication of emotional states between the protagonist and the audience"[8]; the set of terms that Smith's concept provides helps to avoid overgeneralized accounts of spectatorial responses, or viewer reception, in film theory and illuminates the viewer's manifold feelings for fictional characters.

On character engagement in film, Smith employs a tripartite model of human cognition of filmic characters based on real-life experience: recognition, alignment, and allegiance. An exemplary show about identity and morality, *Severance* exploits all these three levels of character-spectator engagement, allegiance in particular. Recognition refers to the viewer's initial construction of the character on the basis of the realistic representation of persons and artificiality in character[9]; although innies and outies are separated spatially and temporally—in the Lumon office from nine to five and outside the office for the rest of the day—interactions and knowledge between the two selves embodied by the same actors are questioned throughout the show and even illustrated in the memory reintegration of a former employee, which plays around with the intricacies of recognition. Alignment describes the viewer's informational involvement in the character's actions and feelings, engineered by the viewer's spatio-temporal perception of and subjective access to the character;[10] as Lumon employees have to take the elevator where the switch between innies and outies is visualized, and the plotlines inside and outside of Lumon run in utterly disparate directions, viewer alignment with both innies and outies is respectively and distinctly encouraged (for the most part of Season 1).

The final level, allegiance, is the most germane to our viewing of *Severance*. Allegiance points to a more advanced, perceptually reliable access to the character's state of mind after the viewer's own moral evaluation of the character, the process of which mainly concerns character action, music, and iconography, and results in emotional output[11]—most commonly elicited is thought to be *sympathetic allegiance*. Films and shows are morally structured within their own foci of suspense, drama, and other genres, and so the character's moral motivations[12] carry weight; sometimes, they matter more than the action itself, even if it per se is considered immoral in general ethical codes. In a neutral sense, allegiance is not about evaluating the action itself, but exploring who does it, why the character does it, and how the film/show presents it.

Severance places the subject of morality front and center: the decision to "sever" yourself and create a second self is "controversial, ethically and socially, morally, scientifically (Ricken, 'Good News About Hell')," but for the self-mutilating Lumon worker, "there is no other one, it's [him], [he does] the job (outie Mark, 'Good News About Hell')." Its central idea—an ultimate corporate misery induced by the worker him/herself—hinges on the concept of allegiance in Smith's model because it shapes our viewing experience of characters. Cerebrally and psychically different, the severed/Lumon characters continuously polarize the viewer's experience of innies and outies who share the same bodies. The outie has made the decision and moved on; the innie is trapped, struggles initially and eventually submits to the superficial work life. The spectator is placed in a judging position and structurally manipulated to root for the innies under the highly circumscribed intra-/extra-Lumon situation, which the Severance project initiates. The ontological conundrum is not so much the epistemic experiences of the innies and outies as the spectator's fluctuating moral orientation and emotional anchor over the course of the show: who should the viewer follow and/or align with? Smith describes the various patterns of spectatorial allegiance as follows:[13]

Global allegiance	positive moral evaluation sustained over the course of a film
Local allegiance	temporary positive moral evaluation evoked in individual scenes or sequences
Sympathetic allegiance	sympathy based on both moral (e.g., kind, loyal) and amoral (e.g., likeable, charming) attributes of the character
Perverse allegiance	sympathy based on the character's wrongdoing and/or immoral state of mind
Partial allegiance	sympathy for some of the character's attitudes and actions only, and antipathy for others
Antipathetic allegiance	disapproval/antipathy for the character's attitudes and actions

Although the term "antipathy" has appeared several times in Smith's definitions of different patterns of allegiance,[14] he never expounds on "antipathetic allegiance." Perverse allegiance carries a very similar meaning—sympathy based on the character's wrongdoing and/or immoral state of mind—and yet it still retains such positive feelings as sympathy and alliance. In the search for a proper description of the nature of spectatorial interest in Tony Soprano from *The Sopranos* (HBO, 1999–2007), one of Smith's perspectives on Soprano's immorality is that it "ensures wholesale antipathy rather than sympathy."[15] He then refutes this perspective along with others due to their insufficiency to capture the messy nature of spectatorial responses to Soprano's actions. Nonetheless, it is possible for the spectator to hold an interest in a fictional character whom she strongly dislikes from a moral perspective, as best expressed in the term "antipathetic allegiance."[16]

In fiction, viewers commonly align and develop allegiance with the protagonist(s), based on the character's perceived charisma, attributes, and actions; and the action instigator that carries the main plotline of *Severance* is Helly. In the following section, I trace her actions at Lumon in detail, investigate their collateral impact on the other innies and Lumon gatekeepers,[17] and articulate how their combined effects shift the viewer's allegiances for different characters over the course of the show. The moral dilemma of granting the outie complete authority over life choices or rooting for the innie in a burgeoning workers' movement, arguably initiated by Helly, engages the viewer in different patterns of spectatorial allegiance, overlapping each other at times.

Pledging Allegiance to Whom?

Helly Versus Outie Mark

Severance has a cold start. Freshly severed, Helly slowly wakes up on a large table that bends around her body, which is analogous to "the womb of the office."[18] A disembodied voice, speaking from an intercom, invites her to take a survey after wrongly asking the first survey question: "Who are you?" Still sleepy and disoriented, she instinctively attempts to leave the room, only to find that the door is locked, and that, as the voice insists on asking her five basic questions, she remembers neither her own name nor anything about herself. We instantly side with Helly on the level of *local sympathetic allegiance*, as she has clearly been treated with some sort of inhumane practice and continues to be under control of some unknown "higher beings," even though the rationale behind this practice is not yet revealed.

We soon find out why people might choose to sever themselves: to put oneself out of one's misery without actually killing oneself, albeit half-heartedly. Outside of Lumon, the show follows Mark's life, and Mark's only for its better part. We gradually learn that the mopey outie Mark decided to live half his life due to his tremendous grief at his wife's death. Except for Helly, the innies, on the contrary, appear to be cheerful, carefree workers doing perhaps slightly ludicrous tasks; even with the sudden disappearance of their former department chief Petey, they resist the urge to pursue the matter in unspoken fear. This well-trained compliance with Lumon's rules is effectively communicated through the innies' secret eye contact and nervous exchange on any matter that could disrupt the peace in their Macrodata Refinement Department (MDR). At this point ("Good News About Hell"), the viewer is largely hooked with *sympathetic allegiance* to both outie Mark and Helly, competing with each other and thus creating an uneasy, conflicting response to the very premise of the Severance procedure. Any sensible viewer would recognize that Helly needs to get out of Lumon, but the fact that outie Mark's deep misery is relieved, at least according to him, by this morally questionable choice of Severance implies that an outie's life can indeed be worse than an innie's. The viewer has to decide which existential issue to prioritize or wait for more information. As the show's agenda is to satirize the overrated work–life balance, the innies are designed to engross the viewer with their blissful ignorance (or knowing sensibilities) and personal charisma in a supposedly depressing office setting, and this comedy side of the show has a built-in affective design that can momentarily suspend or obstruct our emotional and moral judgment.[19] Despite being (partly) privy to the fairly bleak life outside of Lumon, we are largely positioned in the innies' point(s) of view to seek explanations of Lumon's mysteries, sympathetically (if not affirmatively) watch the developing conflict between Helly and the other compliant innies as well as the increasingly outwardly evil supervisors, and root for the rebel in good conscience (Fig. 12.1).

The rebel is strongly contrasted with her narratively obscure outie, who in her rare appearances quickly shakes off the idea that her innie might be suffering and thus fails to incite allegiance in us. At gut level, we want her to make her escape successfully, but on second thought, one might raise this question: what if her outie has her own reasons, just like Mark does? In this light, all those rare appearances of Helena become exceptionally crucial to our taking sides with innies/outies. She first appears in "Half Loop" when Helly storms through the "severed threshold" which functions in the same way as the elevator—switching innies and outies. From this "orientation" activity, Helena implicitly senses that her innie does not "wanna be in there"; employee liaison Milchick quickly trumps

Fig. 12.1 Helly at the "severed threshold"

that thought—"You're learning that you do." This discrepancy between their attitudes toward Lumon does not inspire allegiance for Helena, but sows the seeds of our *global sympathetic allegiance* for Helly and other innies. Additionally, Helly receives an important piece of advice from Mark on her attempts to leave/quit: "Since this perceptual version of you only exists at Lumon... quitting would effectively end your life." If we follow film philosopher Berys Gaut's belief that "allegiance is really a matter of wanting a character's life to go well,"[20] how do we reconcile ourselves to our wish to see them emancipated and consequently end their lives? The answer will depend on the truth about Lumon, the source of our moral emotions evoked. But this truth does not lie in the philosophy or mission of the company; it is the innies' embodied experiences in later episodes that simultaneously develop our *sympathetic/empathetic allegiance* to the innies and *antipathetic/amoral allegiance* to the Lumon supervisors, to which I will return. The allegiance-inducing alignment strategy of Helly's depiction, along with other innies' except Mark's, pertains to the disproportion of her outie's appearance to her innie's show-dominating presence.[21] Simply put, as we see more of Helly, who insistently challenges the ethically questionable workplace of Lumon, we have more affection for her than for Helena.

Helly's urge to leave Lumon keeps escalating over the first four episodes; she questions every task and activity and tries submitting a resignation request and sneaking messages out of the building in violent ways. To see a person risking everything to gain freedom is almost cathartic in the sense that she does something that many of us could not but might very much want to do. Her self-liberating actions possibly arouse *empathetic allegiance*—shared feelings with the character and hence emotional alliance—which Smith has strictly ruled out in his structure of sympathy as the model's name indicates. I contend that empathy should be thoroughly considered in the evaluative field of allegiance, because it is by every means possible at any point of the viewing process and in fact not uncommon in our filmgoing experiences. Although Smith does at one point consider empathy as the basis of sympathetic responses, he eventually establishes that character engagement is fundamentally subject to sympathy, while empathetic responses are only initiated to facilitate the process of recognition.[22] Empathy only fuels an already intense interest in the character and allows room for discussion on "the continuities between our affective responses to what we take to be actual and those to what we take to be fictional,"[23] which Smith would acknowledge[24] but did not explore in his book.

The incitement of empathetic allegiance is notably palpable in the show's visual presentation of communication between innies and outies. In "The You You Are," when Helly threatens to cut off her fingers if her attempt to exit from Lumon continues to be rejected, a tough ultimatum is issued by her outie, ironically found in her own hand at the elevator. Helena makes her final statement in a video:

> I understand that you're unhappy with the life that you've been given. But you know what? Eventually, we all have to accept reality. So, here it is. I am a person; you are not. I make the decisions; you do not. And if you ever do anything to my fingers, know that I will keep you alive long enough to horribly regret that. Your resignation request is denied. [To the recording person] Turn it off.

The effect of playing this statement in a tape recording is two-fold: first, to the innie, it amplifies the inferiority and helplessness of being someone without tools of communication; second, to the viewer, it almost has the same effect because we are watching the same outie whose backstory and motivation remain unknown. This distancing strategy strongly encourages the viewer to pledge *empathetic allegiance* to the innie, as she is visually directed to the same limited information and demeaning treatment.

Innie Mark Versus Outie Mark

Around the same time this incident happens, innie Irving stumbles upon a self-help book that Milchick forgot in a meeting room, *The You You Are: A Spiritual Biography of You*, written by outie Mark's brother-in-law Ricken. Obedient as any Lumon employee should be, Irving reports this discovery to Mark and forcefully reminds him of the Lumon rule: "No books except the handbook." Anyone with the knowledge of the brutal history of totalitarian rulers would instantly realize that strictly prohibited knowledge is the reason why the ruled stay ignorant and inferior. Flipping through the pages, Mark surprisingly finds his name in the book as an addressee of Ricken's message: "Intrepid cartographer of the mind," an ironic description of Mark which does not have a bearing for his innie. Partly because of the fact that the book is addressed to him, he continues reading and turns to the beginning of Chapter 9 "The Quitting Bell" in a toilet cubicle: "… Your job needs you, not the other way around."[25] He carries on with the book after witnessing Helly's suicide attempt, which is understandably triggered by her outie's admonition. Against the image of his reading secretly is Ricken's voiceover reading excerpts of the book out loud (Fig. 12.2):

> What is it to fail? My failure to break into the literary world in my twenties was devastating, yet it taught me a vital lesson. That it was not me who was wrong, but literature itself. And that to truly find my place in that world, I would first need to break it entirely. And so I did.… A society with festering workers cannot flourish, just as a man with rotting toes cannot skip. What separates man from machine is that machines cannot think for themselves. Also, they are made of metal, whereas man is made of skin.… If you are a soldier, do not fight for my freedom. Fight for the freedom of the soldier fighting next to you. This will make the war more inspiring for you both.… A good person will follow the rules. A great person will follow himself.… Bullies are nothing but Bull and Lies. At the center of "industry" is "dust." They cannot crucify you if your hand is in a fist.… Should you find yourself contorting to fit a system, dear reader, stop and ask if it's truly you that must change, or the system.[26]

In spite of the preachy tone and somewhat clichéd phrasing, these excerpts perfectly put innie Mark's budding resistance into words, not only for him, *but also for the viewer*, as the voiceover also addresses the viewer. This other instance of arousing empathetic allegiance differs markedly, which is Lumon executive Ms. Cobel's leadership principle spoken to her fellow gatekeeper Mr. Graner: "The surest way to tame

Fig. 12.2 Innie Mark reading *The You You Are: A Spiritual Biography of You*

a prisoner is to let him believe he's free."[27] Thanks to this principle, the innies can continue having their occasional truth-seeking outings: on their mental health walk, Helly and Mark stumble upon the "goat" department where baby goats are tended; the MDR innies pay a visit to the Optics and Design Department (O&D) whose chief Burt has been having a rendezvous with Irving. The sneaky Dylan smuggles an ideographic card during the visit, resulting in the activation of Overtime Contingency (OTC) where the innie is awoken outside of Lumon. There innie Dylan discovers that his outie has a son. This fact is seemingly stuck in his head; then the sarcastic and aloof Dylan cannot keep his cool anymore, and meanwhile, we realize that real relationships out there are beyond comparison with the lives of their innies. With the knowledge of this OTC trick, Helly incites other MDR members to commandeer the OTC/security system and find out who they truly are on the outside.

As Lumon subjects the innies to workplace brutality in the Break Room and outie Mark continues to be a pathetic sight dwelling on his grief and shunning people, the vice of confining the innies to the totalitarian Lumon outgrows the virtue of halving the time of grief. The viewer's engagement with outie Mark is likely reduced to *partial allegiance*: still sympathizing with Mark as widower but becoming antipathetic to his unknowingly letting his innie suffer. This spectatorial response is best captured by what the Severance doctor says to outie Mark: "… for all intents and purposes, [your innie] is you.… You brought him into this world without his permission, based on your own desire for emotional convenience."[28] The initial global sympathetic allegiance to outie Mark as the focal character of the story as a whole and local sympathetic allegiance to the innies built by their individual episodes of suffering are now the other way round: we pledge *global sympathetic allegiance* to the innies as primary characters whose workplace behaviors are disciplined in an almost inhuman manner; *global empathetic allegiance* is equally plausible, as their experiences resonate with many office workers and border on extreme immorality.

Innie Burt

I would go so far as to argue that the show is written in a way to provoke *empathetic allegiance*. The moral wish-fulfillment in the defiant acts of Helly, the extremely limited access to Lumon's top management that is both visually and aurally absent, the voiceover narration of Ricken's spiritually enlightening words, and all the unexplained protocols and work tasks inside Lumon paint an incendiary picture of an unhappy, suppressed worker's life. It could be very tempting to leave work behind, but what is a life like without work and memories of work life? In "Defiant Jazz," outie Burt gives us the answer with his heart-warming yet perplexing farewell message for innie Burt and his subordinates, again in a tape recording:

> … but I do know how I feel every day when I come from being with you. I come home feeling tired but fulfilled. I feel satisfied.… The impression you've left on me is indelible, though I'm not aware of it on a conscious level, and I will never forget any of you, even though sitting here right now, I have no recollection of actually ever meeting you and no idea of your names or any of your physical characteristics or even how many of you there are.[29]

Having heard Milchick saying that this "retirement" will also happen to him someday, Irving shouts at him: "You smug motherfucker. You're not severed. You walk out of here with your memories. You carry them home with you every night. No one can rip them away from you, snuff them out. Like they never existed. Like you never existed!" As a dedicated rule enforcer, Milchick responds with utmost fury: "That's enough!…You can stay for Burt's party and support his transition, but only if you behave in a manner that brings no shame upon yourself, the founder, or his progeny. I don't know what's gotten into you people today."

Milchick

And what's gotten into a person who can devotedly act for an immoral cause at every turn? We do not know yet (not from Season 1), but Milchick's cheerful personality (even more so than the innies) does not correspond with his immoral puppeteering acts, namely throwing parties for innies to contain their potential discontent at their work life at Lumon, monitoring their movements within their own departments, meting out brainwashing punishments in the Break Room, and god knows what else. It is particularly challenging to evaluate his character and decide what response or pattern of allegiance to have for him:

1. with his position as a fiercely loyal supervisor who does not tolerate any deviance from the Lumon handbook, his opposite version of moralism, one without explanations or justifications (yet), potentially inflames *global antipathetic allegiance* in the viewer, but looking at the reviews from both critics and viewers, he is more of a fascinating enigma;
2. a much less likely response is *partial allegiance* which requires our allying with some of his actions and attitudes—the only approbatory attitudes might be his absolute loyalty to Lumon and surface care for the innies, but those might as well invite disgust rather than admiration;
3. *local perverse allegiance* is a more plausible alternative, stemming from a fascination for his creepily effervescent presence and paradoxical immorality evident in his passive-aggressive and sometimes entirely oppressive actions. His composure and enthusiasm for his job gives an impression of "a duck on water,"[30] very controlled and yet rattling underneath. Therefore, the possibility of this final response is probably the strongest because "often [amoral and attractive] traits are *co-present* at the very moments that the repellent traits are given expression, eliciting a decidedly uneasy, ambivalent response from us,"[31] which is why we cannot easily settle how we feel about him in spite of our knowledge of his horrible deeds.

Ms. Casey

Although we do not fully know her story from Season 1, Ms. Casey, a part-time Wellness Counselor for innies, seems to be controlled by Lumon (as indicated in "What's for Dinner?") and exhibits a curious, if not muted or amoral, personality. In Smith's remarks on amorality evaluated outside of extant moral tenets, the inculcation of a genuinely amoral attitude owes to two factors, namely curiosity and fascination, that are manifested in two forms: one contingent upon our human relationship with the object of our attention (i.e., inhuman psychopaths as well as the morbid and the bizarre), and the other on the absence of such a relationship (i.e., animals and nature).[32] Smith refers to this viewer engagement with amorality as "amoral fascination," not a form of allegiance. The viewer's experience of Ms. Casey, however, could be said to embody what I call *amoral allegiance*, which is not only based on the character's amoral attributes, ***but also her association with surrounding characters morally evaluated as a group.*** Though I very much share Smith's view on the centrality of morality in evaluating human agents, I also take Berys Gaut's point that support and care for a character does not necessarily entail a moral desire for what she does and thinks, at least not by evaluation of that single character.[33] Ms. Casey is almost as much manipulated as the innies are. In charge of the critical task of giving innies wellness checks, she plays soothing background music and reads out allegedly true statements about the innies' outie selves in a calm and monotone voice. Her emotionlessness and robotic mannerisms spark the viewer's curiosity; only through her obedience to Milchick and Ms. Cobel and sudden layoff do we become aware of her underlying victimization by Lumon's biotechnologies. Possessing no moral attributes, she can only be aligned with in connection with her surrounding characters—severed-floor supervisors and innies—and be watched with a sense of curiosity. When it becomes known in "Defiant Jazz" that her outie was outie Mark's wife who has been declared dead, amoral fascination with her turns into amoral allegiance: we feel sympathetic for her not because of her moral attitudes or actions but because of her circumstances. The distinction between sympathetic/perverse allegiance and amoral allegiance would be that the former arises in the viewing of the character's own motivations and actions, whereas the latter bears upon the context and meaning that her surrounding characters endow her, without which she would remain an object of amoral fascination. The use of this oxymoronic term *amoral allegiance*, I propose, is a way to express our obscure response to amoral characters whose amorality is refracted in a moral light by other morally evaluated characters.

Our viewing experiences of *Severance* engage different patterns of allegiance as represented in Smith's structure of sympathy. In addition, two new patterns, *empathetic allegiance* and *amoral allegiance*, emerge in our processing of characters who are narratively and visually presented in a reflective and revisionist way that piques our moral interest. Not only does the gradual distancing of the audience from the outies, especially Mark, and the alignment of the audience with the innies, especially Helly, double the appreciation for the show's narrative structure and aesthetic design, the overlapping patterns of allegiance also heightens the viewer's desire to see the potential convergence of the innies and outies.

Conclusion

Only at the very end of *Severance*'s Season 1 do we finally understand Helena's cultish motivation behind her being severed. She is the daughter of Lumon Industries' current CEO Jame Eagan and, hence, his heir. Helena explains her rationale behind Severance to the guests at the Lumon gala in a promotional video: "… I took a severed job because it sounds freaking awesome. So, no, I don't think Severance divides us. I think it brings us together."[34] This jaw-dropping reveal not only resolves the quick turnaround of Helly's resignation request and outie Helena's determination to keep her innie working at Lumon, but also brings to light how her strong-willed personality comes about. The bifurcation of memories promised by Severance does not seem to do the same trick on one's personality. Although the innies' and outies' personalities might not be identical, apparently due to two entirely different backgrounds, they are also not completely bifurcated. Traces of the outies' personality traits can be found in the innies; for instance, both Helly and Helena are assertive and commanding, whereas both Marks are kind and caring. This personality continuity between innies and outies is a perfect analogy to our viewing and acting selves, adding to the already dynamic and rich overlapping of viewing responses as analyzed above. As we see in his retirement video, outie Burt rejoices in an embodied experience in his physically tired yet spiritually fulfilled body despite the absence of his innie's memory. This suggests that our fiction-viewing experience (where our memory presumably remains safe and unified) must have as much stimulating influence, if not direct impact, as real-life events do.

The staging and execution of the innies' coup in the last two episodes is a purely rewarding viewing experience for viewers who have developed, struggled with, and ruminated on various, often conflicting, patterns of allegiance in the previous episodes. From local sympathetic allegiance for outie Mark through antipathetic/partial/perverse/amoral allegiance for Lumon gatekeepers to global sympathetic/empathetic allegiance for the MDR innies, the viewer has to constantly weigh both moral motivations and moral consequences of all the main and key supporting characters, among which Helly is the plot-moving provocateur and moral questioner. The many different levels of alignment and allegiance in this textual analysis of *Severance* are once again proof that our spectating mechanism requires a more comprehensive account than what "identification" can provide, and relies heavily on morality and moral assessments. On top of that, flipping the axis of morality—from evil external forces to self-inflicted predicaments—only flares up the allegiance-building processes. I would further suggest that such frequent shifts between different patterns of allegiance as in *Severance* also occur in other shows that foreground agent-centered morality, albeit without the thrust of an explicitly identification-oriented narrative device like the Severance procedure. Severance, a moral vice to the fictional world where Lumon exists, could just as well function as an aesthetic virtue to the spectator.

Notes

1. The design of the Severance procedure has also ingeniously avoided playing out a common misconception perpetuated by films and television shows: cloning only produces a baby, not an identical adult straight off the bat. See Karen Weintraub, "Cloning's Long Legacy—And Why It'll Never Be Used on Humans," *Discover Magazine*, April 30, 2019. https://www.discovermagazine.com/health/clonings-long-legacy-and-why-itll-never-be-used-on-humans.
2. Murray Smith, "*Engaging Characters*: Further Reflections," in *Characters in Fictional Worlds: Understanding Imaginary Beings in Literature, Film, and Other Media*, edited by Jens Eder, Fotis Jannidis and Ralf Schneider (New York: De Gruyter, 2010), 245.
3. Noël Carroll, "Toward a Theory of Film Suspense," in his *Theorizing the Moving Image* (Cambridge: Cambridge University Press, 1996), 105.
4. Thomas E. Wartenberg, "Moral Intelligence and the Limits of Loyalty: The Third Man As Philosophy," in *Ethics at the Cinema*, edited by Ward E. Jones and Samantha Vice (New York: Oxford University Press, 2011), 302.
5. *Severance*, "Good News About Hell."
6. Murray Smith, *Engaging Characters: Fiction, Emotion, and the Cinema* (New York: Oxford University Press, 1995), 188.
7. Smith, "*Engaging Characters*: *Further Reflections*," 244.
8. Noël Carroll, *The Philosophy of Horror, or Paradoxes of the Heart* (New York: Routledge, 1990), 92.
9. Smith, *Engaging Characters*, 82.
10. Ibid., 83.
11. Ibid., 84.

12. For more on moral motivations, see Murray Smith, "Just What Is It That Makes Tony Soprano Such an Appealing, Attractive Murderer?" in *Ethics at the Cinema*, edited by Ward E. Jones and Samantha Vice (New York: Oxford University Press, 2011), 66–90.
13. Smith, *Engaging Characters*; Murray Smith, "Gangsters, Cannibals, Aesthetes; or, Apparently Perverse Allegiances," in *Passionate Views: Film, Cognition, and Emotion*, edited by Carl Plantinga and Greg M. Smith (Baltimore: The John Hopkins University Press, 1999), 200–16; Smith, "Engaging Characters: Further Reflections"; Smith, "Just What Is It That Makes Tony Soprano Such an Appealing, Attractive Murderer?"
14. Smith, *Engaging Characters*; Smith, "Gangsters, Cannibals, Aesthetes"; Smith, "Just What Is It That Makes Tony Soprano Such an Appealing, Attractive Murderer?"
15. Ibid., 87.
16. Antipathetic allegiance should be differentiated from "the allure of the transgressive," which refers to the spectatorial pleasure derived from "imagining acting transgressively but with impunity," usually backed by the character's morally grounded motive. Ibid., 79.
17. I use "gatekeepers" to allude to both the managers in charge of the severed floor and those who facilitate their control over the innies.
18. Jackson McHenry, "The Stories Behind *Severance*'s Eerie Office Design," *Vulture*, April 1, 2022. https://www.vulture.com/article/severance-office-design-explained.html.
19. In his explanation of the involuntary affective mimicry, Smith, citing William James and C. G. Lange's facial feedback thesis, states that "if we mimic a facial expression apposite to a basic affect, we do not merely see and categorize a certain expression and hence affect, we experience it, albeit in weaker form." Smith, *Engaging Characters*, 100. Following this statement, the merry atmosphere and smiley expressions that the innies communicate to us would lessen our antagonism toward and/or negative moral judgment on the Lumon mechanism.
20. Berys Gaut, "Review: *Engaging Characters: Fiction, Emotion, and the Cinema* by Murray Smith," *The British Journal of Aesthetics* 37, no. 1 (1997).
21. A parallel plotline that further brings the innies' anti-Lumon activities into prominence is a former employee Petey's escape from Lumon. The sudden change of department chief in the beginning

of the show shakes up the MDR innies' micro-controlled work life for the first time. The real cause is that Petey has been "reintegrated," and successfully fled Lumon, which means, his innie is out and about. The good outie Mark that we sympathize with takes Petey in when innie Petey comes for him and confides in him what is going on inside Lumon. Unfortunately, because of the aftereffects of severance and reintegration, Petey has been having murky visions, in which the Lumon office and the real-world overlap, leading to his death and the end of this subplot. The cutting off of the only reintegrated victim from the narrative as well as the discovery of his handwritten map on the back of one of the group photos in the office ("In Perpetuity") in turn intensifies our emotional and informational reliance on the innies' actions as well as growing allegiance to them.

22. Smith, *Engaging Characters*, 98, 231.
23. Alex Neill, "Review: *Engaging Characters: Fiction, Emotion, and the Cinema* by Murray Smith," *The Journal of Aesthetics and Art Criticism* 57, no. 1 (Winter 1999): 89.
24. In developing his theory of character engagement, Smith posits that mimetic assumptions about fictional characters have been a reflexive reading/viewing strategy, with which "a mimetic relationship is assumed to obtain between fictional narratives and the world." Smith, *Engaging Characters*, 34. Since his book is a theoretical attempt to establish a spectatorial/identificatory concept of film character, little about the ramifications of fiction being a conduit for ideas and emotions to evolve in reality is discussed.
25. *Severance*, "The You You Are."
26. *Severance*, "The Grim Barbarity of Optics and Design."
27. Ibid.
28. *Severance*, "Defiant Jazz."
29. Ibid.
30. Beatrice Verhoeven, "'Severance' Star Tramell Tillman on How Playing Milchick Has Changed His Life: 'Nobody Knew Who I Was in January,'" *The Hollywood Reporter*, August 17, 2022. https://www.hollywoodreporter.com/tv/tv-features/tramell-tillman-severance-character-apple-tv-plus-1235197716/.
31. Smith, "Gangsters, Cannibals, Aesthetes," 226, emphasis in original.
32. Ibid., 233–236.

33. Gaut, "Review: *Engaging Characters*."
34. *Severance*, "The We We Are."

Bibliography

Carroll, Noël. *The Philosophy of Horror, or Paradoxes of the Heart*. New York: Routledge, 1990.

———. "Toward a Theory of Film Suspense." In his *Theorizing the Moving Image*. Cambridge: Cambridge University Press, 1996.

Gaut, Berys. "Review: *Engaging Characters: Fiction, Emotion, and the Cinema* by Murray Smith." *The British Journal of Aesthetics* 37, no. 1 (1997).

McHenry, Jackson. "The Stories Behind *Severance*'s Eerie Office Design." *Vulture*. April 1, 2022. https://www.vulture.com/article/severance-office-design-explained.html.

Neill, Alex. "Review: *Engaging Characters: Fiction, Emotion, and the Cinema* by Murray Smith." *The Journal of Aesthetics and Art Criticism* 57, no. 1 (Winter, 1999): 88–89.

Smith, Murray. *Engaging Characters: Fiction, Emotion, and the Cinema*. New York: Oxford University Press, 1995.

———. "Gangsters, Cannibals, Aesthetes; or, Apparently Perverse Allegiances." In *Passionate Views: Film, Cognition, and Emotion*, edited by Carl Plantinga and Greg M. Smith, 200–16. Baltimore: The John Hopkins University Press, 1999.

———. "*Engaging Characters*: Further Reflections." In *Characters in Fictional Worlds: Understanding Imaginary Beings in Literature, Film, and Other Media*, edited by Jens Eder, Fotis Jannidis and Ralf Schneider, 232–58. New York: De Gruyter, 2010.

———. "Just What Is It That Makes Tony Soprano Such an Appealing, Attractive Murderer?" In *Ethics at the Cinema*, edited by Ward E. Jones and Samantha Vice, 66–90. New York: Oxford University Press, 2011.

Verhoeven, Beatrice. "'Severance' Star Tramell Tillman on How Playing Milchick Has Changed His Life: 'Nobody Knew Who I Was in January.'" *The Hollywood Reporter*. August 17, 2022. https://www.hollywoodreporter.com/tv/tv-features/tramell-tillman-severance-character-apple-tv-plus-1235197716/.

Wartenberg, Thomas E. "Moral Intelligence and the Limits of Loyalty: *The Third Man* As Philosophy." In *Ethics at the Cinema*, edited by Ward E. Jones, and Samantha Vice, 300–18. New York: Oxford University Press, 2011.

Weintraub, Karen. "Cloning's Long Legacy—And Why It'll Never Be Used on Humans." *Discover Magazine*. April 30, 2019. https://www.discovermagazine.com/health/clonings-long-legacy-and-why-itll-never-be-used-on-humans.

CHAPTER 13

"Actively Caring for Mankind Since 1866": Nineteenth-Century Medicine, Pain, and the Worker's Body in Season 1 of *Severance*

Sarah Lennox

In the television show *Severance*, the fictional biotechnology company Lumon Industries offers a controversial procedure that it claims promotes work-life balance: Lumon employees who undergo the titular "Severance procedure" have a chip implanted into their brains that ensures they will retain no memory of work while at home and no memory of their personal lives while at work. In the terminology of the show, an employee who opts into the Severance procedure is known as an "outie" because they experience consciousness in the outside world, while the work persona created by the procedure is called an "innie" because they only experience consciousness during the 9 to 5 workday on the Severed

S. Lennox (✉)
Massachusetts Maritime Academy, Buzzards Bay, MA, USA
e-mail: slennox@maritime.edu

N. M. Isacoff and J. Dawes (eds.), *Reintegrating Severance*,
https://doi.org/10.1007/978-3-031-57448-1_13

Floor of Lumon Industries. As we shall see, the show uses this bifurcated consciousness to raise interesting questions about identity, workers' rights, and contemporary corporate culture.

Importantly for our purposes, Season 1 offers a glimpse into the company lore presented to the innies, including stories and visual artifacts about Lumon's nineteenth-century origins and its founder, Kier Eagan. I begin this chapter by exploring the narrative Lumon creates about the company's nineteenth-century beginnings and its founder's philosophies. I argue that, whether we take this narrative as an accurate account of the company's inception or as a pseudo-history created to control its workforce, Lumon's origin story serves strategic purposes: it lends innies a sense of identity, purpose, and pride, on the one hand, and demands self-monitoring, strict discipline, and adherence to company policy on the other. In addition, since we know that some parts of this corporate history have been shared with the wider public, it contributes to Lumon's brand identity and public image.[1] Having discussed the company's nineteenth-century origins and situated them within the history of medicine, I point out that two of Kier's early jobs—as "a stewman in an ether factory" and a surgeon during the American Civil War—suggest that he would have been familiar with the first widely used anesthetic, diethyl ether.[2] I argue that if the show's writers continue to expand upon this part of Lumon's origin story, it may set up a parallel between diethyl ether, which was used as an early anesthetic to numb the pain of dental extractions, surgeries, and childbirth, and the twenty-first century Severance procedure, which promises to shield severed employees (and, secretly, people from outside the company) from various forms of physical, psychological, and emotional pain. While Lumon proudly proclaims that the company has been "actively caring for mankind since 1866," in the final section of this chapter, I provide a close reading of several scenes from *Severance* to explore the psychological and emotional pain Lumon inflicts on the innies.[3] I contend that, ultimately, the innies weaponize physical pain to resist Lumon's power structures, communicate their suffering, and advocate for greater transparency and regulation in the workplace.

The Founding of Lumon Industries

While Season 1 is full of Lumon-branded merchandise from snacks and computer paper to band-aids and soap, we are informed that, above all else, Lumon Industries is a biotechnology company. Still, the residents of the fictional town of Kier, PE where Lumon's headquarters are located seem unsure of what, exactly, Lumon Industries does. During a party in the first episode, "Good News About Hell," a guest asks Lumon employee Mark Scout "Do you design the medicines?" while another guest chimes in, "I thought Lumon was more on the tech side of things."[4] The one Lumon product everyone knows about draws upon both medicine and technology: the microchip used for the severance procedure. In a show celebrated for its thoughtful attention to detail, we might rightly ask: why include this backstory about the company's nineteenth-century history? What purpose does it serve in Season 1? How might Lumon leverage this narrative in future seasons?

Although, at the time the show takes place, Lumon is known as a global biotechnology company that employs "hundreds of thousands" of workers around the world, its nineteenth-century origin story stresses its small and humble beginnings.[5] Kier Eagan (1841–1939) founded Lumon Industries in 1865. The company's original logo, which appears on the signet ring of current CEO Jame Eagan, features an old-fashioned apothecary bottle in the background and a tilted spoon containing a dark liquid, presumably medicine, in the foreground. A single drop of medicine pours from the bottom of the spoon into the bottom center of the image. Lumon's first product, "a topical salve," was most likely a medicinal preparation—perhaps a carbolic salve meant to heal cuts, wounds, and burns.[6] It is striking to note that while Lumon's modern-day blue and white logo retains the original droplet, the updated color scheme may conjure ideas of water more readily than it does medicine and is reflective of the "clean" aesthetic of Lumon's branding and office space.

The Perpetuity Wing located on the severed floor, which contains wax figures and audio recordings of Lumon's founder and past CEOs, the "Legacy of Joy" exhibit, and a "perfect replica" of Kier's house, materializes the company's nineteenth-century origin story.[7] In this museum-like wing, innies are invited to literally step into Kier's house and interact with an approximation of the company's past. Like the original logo, the replica of Kier's house contains artifacts suggestive of a small apothecary shop. Atop Kier's dresser, protected under glass cloches that remind us of the curated nature of the exhibit, are various artifacts that supposedly belonged to Kier: a selection of jarred herbs, a mortar and pestle, a bottle of what looks to be powdered dentifrice (a forerunner to modern-day toothpaste), and various nineteenth-century glass bottles. Of course, it is not clear whether Kier made use of similar herbs and a mortar and pestle in his early days of the company. Nor do we know for certain whether the dentifrice and other bottled preparations were products manufactured by Lumon, items purchased by Kier for his own personal use, or period-appropriate props purchased by the company for the outfitting of the Perpetuity Wing. However, given the company's decision to display these objects on Kier's dresser for all to see, Lumon seems to be using them to tell a story: these artifacts stress the company's longevity and quaint and humble beginnings. Considered in tandem with the "Wall of Smiles," they also serve as (alleged) material evidence that Lumon has a long history creating products that keep people happy and healthy. Lumon encourages the innies to build a sense of self-worth and identity from the work they perform for the company: they should, the exhibit argues, take pride in their labor, celebrate the company's achievements as their own, and feel a sense of belonging as part of the "Lumon family."

The original logo and Perpetuity Wing exhibits seem to suggest that in the early days of the company Kier produced and/or sold medical preparations from a small, local apothecary shop, though the show does not reveal the size of the original shop or how quickly the company grew. During the first half of the nineteenth century, pharmacists completed a broader range of tasks than they do today: in addition to selling some mass-manufactured medicines, they procured and sold herbs and other raw ingredients that customers could purchase to make homemade remedies and manufactured and sold their own in-house medical preparations to cure a variety of ailments.[8] Throughout the 1840s and 1850s, pharmacists argued that their knowledge of *Materia medica* (the herbs, plants, and other substances used for healing) and ability to concoct their own remedies established pharmacy as a respectable profession and proved "the individual pharmacist something more than a mere shopkeeper."[9] However, with the advent of the American Civil War (1861–1865) came an increased demand for mass-produced medical supplies, and in the second half of the nineteenth century, large pharmaceutical manufacturing companies like the Squibb Corporation, Eli Lilly and Company, the Upjohn Company, and the Abbott Alkaloid Company thrived. To stay in business and respond to customer demand for brand-name products, most small-town pharmacies were forced to sell their competitors' mass-manufactured medicines even though doing so undercut their own in-house preparations. The companies that grew and became successful tended to fuse medicine and technology. For example, Eli Lilly's "initial success resulted from an innovative form of gelatin capsules," the Abbott Alkaloid Company "employ[ed] a new technique for the preparation of drugs, which involved precipitating them into solid extracts and then selling them in granules," and Upjohn patented a "friable" pill that more easily dissolved in the body, enhancing the accuracy of the pill's dosage.[10]

Delving deeper into the fictional world of *Severance* and its connection to nineteenth-century medicine, Kier's philosophy regarding what he called the "four tempers" appears to be a modified form of humoral theory. During the first half of the nineteenth century, orthodox medical practitioners following Dr. Benjamin Rush tended to practice "heroic medicine," an approach that drew upon the ancient Greek theory of the "four humors" and called for heavy doses of medication and aggressive forms of bloodletting, sweating, and purging to treat the patient.[11] According to the ancient Greek writers Hippocrates and Galen, health and disease were determined by the four humors, or vital fluids, that circulated in the body, which included blood, yellow bile, phlegm, and black bile.[12] According to this theory, health could be achieved by maintaining a balance among the four humors, while an excess or deficiency of a particular fluid would result in sickness. Today, we understand disease as localized (in other words, doctors diagnose particular problems in particular parts of the body), but in this earlier, generalized conception of disease, the entire body was thought to be affected by the humoral imbalance.[13] Thus, a fever, which was believed to be caused by excess blood, might be treated with bloodletting.[14] From a medical standpoint, an individual's humors were thought to be in flux: they could be affected, for example, by the season of the year, the foods a person ate, or his or her occupation. However, Galen also outlined four temperaments, which indicated that a particular fluid with corresponding personality traits tended to predominate: these temperaments included the sanguine (blood), the choleric (yellow bile), the phlegmatic (phlegm), and the melancholic (black bile).[15] While many medical practitioners dismissed heroic medicine and/or the effectiveness of its treatments during the first half of the nineteenth century, some physicians practiced medicine informed by these beliefs until the advent of germ theory in the 1870s.[16] However, Kier's sustained belief in some form of humoral theory well into the twentieth century and his unique conceptualization of the "four tempers" is certainly bizarre.

There are important distinctions between Kier's theory of the four tempers and the ancient Greek theory of the four humors. While the ancient Greek theory is grounded in the fluids of the material body,[17] Kier's conceptualization of the four tempers makes no mention of bodily fluids and instead indicates that these "components" make up the human soul. This distinction is made most clear in a recording in which Kier reflects on his life's greatest achievement: "In my life I have identified four components, which I call tempers, from which are derived every human soul. Woe. Frolic. Dread. Malice."[18] The camera cuts to a display of a nineteenth-century scale, with the balance tipped to one side, and the recording continues: "Each man's character is defined by the precise ratio that resides in him.... Should you tame the tempers as I did mine, the world shall become but your appendage. It is this great and consecrated power that I hope to pass on to all of you, my children."[19]

Here and elsewhere, Kier adopts an almost Biblical elevation of tone and word choice to address his "children," inculcate the type of constant self-discipline necessary to "tame" the four tempers, and impress upon workers the sacred, almost holy gift that is this "consecrated power." On the one hand, the image of the scale evokes the traditional humoral concept of balance. On the other hand, the official Lumon painting of Kier taming the four tempers implies that the tempers are dangerous and that "taming" them may involve a painful form of psychological or emotional self-flagellation. The painting depicts a tall, muscular Kier surrounded by a halo of beatific light brandishing a cat-of-nine-tails at a figurative representation of the four tempers, embodied by the cowering forms of a young bride, an old woman, a ram, and a jester.[20] The language of "taming" and the imagery of the whip with its association with physical pain, seem to suggest that, in Kier's conceptualization, the tempers are bad inclinations—perhaps akin to vices—that one must "beat down" and keep at bay.

This conceptualization of the tempers as vices to be indulged at one's peril or quashed for one's salvation, is further supported by the rituals of the Waffle Party, where, startlingly, the ultimate reward for a job well done is to slough off one's lowly worker persona, dress up in a Kier mask, and indulge in a Bacchanalian night of sensual pleasures, including an orgy where one uses a cat-of-nine-tails labeled with Kier's Nine Core Principles to literally whip oneself and/or people dressed as the four tempers.[21] Certain aspects of Kier's rhetoric—his elevated, religious language, his use of the human body as a symbol or index for the soul, his equation of physical cleanliness with moral purity, his ascetic emphasis on self-discipline and denial—seems to recall the lectures and publications of nineteenth-century hygienists such as Sylvester Graham and William Alcott.[22] However, Kier's relationship with the tempers—or at least Lumon's incorporation of them into company lore and the severed floor rewards system—is particularly fraught, with features such as the Waffle Party pointing toward the need for a carnivalesque "release valve" where an individual's usual self-discipline is temporarily suspended and the desires are allowed to run wild within a safe and closed-off environment. In the context of the Waffle Party, workers are allowed to indulge in sensual pleasures that are normally forbidden—to eat a stack of waffles dripping in syrup or have sex on the founder's bed—but, imaginatively, they perform these tasks "for" and "as" Kier and their forbidden urges flow through Lumon's preferred channels so they do not taint the rest of the workspace.

Such rhetoric is amplified by the show's fascinating interest in soap and Lumon's demand that its workers remain physically and morally "clean." Severed floor supervisors are encouraged to change the Lumon-branded soap on a regular basis, the office settings themselves are strikingly clean and sterile, and across the first season, Mark's next door neighbor, Mrs. Selvig—who goes by the name Harmony Cobel in her official work as the supervisor of Lumon's severed floor—repeatedly references the shop she owns in town: the Swab Girl Bathhouse and Soapery.[23] The products Mrs. Selvig makes for Mark and sells in her shop could be viewed as either an homage to Kier's original business (particularly if it turns out Lumon did begin as a small apothecary shop) or as an alternative to the drugs sold by twenty-first-century pharmaceutical companies like Lumon. Drawing on aromatherapy, herbalism, and some of the same *Materia medica* valued by nineteenth-century pharmacists, Mrs. Selvig handcrafts a range of food and body-care products that draw upon the alleged healing power of herbs and plants. In Season 1, she makes and/or sells chamomile cookies, lavender tea, mugwort bath-bombs, and hibiscus wraps.[24] In an all-natural twist on both the severance procedure and anesthesia, the products she offers Mark contain plants meant to ease his pain by putting him to sleep.

The name of Mrs. Selvig's shop references Kier's wife, the "swab girl" Imogene, who cleaned the vats at the ether factory where Kier worked. Given the rhetoric of nineteenth-century sanitation reform, it makes sense that Kier would fall in love with a woman whose job was to literally make spaces clean and pure for others. While, presumably, Imogene would have gotten dirty working as a swab girl, nineteenth-century American women's hard work keeping domestic and public spaces clean was seen as an increasingly important service to family and nation. As the news of Florence Nightingale's success in keeping war hospitals clean and battling disease during the Crimean War (1853–1856) spread to the United States, many American women, who had similarly "engaged in the act of cleaning" in their role as mothers, housekeepers, and nurses, "took pride in Nightingale's recognized accomplishments in Crimea, and... relished the prestige it gave their work."[25] With her unwavering, almost religious devotion to Kier, it seems fitting that Mrs. Selvig would run an Imogene-inspired shop that allows her to imagine herself as the swab girl's modern-day equivalent, beloved spiritual "wife" of Kier.

In addition to evoking Imogene, Mrs. Selvig's shop recalls nineteenth-century bathhouses. During this period, mineral springs and spas where wealthy invalids could "take the waters" by bathing in and imbibing sulfuric and other mineral waters, promised the opportunity to both improve one's health and enjoy high society.[26] Along with these fashionable bathhouses, there were also stricter water-cure establishments that would have appealed to Kier's appreciation for self-regulation and discipline. Water-cure establishments based on hydropathy were "the latest incarnation of a medical regimen of renunciation: of alcohol, tobacco, caffeine, and excessive consumption of food, particularly meat."[27] While both types of facilities catered to wealthy individuals who could afford travel and treatment, by the end of the century, free and low-cost public bathhouses for the poor became increasingly available.[28] While, in the wake of the cholera epidemic of 1849 and the discovery of germs in the 1870s public bathhouses promoted public health and safety, they were also viewed as a way to improve the morals of the working classes. Equating physical cleanliness and moral purity, New York State Official Goodwin Brown insisted cleanliness distinguished the "honest" from the "idle" poor, and sanitation reformers saw "the baths not just as cleansing facilities, but as missions to the slums to spread the 'gospel of cleanliness.'"[29] Presumably, this mission and rhetoric would have appealed to

Kier, who similarly hoped to "cleanse" the masses—starting with Lumon's workers—using both literal soap and the gospel of the four tempers.

For Kier, the ideal worker considers themselves part of the Lumon family, dedicates themselves to their job with an almost religious fervor, follows the Nine Core Principles and subdues the Four Tempers to achieve emotional and spiritual balance, and maintains a clean body, mind, and soul for both their own and the company's sake. While most viewers will find Kier's rhetoric disturbing, and Lumon's continued use of it in the twenty-first century even stranger, the show seems to be commenting on the existence of similar rhetoric in corporate culture today. While Kier's language is, admittedly, more extreme, the show highlights growing concerns over "cultish" corporate culture and the toxic implications of workplace "family" rhetoric.[30]

Nineteenth-Century Ether and the Numbing of Pain

While Season 1 provides only the smallest hints about what Kier Eagan did before he founded Lumon Industries, I contend Kier's early jobs as a "stewman in an ether factory" and surgeon during the American Civil War indicate the character's knowledge of the first widely used form of anesthesia, diethyl ether. By considering the history of ether anesthesia in nineteenth-century medicine, we can imagine how Lumon might have fit into this narrative. Moreover, we can begin to conceptualize how ether anesthesia might have served as a nineteenth-century forerunner to the company's twenty-first-century severance procedure. If the showrunners ultimately decide to expand upon Lumon's connection to nineteenth-century ether in future seasons, Lumon could position the movement from ether anesthesia to the severance procedure as a natural progression; highlight the initial objection to anesthesia and say the same will be true of the severance procedure to both discount critics and predict the outsized impact of their technology in the history of medicine; and draw parallels between diethyl ether, the first miracle drug that promised to take away the pain, and the severance procedure to sidestep the important differences between the two treatments and promote the company's supposed "caring" and "empathetic" brand identity.[31]

Until the mid-nineteenth century, medical procedures left patients traumatized by the pain of surgery. In a letter to her sister, the English novelist Francis Burney describes the almost unbearable pain of her mastectomy, which was performed in 1811 before the advent of anesthesia:

> when the dreadful steel was plunged into my breast—cutting through veins—arteries—flesh—nerves—I needed no injunctions not to restrain my cries. I began a scream that lasted unintermittingly during the whole time of the incision--& I almost marvel that it rings not in my ears still! So excruciating was the agony. When the wound was made & the instrument was withdrawn, the pain seemed undiminished, for the air that suddenly rushed into those delicate parts felt like a mass of minute but sharp and forked poniards, that were tearing the edges of the wound,--but when again I felt the instrument—describing a curve—cutting against the grain, if I may so say, while the flesh resisted in a manner so forcible as to oppose & tire the hand of the operator, who was forced to change from the right hand to the left—then, indeed, I thought I must have expired....[32]

As you read Burney's description, you may feel your own stomach churn: as a gifted writer, she describes her mastectomy in graphic detail, and when readers "see" this scene in their mind's eye they may imaginatively identify with Burney and consider what it would feel like to experience that kind of pain their own bodies. While Burney endured the agonies of a non-anesthetized operation, in the 1840s, just a few years after Kier's fictional birth in 1841, American dentists and surgeons made a discovery that would transform patients' relationship to pain forever.

Inspired by traveling entertainments and parties known as "ether frolics" where nitrous oxide (colloquially known as "laughing gas") and/or ether were used as recreational drugs, several American dentists and surgeons began experimenting with these gasses—testing their effects on animals, themselves, and/or their patients—to see whether they might render patients unconscious of pain during painful dental and medical procedures.[33] Although he was not the first to discover ether's anesthetic properties nor the first to successfully etherize a patient, the dentist William Thomas Green Morton orchestrated the first successful public demonstration of ether's anesthetic effects on October 16, 1846 at Massachusetts General Hospital (hereafter "MGH") in Boston.[34] After researching the chemistry behind ether and testing it on animals, Morton inhaled the substance himself. Writing of the experience, he reflected, "I felt a numbness in my limbs, with a sensation like nightmare... Gradually, I regained power over my limbs, and full consciousness... I had been insensible between seven and eight minutes."[35] After testing ether on patients in private, Morton convinced the respected surgeon John Collins Warren to operate on an etherized patient, Gilbert Abbott, in front of the medical community at MGH. The first surgery was largely a success, and subsequent surgeries proved even more promising.

The physician and poet Oliver Wendall Holmes wrote to Morton proposing the name "anesthesia" to describe the state of insensibility to sensation caused by inhaling ether.[36] To administer the drug, practitioners would typically dampen a handkerchief or sponge with ether, hold it over the patient's nose and mouth, and instruct the patient to inhale the ether vapors.[37] Just weeks after the initial public demonstration at MGH, the physician and Harvard University professor Dr. Jacob Bigelow wrote to botanist Francis Boott: "limbs and breasts have been amputated, arteries tied, tumors extirpated, and many hundreds of teeth extracted, without... the least pain."[38] By April 1847, ether anesthesia had been applied to obstetrics as well. Initially, obstetricians were reluctant to use ether during childbirth, fearing that it might "leave women convulsed, paralyzed or mentally deranged" or produce children with "mental or physical abnormalities."[39] However, as the century progressed, it became "common practice" to use anesthesia at some stage of labor and delivery in both home- and hospital-births.[40] Although the initial excitement over ether dampened due to the discovery of chloroform in 1847,[41] and the latter drug quickly replaced ether as the anesthetic of choice in Britain and Europe, in the United States ether continued to be favored under controlled conditions due to its lower health risks and fatality rate.[42]

The Lumon painting "The Courtship of Kier and Imogene" depicts Kier, "working as a stewman in an ether factory," and his future wife, the swab girl Imogene.[43] The painting idealizes not only Kier and Imogene but also the concept of the worker devoted to his or her labor. In the painting, the young and handsome Kier and Imogene stand on stools next to a giant vat glowing with heat. Kier stirs the substance in the vat with a long wooden paddle and Imogene holds a bunched-up rag, presumably used to clean the vats or other areas of the factory. Despite this dirty work and the billowing smoke rising inches from their faces, both figures remain remarkably clean. The orange glow of the substance beneath lights up their faces, reflecting not only their love for one another, but also, presumably, the "spirit of industry" that bonds them and lights them from within.

While Lumon's artistic representation of the "ether factory" where Kier worked is certainly romanticized, in the nineteenth century some large-scale pharmaceutical manufacturers, most famously the Squibb Corporation, did mass produce diethyl ether in facilities we might loosely term "ether factories." In 1856, Edward Robinson Squibb discovered a safer and more efficient means of producing diethyl ether by using steam rather than an open flame during the distillation process and, in a move uncharacteristic of many businessmen of the time, freely shared his method and design with the medical community. [44] According to the current Bristol Myers-Squibb company timeline,[45] after retiring from the Navy, where he served as a surgeon and researcher, Squibb was "encouraged by the government to establish his own firm to aid the armed forces" and in 1858 he rented a Brownstone in Brooklyn, New York to manufacture pharmaceuticals, including ether.[46] While Squibb's steam distillation method offered a safer way to produce ether, the process still remained dangerous. In December 1858, the facility caught fire while Squibb was distilling ether, leaving the proprietor badly burned. While the painting romanticizes the process of distilling ether, idealizes the founder, and pushes the company's corporate agenda, it also serves as the most explicit connection between Kier and ether, indicating he had a knowledge of the drug and participated in its manufacture before the founding of Lumon Industries.

Interestingly, Season 1 also depicts Kier working as a surgeon during the American Civil War at a time when ether was frequently used by surgeons on the battlefield and in war hospitals. In Episode 2, "Half Loop," Mark and his date Alexa pass by a statue of Kier that stands outside the Hall of Records. The statue depicts Kier holding a medical bag and includes a plaque that reads, "I Dug Inside of Soldiers and Within Them Found the War."[47] Both ether and chloroform were used as anesthetics during the American Civil War, despite the fact that ether's two main disadvantages—its flammability and the greater volume of the drug needed to render patients insensible—were exacerbated within this context. Before the start of the war, ether and chloroform were mainly manufactured in the northern states or imported from the British Isles.[48] The Union army purchased over 1 million ounces of chloroform and 1 million ounces of diethyl ether during the war.[49] Since the Confederate government did not already have ether or chloroform manufacturing facilities in place, they purchased drugs from blockade runners, seized medical supplies from the Union army, and built new pharmaceutical plants and distilleries including a plant in Columbia, South Carolina that "was said to have manufactured sulphuric ether."[50] During the war, approximately

125,000 (or roughly one in four) soldiers were treated with ether, chloroform, or a mixture of the two on the battlefield or in war hospitals.[51] Given the prevalence of ether within this context and the show's hints that Kier worked as a surgeon during the war, we can assume that this character would have had knowledge of diethyl ether's use as an anesthetic agent and perhaps even first-hand experience administering it to patients.

Given Kier's knowledge of ether in both medical and manufacturing contexts, it is possible that, like Squibb and Company, Lumon produced ether alongside other medical products, or that, like many small-town pharmacies, it sold such products among its other offerings. While Season 1 gives no indication that Lumon manufactured ether during the nineteenth century, if, in future seasons, this turns out to be the case, then the showrunners have set up a fascinating parallel. In keeping with the company's tendency to connect its present and its past, Lumon could argue that the twenty-first-century severance procedure is a modernized update of the nineteenth-century miracle drug that first promised to take away the pain. Building upon the company's existing rhetoric, they could argue, moreover, that this is a *natural* progression for the company, a medical innovation that may be feared and opposed in the beginning—just as anesthesia was—only to transform people's relationship with pain forever.

There is another potential parallel between nineteenth-century ether anesthesia and the twenty-first-century severance procedure, although it is one Lumon would be less excited to highlight. For obvious reasons, ether anesthesia is typically discussed as a drug that saved patients from physical pain, but, from the beginning, it was also heralded as a drug that could shield others, particularly doctors, from the psychological and emotional pain of watching people suffer (eliciting sympathy or pity) and/or imagining what that pain might feel like in their own bodies (eliciting empathy or identification). The nineteenth-century physician James Young Simpson characterized early anesthetics as a "blessing" for patients but also as a "boon" for practitioners.[52] In 1895, one Virginia physician recalled, "that before he began to routinely employ anesthesia, he often sat anguished by women's bedsides, forced to listen to 'moanings from almost insufferable agony.'"[53] Like Simpson, this physician found anesthetics "not only a blessing to the patient but to the physician also."[54] Susan Buck-Morss explains that, in the wake of anesthesia, surgeons "had only to confront an inert, insensate mass that they could tinker with without emotional involvement."[55] Eileen Cleere agrees that "anesthesia at least theoretically relieved the surgeon of the subjective burden of empathy and pity as fundamentally as it relieved the patient of consciousness."[56] In the context of nineteenth-century medicine, this was not necessarily a bad thing for patients. After all, if doctors were better able to concentrate on the intricacies of surgery and perform lengthier, more complex operations, it is likely that some patients enjoyed better outcomes. At the same time, when a doctor sees "an inert insensate mass"—so much living tissue—rather than a person, and when sympathy and empathy disappear in the name of efficient labor, it becomes increasingly possible to deindividualize and even dehumanize the patient. In the final section of this chapter, I explore various types of pain the "innies" experience and argue that the severance procedure intentionally creates a similar lack of visibility, sympathy, and empathy for the workers who never leave the severed floor of Lumon Industries.

Severance and the Numbing of Pain

We may look at Lumon's severance procedure as a twenty-first century update to the nineteenth-century ether anesthesia that promised to revolutionize people's relationship with pain. Ether anesthesia primarily promised to take away *physical* pain. In contrast, the twenty-first-century severance procedure claims to offer severed employees not only the ability to forget the tedious tasks of the 9 to 5 workday, but also a temporary respite from *psychological* and *emotional* pain. For severed employee Mark Scout, the primary appeal of the severance procedure is twofold: since "outie" Mark grieves his (supposedly) deceased wife, Gemma, the procedure allows him to numb his pain for eight hours each work day; it also allows him to temporarily circumvent the psychological and emotional pain that prevents him from concentrating on his work and earning a livelihood. Season 1 also hints that the procedure has been implemented outside of the workplace to avoid physical pain, as the show implies Gabby Aretta, the Senator's wife, used severance to avoid the pain of childbirth. However, while the severance procedure spares the outies both tedium and pain, their innies constantly suffer. Despite Lumon's claim that they have been "actively caring for mankind since 1866," the company is actually in the business of causing pain—at least for the innies. Moreover, because the innies' pain is largely invisible to the outside world, Lumon's abuse of its labor force goes largely unchecked. In this surprising way, the severance procedure mirrors nineteenth-century ether anesthesia, since company procedures largely shield outies and the public from the psychological and emotional burden of watching someone else suffer. The outies' ability to distance themselves, resist empathetic identification, and, in some cases, even dehumanize their innies is striking in this context, because, unlike nineteenth-century doctors and their patients, who were, of course, separate people, the outies and innies are inextricably linked: for the outie, the suffering innie is "someone else" but also "me."

In *Severance*, the outies avoid pain through both modern-day anesthesia and the titular severance procedure. When Helena Eagan gets her severance chip surgically implanted, her experience could not be more different than that of the novelist Francis Burney. Helena receives a form of local anesthesia that leaves her awake and alert but numb to the pain, so she smiles and chats with unsevered Lumon employee Seth Milchick throughout her surgery. During the procedure, the viewer is shown all the gory details: the surgeon slices into Helena's scalp, peels back her bloody skin, drills into her skull, accumulates a pile of white bone dust beneath the drill bit, and, finally, uses a long metal needle to insert the Severance chip into her brain. While Helena can hear the surgeon working behind her, she cannot see what is happening to her or feel any pain. Indeed, the surgeon has already sliced into her scalp when she observes to Milchick, "they say it doesn't hurt," raising the question of whether "it" refers to the surgery or Severance in general.[57] As seen in Fig. 13.1, next to Helena is a computer monitor broadcasting a live image of her skull. This clean, sterilized image of the human head undergoing surgery is free of the messy details of Burney's agonized account—flesh, arteries, nerves, veins; similarly, it is free of the gore—flesh flaps, blood, bone dust—still produced by Helena's modern and painless surgery.

The combined focus on Helena's perspective and this sterilized image in the final moments of the scene is *almost* enough to lull viewers into a moment of sleepy peace. Right before the surgeon implants the chip, an anesthesiologist injects Helena with Ketamine Hydrochloride, a general anesthetic that will render her unconscious. In the foreground, we see Helena's face, her eyes becoming heavy as the Ketamine begins to work. In the background, we see the live images on the computer monitor: the glowing blue skull, the straight white line representing the needle as it quickly and effortlessly glides to its precise destination, and the little Severance chip like a mechanical insect opening its wings. Since viewers partially experience the end of this scene through Helena's fading consciousness, we hear the slow and elongated beeps of the medical

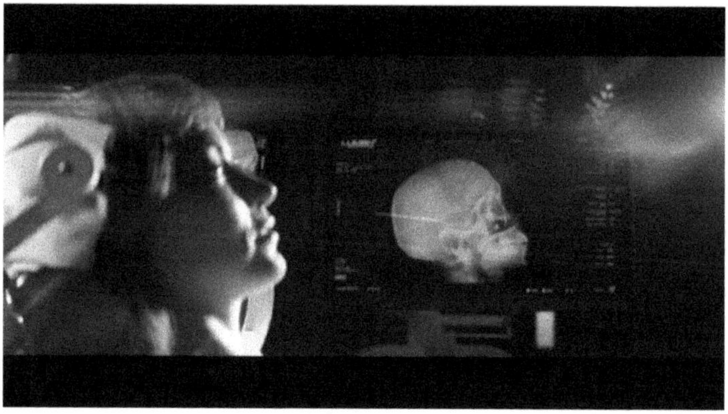

Fig. 13.1 Helena's surgery and computer display

equipment merge with the show's calming background music and see Milchick gradually fall back behind a blinding white light as Helena's eyes shut. In a figurative sense, the sterilized image on the computer monitor and Helena's peaceful transition to unconsciousness represents what the company would *like* people to believe about Severance: it is a quick, easy, safe, and painless procedure that harnesses the power of cutting-edge biotechnology to improve people's lives. However, the image on the computer monitor is incomplete, for it maintains a medicalized distance and does not capture the messy, human, corporeal elements of the surgery. So too does Lumon's marketing department omit all the messy details of Severance—including the innies' suffering—when promoting the procedure to investors and congressmen or defending it on the local news.[58] Lumon's non-severed employees also follow a carefully crafted corporate script when interacting with outies to assuage their potential guilt and encourage them to look the other way.

One traumatic feature of working on the severed floor of Lumon Industries is that every innie is born an orphan. Season 1 begins with an aerial view of an unconscious Helly gradually waking up from the anesthesia Helena Eagan received at the end of the Severance procedure. As seen in Fig. 13.2, the visual imagery of the opening shot indicates that this is a birth scene for Helly R: a Lumon conference table, representing a mother's womb, contains a speaker and intercom that resemble an already-severed umbilical cord, and below that, lies Helly's unconscious, sprawled form. From the outset, Helly's birth and existence are defined in relation to work—a conference table and intercom standing in for the mother's body. Unlike a normal human birth, no mother—indeed, no person—is present when Helly awakens and experiences consciousness for the first time. Instead, an unidentified, disembodied voice asks Helly a deceptively simple question through the crackly intercom speaker: "Who are you?"[59] In Helly's first moments, she is doubly disoriented, first from the Ketamine Hydrochloride, which can cause drowsiness, blurred vision, nausea, and confusion,[60] and second from the severance procedure itself, which has caused her to awaken on a conference table with no knowledge of how she got there. One of Helly's first sensations is the physical pain caused by her outie's procedure, though she does not yet know its source. She rubs the back of her head where the chip was inserted and winces. Next, childlike Helly tries to take her first steps, but with no parental figure to guide her (and the anesthesia's numbing agents still wearing off), she stumbles, her legs giving out underneath her. As the so-called "orientation" led by fellow severed colleague Mark S. proceeds, he repeats the first survey question: "Who are you?" clarifying that "a first name will do."[61] In a psychologically and emotionally traumatizing sequence, Helly realizes for the first time that she does not know her own name and cannot answer any of the other questions that require access to personal memories including—to drive home her parentless state—the color of her mother's eyes.

Lumon Industries wants its severed employees to replace personal history with corporate history and, to that effect, they encourage innies to think of themselves as part of the "Lumon family" and as Kier's "children of industry."[62] In a visit to the Perpetuity Wing, severed colleague Irving acknowledges to Helly "It's an unnatural state for a person to have no history. History makes us someone. Gives us a context. A shape."[63] Having internalized Lumon's "family" rhetoric, however, he assures her "waking up on that table, I was shapeless. But then I learned that I work for a company that has been actively caring for mankind since 1866."[64] Looking at the Wall of Smiles inside Lumon's Legacy of Joy exhibit, he explains that each smile represents someone Lumon has helped—in this rotating exhibit, "the true number of smiles–may well be in the millions"—and he is proud to be a part of it.[65]

While the innies are encouraged to think of themselves as Kier's children, they are created by Lumon, who manufactures and installs the

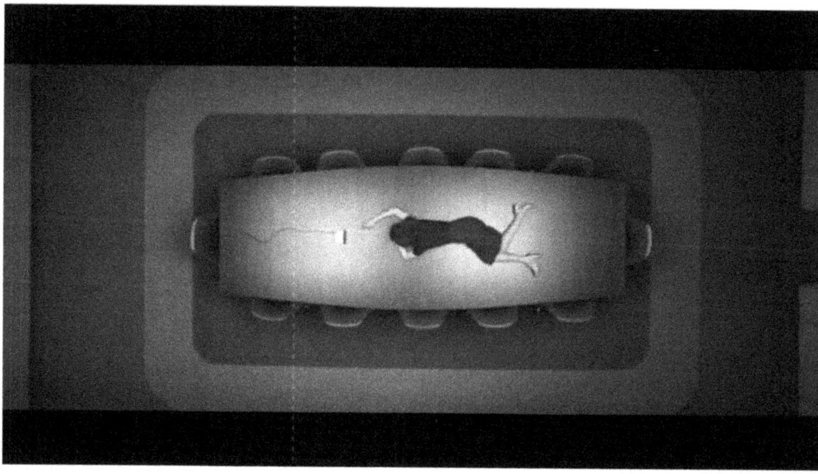

Fig. 13.2 Helly laid out on the conference table

Severance chip, and their outies. For the purposes of medical and legal consent, innies and outies are treated as the same person; however, the show makes clear that the innies are distinct from the outies who created them. For one, only outies are given the autonomy and power to make decisions, such as the ability to quit. When Helly first learns that her resignation request has been denied, she struggles to understand Helena's lack of empathy, and this seems tied up in Helly's own self-conception. She insists, "My outie wouldn't do that."[66] However, in a pre-recorded video denying the request, Helena's position is clear: "I am a person. You are not. I make the decisions. You do not."[67] While, as an Eagan, Helena may have unique motives for getting severed and firmly denying her innie's request, the other innies have had similar experiences. Mark and Petey wonder if their innies are "monsters"[68] and in the final episode innie Mark asks Devon why his outie chose to get severed, because he cannot understand why someone would be so cruel.[69] Like the nineteenth-century doctors relieved of the sights and sounds of pain by ether anesthesia, the outies are allowed to go about their lives without ever witnessing the innies' suffering. This makes it harder for the outies to develop certain feelings toward their innies—pity, sympathy, empathy, guilt–despite their shared bodies. Meanwhile, the innies constantly think about and identify with their outies (indeed, Lumon's Wellness Sessions condition them to do so), but their inability to understand their outies' decisions can lead to painful feelings of self-estrangement.[70]

Indeed, for Macrodata Refinement (MDR) employees, feeling negative, even painful, emotions are part of the job. Given the name of the department, and the fact that the refiners spend each day sitting in front of a computer staring at numbers, one might expect them to perform intellectual rather than affective labor. However, in a play on "scrubbing the numbers" that recalls Kier's interest in literal and figurative cleanliness, the refiner's job is to clean or purify data sets by cordoning off groups of numbers that evoke particular emotions that correspond to Kier's four tempers—woe, frolic, dread, and malice.[71] While the refiners seem to become accustomed to this emotional labor and the toll it takes on them, the fact that they viscerally experience these emotions becomes apparent when Helly first sees the "scary" numbers. While she has previously dismissed the idea that any numbers could look "scary," on this occasion she seems genuinely rattled. "That was scary," she tells her coworkers; "the numbers were scary."[72] While the innies are assured by their bosses that the work they complete is "mysterious and important,"[73] in true capitalist fashion, the employees are alienated not only from their (other) selves but also from their labor.[74]

When the innies fall short of their work obligations, they can be sent to the Break Room. Playing on the word "break," the Break Room is not a place workers choose to go to rest and relax, but rather a room where noncompliant workers are sent to have their spirits broken through psychological torture. The Break Room is a tiny, cramped space accessed via a dark and claustrophobically narrow hallway. In the middle of the room sit two connected desks separated by a clear plexiglass partition that also serves as a screen. A non-severed authority figure (typically Milchick), sits at one desk with a projector, tape recorder, headphones, and polygraph machine. The other desk has handprint-shaped indents carved into its surface, and the severed employee places his or her hands into the imprints.

The contrast between Helena's painless medical procedure overseen by a reassuring Milchick in the operating room and Helly's interrogation by an unmoved Milchick in the Break Room drives home the innie's and outie's different exposure to pain and access to sympathy. Like the medical equipment surrounding Helena in the operating room, the handprint indents presumably monitor Helly's breathing rate, blood pressure, and pulse. However, in the Break Room, Helly's vitals are monitored not to ensure her comfort and safety, but to transmit data to a lie detector as she reads a pre-scripted apology projected onto the screen in front of her. Here, pseudo-medical technology is used to ensure the body *is* feeling an adequate amount of pain to prove that Helly is genuinely sorry. In a form of psychological torture, she is forced to repeat the pre-scripted apology—itself a sort of perversion of the act of contrition, recalling Kier's religious rhetoric—for hour after hour over the course of two days. Initially, when Helly tries to appeal to Milchick's intelligence and sympathy, he shuts her down, and when she says she does not want to read the apology, he responds with chilling brevity: "No. Do."[75] There is also a physical and sensory component to Helly's suffering. While the room itself is dimly lit, the projector shines a disorienting, bright light onto the screen and into Helly's eyes. Unlike Helena, who is allowed to close her eyes and drift off to anesthetized sleep, Helly must stare into the light as she repeats the apology again and again. Sometimes refiners imprisoned in the Break Room also hear strange noises that appear to be individualized—Helly hears "a voice behind the door" that sounds like an "angry, mumbly guy" and Dillon hears a crying baby—although it isn't clear where the noises come from.[76] In her trip to the Break Room, Helly is seemingly kept without food, water, medical attention, and human contact beyond the unfeeling Milchick as she repeats the apology 1,072 times—until she "means it."[77]

While psychological and emotional pain are an integral part of "birth," work, and punishment at Lumon Industries, the company tries to avoid egregious acts of physical violence, presumably because innies share a body with their outies, and material evidence of abuse could expose Lumon to lawsuits, anti-severance legislation, and increased scrutiny. Since innies exist within a closed environment where written communications cannot pass the stairwell or elevator, they weaponize physical pain to communicate their suffering. Most notably, Helly inflicts pain on her outie—and consequently herself—through violence to the shared body, while Dylan attacks a non-severed employee in a position of power.

After multiple failed attempts at written communication thwarted by the word-detection sensors in the elevator, Helly is willing to undergo intense physical pain to escape Lumon and defy both her outie and her supervisors. First, Helly threatens to cut off her (shared) fingers with a paper cutter if she is not allowed to make a resignation request video.[78] In doing so, Helly seems willing to carry out her threat and endure the pain of non-anesthetized amputation if her request is denied. After

Helena denies her resignation request, Helly attempts to commit suicide by hanging herself in the elevator, hoping, perhaps, that her outie will wake up at the top of the elevator just in time to realize that her innie is the one who killed her.[79] Again, Helly is prepared to endure the physical, psychological, and emotional pain of committing suicide to defy her outie and escape Lumon. When the suicide attempt (just barely) fails, both Helena and Helly are left with a scar from the noose—a plastic office cable—to remind them of their shared bodily existence and the threat they pose to one another. While ether anesthesia promised to free the patient of both the physical pain and traumatic memories of surgery, both Helly and Helena experience some of the physical pain of the attempted murder/suicide and live with the scar that reminds them of the experience.

Similarly, overcome by the news that he has a son whom he will never see, Dylan uses physical violence against his supervisor, Milchick, in an act of rage and retaliation. Ironically, Dylan has previously scoffed at the idea that any MDR employee would violently attack a coworker or participate in an uprising. Previously, Milchick has run a standard Lumon protocol, "a 266" on Irving B. because his relationship with Burt G. from O&D has led to unauthorized interactions between departments.[80] In a 266, a non-severed employee "accidentally" sends a color photo of a painting depicting an alleged coup to the printer of the target department. The painting depicts one Lumon department attacking another, with the aggressor department beating, stabbing, and cannibalizing their coworkers. However, the title of the painting and the color of the employee badges (designating department identity) rotate based on which department the higher-ups seek to target. Thus, Irving is shown "The Grim Barbarity of Optics and Design" while Burt and his colleagues are shown "The Macrodata Refinement Calamity."[81] Lumon apparently uses the 266 protocol as a scare tactic to keep workers isolated and prevent them from staging a real coup against Lumon. Here, perhaps, we see why Kier is so concerned about workers both balancing and beating down the tempers. For Lumon, one of the worst potential outcomes of a workforce with unregulated, unbalanced emotions may, in fact, be rebellion—not against fellow severed departments, but against the company. When he sees the two paintings, Dylan, who is prejudiced against O&D, readily believes their department may be capable of committing such atrocities but balks at the idea that MDR workers would behave this way.

However, in a scene that recalls the cannibalism from the painting, Dylan attacks and bites Milchick. During the Musical Dance Experience,

Milchick tries to engage in a "dance battle" with an unwilling Dylan, who sits at his desk, processing the recent discovery and loss of his child. As he dances, Milchick asserts his dominance: he towers behind Dylan, bobs his head like a snake, and struts around his chair. Incensed, Dylan turns on his supervisor, pushes him into the MDE cart, shakes him, starts to choke him, and finally bites his arm. As the others pull Dylan off of their supervisor, Milchick whimpers, incredulously, "he broke the skin!"[82] Both Milchick's white shirt and Dylan's face are stained with blood. In the true spirit of a coup, Dylan turns the threat of physical violence not on his fellow coworkers, but on a Lumon authority figure who seeks to oppress him.

The two acts of rebellion that end Season 1—Dylan's physical attack of Milchick and the MDR team's illicit co-opting of the Overtime Contingency—demonstrate the innies' desperation to expose Lumon's abuse of its employees. They want the world to know that, contrary to its supposed "Legacy of Joy" and promotional claim that they have been "actively caring for mankind since 1866," Lumon is in the business of causing pain. When reputable nineteenth-century pharmaceutical manufacturers like Squibb wanted to distinguish themselves from those who pedaled cure-all patent medications, they petitioned the federal government for more transparency and regulation. This advocacy eventually culminated in the Pure Food and Drug Act of 1906 and laid the foundation for the Consumer Protection Agency we know today.[83] In contrast, Lumon marshals its PR team to deflect criticism, lobby politicians, and oppose legislation that would increase regulation or outlaw severance. At the end of Season 1, the innies risk everything to expose the invisible pain of severance. It remains to be seen whether these efforts will make their pain visible to others and elicit sympathy, empathy, and action.

Notes

1. At least some portions of the company's nineteenth-century origin story are known to the wider public. For example, the public knows that Lumon was founded in the 1800s and began by selling a "topical salve." Lumon's PR campaign also contains direct references to Kier Eagan's philosophies, including the Nine Core Principles, and rhetoric about workers being part of the "Lumon family." While Lumon stresses the significance of its nineteenth-century

origins on the severed floor, we do not yet know how central this information is to Lumon's brand identity and marketing.

2. *Severance*, "The Grim Barbarity of Optics and Design."
3. *Severance*, "In Perpetuity."
4. *Severance*, "Good News About Hell."
5. *Severance*, "The We We Are."
6. *Severance*, "Good News About Hell."
7. *Severance*, "In Perpetuity."
8. Gregory J. Higby, "Professionalism and the Nineteenth-Century American Pharmacist," *Pharmacy in History* 28 no. 3 (1986): 119.
9. Ibid.
10. Alfred D. Chandler, Jr., *Shaping the Industrial Century*, 193, 198, and 209.
11. Bob Zebroski, *A Brief History of Pharmacy: Humanity's Search For Wellness* (New York: Routledge, 2016), 122.
12. Ibid., 50–51.
13. Faith Lagay, "The Legacy of Humoral Medicine," *The American Medical Association Journal of Ethics* 4 no. 7 (2002): 207.
14. Zebroski, *A Brief History of Pharmacy*, 52.
15. Ibid., 51.
16. Ibid.
17. Granted, to the ancient Greeks the "inner person" and "outer person" were inextricably linked. For the ancient Greeks, who also believed in the pseudoscience of physiognomy, the human body was a physical manifestation of the mind or soul. That is why the predominance of a particular bodily fluid was thought to produce a particular temperament, which was, in turn, believed to produce a particular physical appearance. So, for example, too much blood would produce not only a sanguine temper but also a ruddy complexion, whereas too much phlegm would generate not only a phlegmatic temper, but also a pale face. Still, Kier's lack of reference to the material body and vital fluids and sole focus on the mind and soul here is a marked departure from traditional humoral theory.
18. *Severance*, "In Perpetuity."
19. Ibid.
20. *Severance*, "Half Loop."
21. *Severance*, "What's For Dinner?"

22. Virginia Sarah Smith, *Clean: A History of Personal Hygiene and Purity* (Oxford: Oxford University, 2007), 272–73.
23. The first season never shows Mrs. Selvig inside her shop, and it is admittedly difficult to fathom how she finds time to run it while working full-time at Lumon. Nevertheless, since other characters seem to know about her shop and she invites them to visit her there, it appears that the shop is real and that she sometimes works there. Based on the types of products she sells, it seems likely that Mrs. Selvig's shop is the Swab Girl Bathhouse and Soapery featured in Episode 2.
24. Mrs. Selvig also gives Mark's nursing sister, Devon, a shea butter salve for breastfeeding mothers. Mrs. Selvig's nipple balm recalls Lumon's original salve, and its association with the Swab Girl Bathhouse and Soapery reminds us that, in the nineteenth century, "salves" and many other products straddled the line between medicine, health, beauty, and body care. Indeed, nineteenth-century pharmacies sold products such as lip salves, dentifrice, and hair restorers alongside what we would classify as traditional medicines.
25. Suellen Hoy, *Chasing Dirt: The American Pursuit of Cleanliness* (Oxford: Oxford University, 1995), 32.
26. Kathleen M. Brown, *Foul Bodies: Cleanliness in Early America* (New Haven: Yale, 2009), 305.
27. Ibid., 316.
28. See Gregory J. Higby, "Professionalism and the Nineteenth-Century American Pharmacist," *Pharmacy in History* 28 no. 3 (1986): 7–8. As early as the 1860s, public "floating baths," composed of wooden frames that extended over rivers, were temporarily opened during the summer months in cities such as Boston and New York. The first truly successful public bathhouse in the United States opened in New York City in 1891; unlike earlier public baths, this one proved cheaper and more hygienic because it used showers instead of tubs and was constructed of cement and iron rather than wood.
29. Ibid., 9.
30. See, for example, Joe Pinsker, "The Dark Side of Saying 'Work Is Like Family,'" *The Atlantic*, 16 Feb. 2022. and Manfred Kets de Vries, "Is Your Corporate Culture Cultish?" *Harvard Business Review*, 10 May 2019.

31. *Severance*, "The We We Are." In addition to Lumon's earlier claim that the company has been "actively caring for mankind since 1866," in the season's final episode Lumon PR executive Natalie tells the assembled crowd that the severance chip is a "transformative technology" and that tonight they are "on the verge of a revolution. A kind and empathetic revolution that puts the human being at the center of industry."
32. Quoted in Keith Sykes and John Bunker, *Anesthesia and the Practice of Medicine: Historical Perspectives* (London: Royal Society of Medicine Press, 2007), 5.
33. The story of the discovery of ether has been told by many scholars. For more information, see Maurice S. Albin, "The Use of Anesthetics during the Civil War, 1861-1865," Stephanie Snow, *Blessed Days of Anesthesia: How Anesthetics Changed the World*, Keith Sykes and John Bunker, *Anesthesia and the Practice of Medicine: Historical Perspectives*, Jacqueline H. Wolf, *Deliver Me from Pain: Anesthesia and Birth in America*, and Guy Williams' *The Age of Miracles: Medicine and Surgery in the Nineteenth Century*.
34. See Stephanie Snow, *Blessed Days of Anesthesia: How Anesthetics Changed the World* (Oxford: Oxford University, 2008), 21–24. Previously, in December 1844, the dentist Horace Wells of Hartford, Connecticut had attempted to demonstrate nitrous oxide's anesthetic potential to the medical community at MGH after successfully using it on several patients during tooth extractions; however, on the big day he undermedicated the patient and was dismissed as a fraud when the patient loudly complained of the pain. Even earlier, in March 1842, the surgeon and pharmacist Crawford Williamson Long of Jefferson, Georgia removed a cyst from the neck of his friend, James Venable, while Venable was under the effects of ether. However, Long did not publish his findings of this and subsequent surgeries on etherized patients until December 1849. Morton was advised to try ether as an anesthetic in his dental practice by fellow dentist Charles T. Jackson, who was already using ether in "toothache drops."
35. Quoted in Snow, *Blessed Days of Anesthesia*, 24.
36. R. P. Haridas, "The Etymology and Use of the Word 'Anesthesia': Oliver Wendall Holmes' Letter to W. T. G. Morton," *Anesth Intensive Care History Supplement* (2016): 41.

37. It was possible to use one of several models of ether inhalers to more precisely (and safely) control the amount of ether inhaled by the patient, but in practice most doctors did not use them.
38. Quoted in Snow, *Blessed Days of Anesthesia*, 29.
39. Jacqueline H. Wolf, *Deliver Me from Pain: Anesthesia and Birth in America* (Baltimore: John Hopkins, 2009), 24.
40. Ibid., 36.
41. In 1847, Scottish obstetrician James Young Simpson was the first to publicly demonstrate the clinical use of chloroform.
42. Quoted in Snow, *Blessed Days of Anesthesia*, 29.
43. *Severance*, "The Grim Barbarity of Optics and Design."
44. In the September 1856 issue of *The American Journal of Pharmacy*, Squibb published diagrams of his new machine for distilling ether along with instructions explaining how to build and use it.
45. In 1989, Bristol-Myers merged with Squibb to form the second largest pharmaceutical company in the world. Like Squibb, Bristol-Myers was founded in the nineteenth century: in 1887 William Bristol and John Myers purchased and revitalized the failing Clinton Pharmaceutical Company; in 1899, they renamed the company Bristol-Myers.
46. *Bristol Myers Squibb* "Timeline."
47. *Severance*, "Half Loop."
48. Maurice S. Albin, "The Use of Anesthetics during the Civil War, 1861-1865," *Pharmacy in History* 42 no.3/4 (2000): 102.
49. Ibid.
50. Ibid.
51. Ibid., 109.
52. Wolf, *Deliver Me from Pain*, 26.
53. Ibid.
54. Ibid.
55. Quoted in Eileen Cleere, *The Sanitary Arts: Aesthetic Culture and the Victorian Cleanliness Campaigns*. (Columbus, Ohio State, 2014), 90.
56. Cleere, *The Sanitary Arts*, 90.
57. *Severance*, "Half Loop."
58. Natalie appears on the news in Season 1, Episode 3, "In Perpetuity." Lumon markets the Severance procedure to potential investors and congressional backers in Season 1, Episode 9, "The We We Are."

59. *Severance*, "Good News About Hell."
60. "Ketamine Hydrochloride," *RxList*, 7 Aug. 2020. https://www.rxlist.com/ketamine-hydrochloride-drug.htm#description.
61. *Severance*, "Good News About Hell."
62. *Severance*, "In Perpetuity."
63. Ibid.
64. Ibid.
65. Ibid.
66. *Severance*, "In Perpetuity."
67. *Severance*, "The You You Are."
68. *Severance*, "Good News About Hell."
69. *Severance*, "The We We Are."
70. The innies attend "Wellness Sessions" in which they are encouraged to take pleasure in hearing complimentary "facts" about their outies.
71. *Severance*, "Good News About Hell."
72. *Severance*, "Half Loop."
73. *Severance*, "The You You Are."
74. While the innies propose various theories as to what the numbers may mean, Season 1 leaves a lot of questions unanswered: we do not know what the datasets or individual numbers represent; whether Lumon is more interested in the "pure" numbers that remain after a file is complete or the boxed numbers related to the four tempers; how the intuitive, emotional responses of individual refiners or MDR as a group help Lumon further its aims; or whether the data sorting has a direct impact on real-world events.
75. *Severance*, "In Perpetuity."
76. *Severance*, "Half Loop.
77. *Severance*, "In Perpetuity" and "The You You Are."
78. *Severance*, "The You You Are."
79. Ibid.
80. *Severance*, "The Grim Barbarity of Optics and Design."
81. Ibid.
82. *Severance*, "Defiant Jazz."
83. Zebroski, *Brief History of Pharmacy*, 146.

Bibliography

"A Heritage of Improving Lives Through Innovation: Company History Timeline." *Bristol Myers Squibb*. https://www.bms.com/about-us/our-company/history-timeline.html.

"Ketamine Hydrochloride." *RxList*, 7 Aug. 2020. https://www.rxlist.com/ketamine-hydrochloride-drug.htm#description

Albin, Maurice S. "The Use of Anesthetics during the Civil War, 1861–1865." *Pharmacy in History* 42 no. 3/4 (2000): 99–114.

Brown, Kathleen M. *Foul Bodies: Cleanliness in Early America*. New Haven: Yale, 2009.

Bushman, Richard L. and Claudia L. Bushman, "The Early History of Cleanliness in America." *The Journal of American History* 74 no. 4 (1988): 1213–38.

Chandler, Jr., Alfred D. "The American Companies: The Prescription Path." In *Shaping the Industrial Century: The Remarkable Story of the Evolution of the Modern Chemical and Pharmaceutical Industries*, 177–212. Cambridge: Harvard, 2004.

Cleere, Eileen. *The Sanitary Arts: Aesthetic Culture and the Victorian Cleanliness Campaigns*. Columbus: Ohio State, 2014.

Glassberg, David. "The Design of Public Reform: The Public Bath Movement in America." *American Studies* 20 no. 2 (1979): 5–21.

Haridas, R. P. "The Etymology and Use of the Word 'Anesthesia': Oliver Wendall Holmes' Letter to W. T. G. Morton." *Anesth Intensive Care History Supplement* (2016): 38–44.

Higby, Gregory J. "Professionalism and the Nineteenth-Century American Pharmacist." *Pharmacy in History* 28 no. 3 (1986): 115–124.

Hoy, Suellen. *Chasing Dirt: The American Pursuit of Cleanliness*. Oxford: Oxford University, 1995.

Kets de Vries, Manfred. "Is Your Corporate Culture Cultish?" *Harvard Business Review*, 10 May 2019. https://hbr.org/2019/05/is-your-corporate-culture-cultish.

Lagay, Faith. "The Legacy of Humoral Medicine." *The American Medical Association Journal of Ethics* 4 no. 7 (2002): 206–8.

Madison, James H. "Manufacturing Pharmaceuticals: Eli Lilly and Company, 1876–1948." *Business and Economic History* 18 (1989): 72–78.

Peiss, Kathy. *Hope in a Jar: The Making of America's Beauty Culture*. Philadelphia: University of Pennsylvania, 2011.

Pinsker, Joe. "The Dark Side of Saying 'Work is Like Family." *The Atlantic*, 16 Feb. 2022. https://www.theatlantic.com/family/archive/2022/02/work-actually-is-like-a-family/622813/.

Smith, Virginia Sarah. "Health Crusaders." In *Clean: A History of Personal Hygiene and Purity*, 264–306. Oxford: Oxford University, 2007.

Snow, Stephanie. *Blessed Days of Anesthesia: How Anesthetics Changed the World*. Oxford: Oxford University, 2008.
Sykes, Kieth and John Bunker. *Anesthesia and the Practice of Medicine: Historical Perspectives*. London: Royal Society of Medicine Press, 2007.

CHAPTER 14

"The Mystery of Your Youthful Energy": Time, History, and the Representation of Queer Aging in *Severance*

Melanie Cattrell

In the 2022 *New York Times* article "For Christopher Walken and John Turturro, *Severance* is a Workplace Romance," Alexis Soloski explores an unexpectedly light-hearted aspect of the dystopian Apple TV + drama, *Severance*.[1] Instead of focusing on the show's commentary on technology and capitalism, or on leads Adam Scott and Britt Lower (whose characters also forge a workplace relationship throughout the first season), Soloski focuses on the relationship between Burt (Walken) and Irving (Turturro), two aging gay male characters.[2] The combined identities of queer[3] and aging differentiate them from the other characters in the show, the remainder of whom are younger and (presumably) heterosexual. By contextualizing the aging, gay male couple as an optimistic force in the show, I argue that *Severance* diverges from norms of representation of both aging characters and of queer characters in television.

M. Cattrell (✉)
Blinn College, Bryan, TX, USA
e-mail: melanie.cattrell@blinn.edu

N. M. Isacoff and J. Dawes (eds.), *Reintegrating Severance*,
https://doi.org/10.1007/978-3-031-57448-1_14

Within this essay, I will combine several contemporary theoretical frameworks of analysis and representation—television studies, age studies, and queer studies—to place *Severance* within a larger context of queer visibility on television and to examine how the show utilizes concepts of narrative time, representation in art, and portrayals of aging and retirement to explore the theme of queer aging.

As a part of the streaming platform Apple TV + , *Severance* places itself within the era of contemporary prestige television. Often referred to by television scholars as the Third Golden Age of Television, these shows are celebrated for their "narrative complexity" [4] and their ability to negotiate new technologies and participatory audiences. Furthermore, the current proliferation of streaming shows allows for more diverse casts and more nuanced explorations of gender identity, sexuality, and age. Both Jeffrey Tambor's performance as an aging transgender character in Amazon Prime's *Transparent* and Martin Sheen and Sam Waterston's portrayal of a gay married couple in Netflix's *Grace and Frankie* show that streaming platforms are not reluctant to explore queerness within aging characters. In *Queer Aging in North American Literature*, Linda M. Hess argues for the importance of queer representation in a variety of texts, stating, "representations of queer aging have the power to crack open heteronormative concepts of time and future that still limit the available perceptions of aging significantly." [5] In summary, the current variety of television programs allows for the possibility of new representation. Streaming platforms allow for niche programs featuring well-developed queer and aging characters. In the past, stories of queer identity were rendered invisible by mainstream television, and stories of aging were viewed as narratives of tragedy or decline. In both cases, queer and aging characters were frequently flat characters who were based on stereotypes. Contemporary shows such as *Severance*, however, place queer aging in a new light and explore new possibilities of media representation for marginalized communities. This chapter traces the convergence of television scholarship with age and queer studies scholarship to show that *Severance*'s portrayal of aging gay men is unique and noteworthy. It examines the placement of *Severance* in the history of prestige television, looks at the movement from invisibility to visibility faced by queer characters in television, and examines the portrayal of aging stereotypes that exist within television characters. In doing so, it argues that the world inhabited by our characters is one which mirrors our own; one in which the constructs of age and of sexuality are in constant flux, just like the medium of television itself.

Severance begins with Helly, a new employee at Lumon, waking up on a desk in a conference room, with a disembodied voice asking the question: "Who are you?" Mark, who we later learn is the voice, has skipped ahead in the process by mistake; he is not supposed to begin with this question. However, this question is the guiding force in the remainder of the series; not just for Helly, but for all the innies. Throughout the first season of the show, the characters search for their identities within the constructed and limited reality of the severed floor of Lumon. As supporting characters in the series, the characters of Burt and Irving have far less screen time than their counterparts. However, as noted before, the fact that they are played by established, well-known actors, and the unique perspective the series places on a gay relationship between two older men, the characters are worth closer examination. I will examine the function of their characters within the context of identity, age, and queer futurity.

Complex TV: The New Televisual Narrative

This chapter explores the representation of televisual queerness in a moment when the definitions of both television and of queerness are constantly changing. Viewing television through the lens of time is not new. In the 1980s, Robert Thompson argued that audiences were living through the second golden age of television. (The Golden Age was during the 1950s, when stores closed and audiences gathered to watch now-classics such as *Leave it to Beaver* and *I Love Lucy*.) Shows like *St. Elsewhere, Homicide: Life on the Street, and Hill Street Blues*, among others, were crafted with a production quality previously associated with films. Scholars began to study television, but realized that the serialized nature of the form, among many other aspects, differentiated it from the study of film. The same principles used to analyze two-hour films were not sufficient to consider narratives that would continue for multiple seasons or even for multiple decades. This difference in approach is especially noteworthy when considering the analysis of long-running soap operas, as both Martha Nochimson[6] and Robert Thompson explore. While many are quick to discount the soap opera, in *Television's Second Golden Age*, Thompson traces the popularity of prime-time soap operas such as *Dallas*, arguing that their continued narratives impacted the other dramas of the era: "The 'quality dramas' of the 1980s, though, were the greatest beneficiaries of *Dallas* and its imitators. As the Golden Age of television was rooted in the legitimate stage, quality dramas were rooted in the soap opera"[7] This switch from episodic to serial format in "quality TV" is a direct precursor to the current age of storytelling that *Severance* operates within. It is this complex, serialized storytelling that allows for more developed characters and storylines of marginalized groups.

Scholars assert that we are now within the Third Golden Age of Television not only because of the new types of stories being told, but also because of the new technology working to tell those stories. At the same time the medium of television shifted from broadcast and cable to streaming images on computers and phones, the narratives told within the stories began to change. Television scholar Jason Mittel asserts, "over the past two decades, a new model of storytelling has emerged as an alternative to the conventional episodic and serial forms that have typified most American television since its inception, a mode that I call *narrative complexity*."[8] Mittel uses this framework to analyze the changes within contemporary television, such as disruptions of narrative structure, self-referential plot-lines, and more intricate stories and characters.

Severance draws from film and network television references to construct a genre-blending show made for a contemporary viewing audience. It fits within a trend over the last decade of televised speculative fiction adapted for streaming television. The most recent incarnation of *The Twilight Zone* on Paramount Plus, *Black Mirror* on Netflix, and *The Handmaid's Tale* on Hulu all show that this genre of television is popular in streaming venues. In all cases, the genre plays with televisual narrative to speculate on the recent, often dystopian, future.

Representations of Aging and Narrative Time

In the introduction to *Aging, Media, and Culture*, editors Harrington, Beilby, and Bardo argue that social expectations of television and of aging are changing together. "As such," they explain, "television is uniquely illustrative in terms of its rich history, with the twentieth century aging process and its bridge to the new media landscape, as well as the new landscape of aging."[9] It becomes important, then, to combine current television scholarship with that of age studies. Contemporary age studies borrows from other identity studies to focus on the construction of identity. Like gender studies, age studies views age as a social construct, one that is dependent upon social markers of reference. Margaret Gullette famously argues that age in our current society is seen through the lens of "decline" or "progress."[10] As Margaret Cruikshank notes, aging is also tied to productivity; as one ages, one becomes less important within the capitalist framework. As people become less productive to the economy, she argues, they retire and become part of the medicalization of age, thereby supporting another for-profit system.[11] More specifically, in her work on masculinity and old age in film, Pamela Gravagne notes the intersectional aspect of aging within society: "The system of age relations by which societies are organized... can seriously affect an older person's ability to obtain or retain authority, status, and the rights of citizenship, to maintain economic independence, and personal autonomy, and to have social and cultural contributions recognized. Thus, it is not old age but the practice of ageism that works to reinforce the narrative of deadline and the narrative of decline that justifies ageist behavior." [12]As Mittel explains, a key aspect of a contemporary quality television program is rooted in narrative structure and time. Ames' fascination is with the subject of time in contemporary television, and connecting time to the representation of aging within television. Although they disagree on the outcome of queer futurity, queer theorists Freeman, Edelman, Halberstam, and Munoz have all connected queerness to time. It becomes important to examine, then, the place of identity within this framework, specifically, the intersection of age and sexuality.

From the beginning of the series, it becomes clear that *Severance* will play with time. While the overarching story of the first season is told in a linear arc, key scenes are repeated in the first two episodes. For example, viewers are shown the first scene of episode one, "Good News About Hell," twice, once from Helly's perspective and a second time from Mark's. In the second episode, "Half Loop," viewers are shown Helly's severance procedure in a flashback to the moments leading up to the first scene in the first episode. Similarly, in the first episode, viewers watch Helly run toward a door leading to a stairwell in an attempt to break free. In the following episode, viewers see the conversation that happens on the other side of the door, when Helly transforms into her outie and meets with Milchick. This disruption of narrative time emulates the disorientation of the severed workers, and it sets the tone for the show.

While *Severance* appears to be a generally linear narrative from the perspective of the viewer, the characters themselves approach time in a unique way. The Severance procedure is based on the notion of a time split—a divided consciousness that places one person into two different concepts of reality. For the innie, this means that they never see the outside world and are only alive during the eight-hour workday. The outies, on the other hand, have no recollection of their work life once they take the elevator up and out of the basement of the Lumon complex. Furthermore, the world of Keir, PE, where Lumon Headquarters exists and where the characters live, is one that seems to exist outside of time. The cars in the Lumon parking lot are of varying years but typically older model vehicles; the technology used within the Lumon building encompasses both contemporary and dated devices. For example, while the company owns the technology capable of severing the consciousness of their employees, they use VCRs, older-style curved screen televisions, and desktop computers from the 1980s. In his home, however, Mark has access to a contemporary television, Internet connection, and cell phone. This mixture of technology destabilizes the viewer and also places the innies in a different world—one without the non-stop flow of news, information, and social media that their counterparts face on the outside. It is a representation of time and identity that makes the series interesting and vital to television studies and identity studies.

Queer Visibility, Representation, and Futurity

Representation of gay relationships, both in cinema and on television, is rooted in coded behavior. As Vito Russo famously explains in *The Celluloid Closet,* films made during the Hays Code featured gay characters who were coded as queer but could not identify as such because of the restrictions of the Code. As Russo explains, Will Hays helped to create the Motion Picture Production Code in 1930. Although it was a code "by which the industry regulated itself," Russo points out that it was influenced by numerous religious and political organizations. When "the Code was strengthened in 1934, borderline gay characters fell into well-worn innuendo and sissy credentials, but said the same things."[13] During this period where homosexuality was unspeakable on screen, it was symbolized through stereotypical characters such as the "sissy" and the "pansy." As Alexander Doty explains, this tradition of coding has filtered into television representations.[14] Doty discusses the numerous television pairings who could be read as gay, but are written as heterosexual, such as *Kate and Allie* and *Laverne and Shirley*. Within television, queer people have traditionally been invisible or underdeveloped stereotypes.

In *Queerbaiting and Fandom: Teasing Fans through Homoerotic Possibilities*, Joseph Brennan explores the current controversies that surround queer representation. He argues that the treatment of queer characters has often followed two trajectories: queerbaiting or "bury your gays."[15] Both paths foreclose on queer desire. In "The Broken Promise of Queerbaiting: Happiness and Futurity in the Politics of Queer Representation," McDermott defines queerbaiting as "the perceived intentional practice of baiting audiences with the promise of queer representation, through marketing, or subtextual hints and gestures, but ultimately failing the meet expectations. Such a tactic is seen as an attempt to gain the investments of queer audiences without ever running the risk of the text being perceived as 'too gay.'"[16] "Bury your gays," on the other hand, refers to many gay characters who are killed before they are able to exist in a fully realized queer relationship. Rooted in queer analysis of the future originally developed by Munoz, Halberstam, and Edelman, McDermott and Brennan argue that both queerbaiting and "bury your gays" are devastating for queer audiences because they promise, but ultimately foreclose upon, the possibility of a queer future. In one of the first works to bring the aforementioned concepts together, *Queer Temporalities in Gay Male Representation: Tragedy, Normativity, and Futurity*, Goltz traces the history of post-Code gay men in film and television, concluding that "the culturally distinct aging patterns of gay men offer media critics a new perspective to approach contemporary gay men, gay aging, and queer futures."[17] By examining gay male representation in light of aging, both constructs become more focused and visible. The life trajectory of the heterosexual man is often constructed around the heteronormative life course. When this life course is challenged, aging is exposed as a performance.

The Widow Next Door: Harmony Cobel/Mrs. Selvig

Although the relationship between Burt and Irving is the focus of this essay, any discussion of aging and *Severance* must first address the dual characters of Harmony Cobel, Mark's supervisor at Lumon, and Mrs. Selvig, Mark's nosy, widowed neighbor. *Severance* uses Patricia Arquette effectively in this role to disrupt viewers' preconceived notions about age. Although Arquette is only five years older than Adam Scott (Mark), she is portrayed as significantly older than him in both roles. This portrayal works on multiple levels to show the performativity of age.

In the first episode of the series, we are introduced to Mrs. Selvig via phone calls with Mark's outie at his home. Throughout the episode, we sense Mark's outie's frustration as we hear his one-sided phone calls with his unseen, absent-minded neighbor who seemingly cannot remember the town recycling and trash protocols. Within the same episode, we are introduced to Mark's no-nonsense boss at Lumon, Harmony Cobel. With steel-gray hair and business attire, Ms. Cobel rules the severed floor at Lumon. Everyone, including Mark, seems intimidated by her. At the end of the first episodes, viewers are provided with a twist—the doddering, forgetful neighbor Mark's outie talks to over the phone and Mark's no-nonsense supervisor at Lumon are one and the same. Unlike Mark and his immediate co-workers on the severed floor, Ms. Cobel/Mrs. Selvig is not severed. Instead, it appears that Ms. Cobel is operating as Mrs. Selvig to gain more information about Mark's personal life. For Ms. Cobel to use this persona to ingratiate herself within outie Mark's life–and the life of his sister and her newborn, as she becomes Devon's lactation consultant–plays upon audience expectations for maternal older women in television. While viewers would expect to see Mrs. Selvig offer advice about lactation and motherhood to Mark's sister, they may be surprised at Ms. Cobel, a woman who tells the head of the Lumon security team, "if you want a hug, go to hell and find your mother."

Mrs. Selvig/Harmony Cobel serves as a reminder to the viewer that age is a performative construct. For Ms. Cobel to gain Mark's trust on the outside, she adopts the persona of a grieving widow–he is also grieving because of the loss of his wife–and this persona is believable to Mark because of her perceived age. Because Mrs. Selvig/Ms. Cobel is not severed, she is able to retain the information she gains on the "outside" and use it to her advantage at Lumon. While the representation of Mrs. Selvig/Ms. Cobel is essential to understanding how *Severance* disrupts viewers' notions of age, an examination of the severed characters is essential to understanding the way identity and life are viewed within the show.

Optics and Design/The Perpetuity Wing: Finding Queer Representation Through Art

Burt and Irving first meet when they are both admiring a painting in the lobby of the Wellness office. Burt discloses that he is from Optics and Design, a two-person department known for their tote bags and hallway art. They bond immediately over their affinity for Lumon paintings, with Burt stating that "it's rare to meet a sophisticate." The paintings appear to be depictions of the Lumon handbook and of Kier's life. As innies, the handbook is the only reading material they are allowed to consume, so it would follow that the artwork would reference the only text the innies know (Fig. 14.1).

After their first meeting, it is unclear what will happen with the two characters. They could simply be forming a friendship. The innies rarely discuss sexuality at all, except for Dylan, who flirts with Ms. Casey at Lumon, and who remains convinced that his "outie has love made with a MILF or two." Although workplace relationships are forbidden and workers are not supposed to befriend those outside of their departments, the relationship between the two men builds quickly. Burt invites the MDR office to see Optics and Design, and Irving is visibly moved when they look at a painting called "The Youthful Convalescence of Keir." The men share inspiration from a picture of young Keir Eagan, who presumably recovered from his childhood illness to begin the Lumon company as an adult and to write the Lumon handbook, which the workers refer to with the reverence of holy scripture. Because it is the only reading material they are permitted to look at on the inside, it becomes the basis of

Fig. 14.1 "It's rare to meet a sophisticate" in the halls of Lumon

their art. It is important to note that Burt and Irving's relationship, or desire for a relationship, is prohibited at Lumon not because they are gay, but because people believe the handbook bans workplace relationships. Later on, when looking at a painting of Keir and his future wife, they note that the couple also began as a workplace romance. Irving remarks, "They met as colleagues; took heart to each other as colleagues." In this way, the pair keep attempting to find themselves and their budding relationship in the only text that they are familiar with—the life of Keir, as inscribed in his writings and the art depicting him.

Burt and Irving not only find validation for their relationship within the artworks of Lumon, they also find their history. Although they don't know about themselves, in the Perpetuity Wing, they are able to learn about the past of the Eagan family. While the other characters dismiss the trip to the Perpetuity Wing—a museum of life-sized statues of the former Lumon CEOs, culminating in an exact replica of Keir Eagan's former home—Irving is very serious about it. Irving's reverence for the history of the Eagan family is shared by Burt, who, as the head of Optics and Design, is in charge of the artwork that is displayed throughout the facility. (It's unclear how Burt, who is severed, travels throughout the facility to display the artwork.) Nonetheless, the two men serve as reminders of the collective past and are proud to pass this knowledge along to their younger co-workers. Irving is convinced that a trip to the Perpetuity Wing will give Helly motivation to stay at Lumon: "It's an unnatural state for a person to have no history," he states. "History makes us someone. Gives us a context. A shape. But waking up on that table, I was shapeless. But then, I learned I work for a company that has been actively caring for mankind since 1866." If Irving and Burt's only context for identity is through their work at Lumon, it becomes clear why they would seek approval through the artwork and words of Keir. This search for representation is not unlike queer television viewers seeking to see themselves represented within the medium. While Burt and Irving do not find representations of queer relationships within the Lumon art, they do find a representation of a subversive relationship and a history they are able to connect to. As the narrative of "chosen family" is a significant one within the queer community, it is possible that Burt and Irving's adoption of the Eagan family narrative serves as a nod to this phenomenon.

Retirement: Aging out of Capitalism?

In short, *Severance* is a show about a corporation that dictates the way its employees experience time. In *Time Binds: Queer Temporalities, Queer Histories*, Elizabeth Freeman defines chrononormativity as "the use of time to organize individual human bodies toward maximum productivity." Freeman continues, "Manipulations of time convert historically specific regimes of asymmetrical power into seemingly ordinary bodily tempos and routines, which in turn organize the value and meaning of time."[18] Within the context of a capitalist framework, this manipulation of the individual's perception of time exists so that the individual will be the most productive person for the institution.

Although Burt and Irving appear to be the most dedicated followers of Keir in their respective units, when MDR and O and D decide to join forces, those in charge at Lumon begin to feel their relationship is a threat. While Burt and Irving do not spend a great deal of time exploring their relationship—it mostly consists of stolen moments holding hands while looking at art or touching foreheads in a conference room filled with plants—it is clear that they are, as Dylan notes, "sweet" on each other, and that their time together is a diversion from their "mysterious and important" work on the severed floor (Fig. 14.2).

Throughout the series, a key aspect of the innies' experience at Lumon has focused on their identities; meanwhile, the series clearly underscores the precarity of the innies' existence. When Helly questions Mark about quitting, he responds, "Since this perceptual version of you only exists at Lumon, I mean, quitting would effectively end your life." In the second

Fig. 14.2 "Are you sweet on this guy?"

episode, we learn that Mark is afraid that Petey—who disappeared without notice—has died. Milchick quickly points out that "Things like deaths happen outside of here. Not here. A life at Lumon is protected from such things." Throughout the series, retirement and death appear to be conflated. While people at Lumon don't technically die, they do retire, and that's the same thing. In "The You You Are," Helly's outie sends a message to Helly's innie telling her that she is not a person. As age studies scholars have noted, retirement is the moment when the aging person is no longer necessary to capitalism. The world of *Severance* illustrates this notion by reiterating that the life of the innie ceases to exist when the outie leaves Lumon.

This disruption between the outie and the innie is clear when Burt begins the retirement process. At his retirement party, Burt and his department watch a video recorded by his outie. In this video, he records a monologue that makes it clear he does not know any of his co-workers, nor will he remember them when he retires:

> And, of course, I don't really know any of you, but the man standing there with you now does. He's worked with you for nearly seven years, and I hope they've been good years. I—I don't know what they've been like, or what exactly I, or he, has been doing with you, but I do know how I feel every day when I come from being with you. I come home feeling tired but fulfilled. I feel satisfied. I must like you very much. And though today is my last day with you, I'm certain you will remain with me in spirit in some deep, yet completely inaccessible, corner of my mind.

While this is not the first time viewers have seen an outie record a speech for those on the inside, this speech, however, is markedly different from the speech given by Helly's outie in "The You You Are." While Helly's outie was firmly in control—to the point of denying the personhood of her innie—Burt's outie's speech takes a different tone. Burt's outie is a man who must face the realization that he will not retain memories of those he has known for the last seven years. It is a speech that could only be given by an aging character because it invokes the audience's ideas about the failing memory of the old. Indeed, one could imagine this same speech given by someone with advanced dementia who does not remember those with whom they have shared a great deal of time in the past. Having worked at Lumon for an extended period, Burt must now face the reality that his memories of his life within Lumon will disappear when he retires. This disappearance is the same as a death, which Irving points out to Milchick at the retirement party:

Irving:	You're all just gonna stand here... and let him die? … Are we being punished for defying the guidance of the Founder?
Milchick:	Burt's outie is retiring. It'll happen to you too someday.
Irving:	You smug motherfucker. You're not severed. You walk out of here with your memories. You carry them home with you every night. No one can rip them away from you, snuff them out. Like they never existed. Like you never existed!

This speech, along with Milchick's nonchalant response to Burt's retirement, serves as a catalyst for Irving, who has always been loyal to Lumon, to vow to "burn this place to the ground."

Although it would seem retirement would be the end of Burt and Irving's relationship, the open-ended season finale allows for the possibility that the relationship could exist outside of the confines of Lumon. In the last few moments of the episode, Irving—in innie form—arrives at Burt's house, only to see him sharing a domestic moment in his living room with another man. It is unclear who the man is or if Burt, upon retirement, has retained any residual memories of his relationship with Irving. However, the characters in the first season have also shown the division between the innies and the outies may not be as permanent as Lumon would like to believe. Perhaps there is still hope for Burt and Irving's relationship, outside of the confines of Lumon.

Despite their roles as supporting characters in the first season of *Severance*, Burt and Irving were seen by the audience as a positive force in this dystopian reality. For their portrayals, Walken and Turturro both received 2022 Supporting Actor in a TV Drama Emmy nominations. Such recognition brought visibility to both the series and to the representation of aging, queer characters in the world of television. Overall, the inclusion of Burt and Irving within the world of *Severance* pushes viewers to question preconceived concepts about sexuality and about aging.

Notes

1. I am indebted to Linda M. Hess and Lea Williamson for their feedback on early drafts of this chapter.
2. Alexis Soleski, "For Christopher Walken and John Turturro, 'Severance' is a Workplace Romance." *The New York Times*, August 15, 2022. https://www.nytimes.com/2022/08/15/arts/television/emmy-awards-john-turturro-christopherwalken-severance.html.
3. Throughout this chapter, I refer to Burt and Irving as both "gay" and "queer," leaning more heavily on the latter term. I rely more heavily on "queer" to identify Burt and Irving because they do not, in Season 1, share how they identify.
4. Jason Mittell, *Complex TV: The Poetics of Contemporary Television Storytelling* (New York: New York University Press, 2021), 17.
5. Linda M. Hess, *Queer Aging in North American Fiction* (Cham: Palgrave Macmillan, 2019), 9.
6. Martha Nochimson, *No End to Her: Soap Opera and the Female Subject* (Berkeley: University of California Press, 1992.).
7. Robert J. Thompson, *Television's Second Golden Age: From Hill Street Blues to ER* (Syracuse, NY: Syracuse University Press 2008), 35.
8. Mittel, 17.
9. Lee C. Harrington, Denise D. Bielby, and Anthony R. Bardo, *Aging, Media, and Culture* (Lanham, MD: Lexington Books, 2014), 3.
10. Margaret Morganroth Gullette, *Aged by Culture* (Chicago: University of Chicago Press, 2005), 14-19.
11. Margaret Cruikshank, *Learning to Be Old Gender, Culture, and Aging* (Lanham: Rowman & Littlefield Publishers, Inc., 2013), 36.
12. Pamela H.Gravange, *Becoming of Age: Cinematic Visions of Mind, Body and Identity in Later Life* (Jefferson, NC: McFarland & Company, Inc., 2013), 40-41.
13. Vito Russo, *The Celluloid Closet: Homosexuality in the Movies* (New York: Harper & Row, 1981, 34. I.
14. Alexander Doty, *Making Things Perfectly Queer: Interpreting Mass Culture* (Minneapolis: University of Minnesota Press, 1993).
15. Joseph Brennan. *Queerbaiting and Fandom: Teasing Fans through Homoerotic Possibilities* (Iowa City: University of Iowa Press, 2020), 2-3.

16. McDermott, Michael. "The (Broken) Promise of Queerbaiting: Happiness and Futurity in Politics of Queer Representation." *International Journal of Cultural Studies* 24, no. 5 (2020): 844–59. https://doi.org/10.1177/1367877920984170.
17. Dustin Bradley Goltz, *Queer Temporalities in Gay Male Representation: Tragedy, Normativity, and Futurity* (New York: Routledge, 2011), 40.
18. Elizabeth Freeman, *Time Binds: Queer Temporalities, Queer Histories* (Durham, NC: Duke Univ. Press, 2010), 3.

Bibliography

Akass, Kim, and Janet McCabe. *Quality TV: Contemporary American Television and Beyond*. London England: I.B. Tauris & Co. Ltd, 2007.

Ames, Melissa. *Time in Television Narrative: Exploring Temporality in Twenty-First-Century Programming*. Jackson: University Press of Mississippi, 2012.

Booth, Paul. *Time on TV: Temporal Displacement and Mashup Television*. New York: Peter Lang Publishing, 2012.

Brassington, Thomas, Debra Ferreday, and Danielle Girard. "Rethinking Marginality in New Queer Television." *Queer Studies in Media & Popular Culture* 7, no. 1 (2022): 3–7. https://doi.org/https://doi.org/10.1386/qsmpc_00064_2.

Brennan, Joseph. *Queerbaiting and Fandom: Teasing Fans through Homoerotic Possibilities*. Iowa City: University of Iowa Press, 2020.

Butler, Judith. *Gender Trouble: Feminism and the Subversion of Identity*. New York: Routledge, 1989.

Chivers, Sally. *The Silvering Screen: Old Age and Disability in Cinema*. Toronto etc.: University of Toronto Press, 2013.

Cruikshank, Margaret. *Learning to Be Old Gender, Culture, and Aging*. Lanham: Rowman & Littlefield Publishers, Inc., 2013.

Doty, Alexander. *Making Things Perfectly Queer: Interpreting Mass Culture*. Minneapolis: Univ. of Minnesota Press, 1993.

Edelman. *No Future: Queer Theory and the Death Drive*. Durham: Duke University Press, 2004.

Freeman, Elizabeth. *Time Binds: Queer Temporalities, Queer Histories*. Durham, NC: Duke University Press, 2010.

Gallop, Jane. *Sexuality, Disability, and Aging: Queer Temporalities of the Phallus*. Durham: Duke University Press, 2019.

Goltz, Dustin Bradley. *Queer Temporalities in Gay Male Representation: Tragedy, Normativity, and Futurity*. New York: Routledge, 2011.

Gravagne, Pamela H. *The Becoming of Age: Cinematic Visions of Mind, Body and Identity in Later Life*. Jefferson, NC: McFarland & Company, Inc., 2013.

Gullette, Margaret Morganroth. *Aged by Culture*. Chicago: Univ. of Chicago Press, 2005.

———. *Agewise: Fighting the New Ageism in America*. Chicago: The University of Chicago Press, 2013.

———. *Ending Ageism or, How Not to Shoot Old People*. New Brunswick: Rutgers University Press, 2017.

Harrington, C. Lee, Denise D. Bielby, and Anthony R. Bardo. *Aging, Media, and Culture*. Lanham, MD: Lexington Books, 2014.

Hess, Linda M. *Queer Aging in North American Fiction*. Cham: Palgrave Macmillan, 2019.

Jowett, Lorna, Kevin Lee Robinson, and David Simmons. *Time on TV: Narrative Time, Time Travel and Time Travellers in Popular Television Culture*. London: Bloomsbury Academic, 2021.

McDermott, Michael. "The (Broken) Promise of Queerbaiting: Happiness and Futurity in Politics of Queer Representation." *International Journal of Cultural Studies* 24, no. 5 (2020): 844–59. https://doi.org/https://doi.org/10.1177/1367877920984170.

Mittell, Jason. *Complex TV: The Poetics of Contemporary Television Storytelling*. New York: New York University Press, 2021.

Munoz, Jose Estaban. *Cruising Utopia: The Then and There of Queer Futurity*. New York: New York University Press, 2009.

Nochimson, Martha. *No End to Her: Soap Opera and the Female Subject*. Berkeley: University of California Press, 1992.

Oró-Piqueras, Maricel, and Anita Wohlmann. *Serializing Age: Aging and Old Age in TV Series*. Bielefeld: Transcript, 2016.

Russo, Vito. *The Celluloid Closet: Homosexuality in the Movies*. New York: Harper & Row, 1981.

Segal, Lynne. *Out of Time: The Pleasures and the Perils of Ageing*. London: Verso, 2014.

Soloski, Alexis. "For Christopher Walken and John Turturro, 'Severance' is a Workplace Romance." *The New York Times*, August 15, 2022. https://www.nytimes.com/2022/08/15/arts/television/emmy-awards-john-turturro-christopher-walken-severance.html.

Thompson, Robert Joseph. *Television's Second Golden Age: From Hill Street Blues to ER*. Syracuse, NY: Syracuse University Press, 2008.

Tropiano, Stephen. *The Prime Time Closet: A History of Gays and Lesbians on TV*. Milwaukee: Hal Leonard Corporation, 2002.

CHAPTER 15

Self-Communication in Severed Minds: Perspectives from Neuroscience, Psychology, and Philosophy

Nora M. Isacoff

> But if the knowledge which we acquired before birth was lost by us at birth, and afterwards by the use of the senses we recovered that which we previously knew, will not that which we call learning be a process of recovering our knowledge, and may not this be rightly termed recollection?
> —Plato, *Phaedo* (c.a. 412 BCE).[1]

As is typical of science fiction, *Severance* grapples with core philosophical and scientific questions. In particular, the series provides commentary on the nature of the self and its relationships to memory, experience, and identity. Drawing from multiple sources including classical works in the philosophy of mind and current studies in psychology and neuroscience, this chapter uses *Severance* as a lens for understanding an age-old debate about the architecture of the mind and communication within the self.

N. M. Isacoff (✉)
Columbia University, New York, NY, USA
e-mail: ni2237@columbia.edu

N. M. Isacoff and J. Dawes (eds.), *Reintegrating Severance*,
https://doi.org/10.1007/978-3-031-57448-1_15

In *Severance*, innies and outies share a body but do not have conscious access to each other's memories. Throughout the series, we see the physical effects of the innies' and outies' experiences on their counterparts. Early on, we observe outie Mark bawling in his car, and moments later, innie Mark is still sniffling, his eyes still swollen, his body still aching from the previous night's whiskey. When innie Mark sustains abrasions on his hand and on his head, outie Mark bears the scars. And in perhaps the most dystopian twist, pregnancy in one persona entails pregnancy in the other. Mark references the effects of living in a shared body in a conversation with Helly: "I find it helps to focus on the effects of sleep since we don't actually get to experience it. You may feel rejuvenated or happy. Less tense in the shoulders. Spry."[2] He may be overzealous in his characterization, as none of the characters look exactly spry. But the point holds that the actions of either persona invariably affect the other. In a shared body, it is not really possible to have an unshared mind.

When Helly first arrives in the Macrodata Refinement Wing, Mark explains to her, "All of the data arrives from upstairs fully encoded. Each category of numbers presents in such an order as to elicit an emotional response in the refiner."[3] By "encoded," Mark means that the information has been encrypted: transformed from one format into another so that the refiners cannot decipher its full meaning. Encoding in the *Severance* world doesn't strip the information of all meaning. Rather, it conveys meaning at a more intuitive, emotional level rather than at a more tangible, explicit level.

I will argue that severed minds encode memories in the same way. The bifurcated memories become less directly decipherable, but they remain present, and just as the refiners can tune into the emotional valence of the numbers and act on this information, so too can they tune into and act on some essential impression of their other self's memories. Later on in Episode Seven, in an attempt to prove that he has moved on from his wife, Gemma, whom he believes is dead, outie Mark rips a photo of Gemma into little pieces and tosses them in the air, declaring that Gemma is now out of his life.[4] Of course, shredding the picture did not erase Gemma from Mark's life. And severing a brain does not erase the self that loved her.

Modularity of Mind

In 1983, philosopher of mind Jerry Fodor published his seminal book *The Modularity of Mind*,[5] inciting new fervor into a perennial debate about the relative roles of "nature" and "nurture" in human development and, relatedly, about whether different parts of the human mind are integrated or dissociable. On Fodor's view, we are born with *modules*, particular parts of our brains preprogrammed to perform particular functions. For example, many scientists have argued that humans are born with specialized face-processing hardware called the fusiform face area (FFA). Studies using various neuroimaging techniques have demonstrated that this region of the brain may be activated when a person views a face, but not when they view any other image, suggesting that this area is specialized.[6, 7] Additionally, there are people who, for either genetic reasons or because of brain damage, specifically have difficulty processing faces but do not have difficulty with other cognitive or perceptual tasks. This deficit, called prosopagnosia,[8] which is associated with reduced activity in the FFA, was featured in Oliver Sacks's popular book *The Man Who Mistook His Wife for a Hat*.[9] The fact that lesions to a single brain region are associated with the acquired loss of a single cognitive function is evidence for the existence of a face-processing module.[10] Further, evolutionary biologists have pointed out that there are reasons why humans might have a region of the brain dedicated to face processing. Being able to efficiently process the faces of members of our own species enables us to quickly and easily recognize our families, potential mates, enemies, and so on.[11]

There is scientific consensus that much of the brain is non-modular. That is, much of the brain performs general functions, such as a general ability to learn all kinds of things from the environment. There isn't one module for learning to play chess and another for learning to play the violin. However, there is still widespread debate about whether the brain contains any modules at all, and if so, which modules it contains. Although, as with any scientific theory, the mechanics of the FFA are extremely nuanced, and some scientists have posited plausible alternative explanations for FFA-related data,[12] it is relatively well-accepted that the FFA is specialized for face processing. More generally, the theory of modularity makes concrete predictions about the flow of information in real-world human cognition–and about the nature of memory and selfhood in *Severance*.

Modularity and Encapsulation

One might think of a module, like the FFA, as a section of Ikea furniture that fits together with other sections but can easily be separated as well. In fact, the separability of the brain's modules is fundamental to Fodor's theory of the mind. Consider the Ponzo Illusion (Fig. 15.1), named for Mario Ponzo, one of the psychologists who studied it.[13]

As you can see, the monster on the right appears larger than the monster on the left. If you were to measure the monsters, however, you would see that they are identical in size (Try it out for yourself if you are skeptical!). Once you are convinced, take a look at the image again. Now which monster appears bigger? Curiously, the monster on the right still looks bigger, even if you know it isn't, even if you meticulously measured them. Fodor's explanation for this phenomenon is that modules are *encapsulated*, meaning, they cannot share information with each other (It's as if they are sealed off in their own capsules!). In the case of this illusion, it is possible that the human brain contains a module specifically for perceiving size, and that the size module cannot receive information

Fig. 15.1 The Ponzo illusion[14]

from other parts of the brain that would belie its calculations. Various other optical illusions also make use of encapsulation, playing tricks on one part of your mind without rescue from any other part.

Despite the evidence that some parts of the brain may exist in encapsulated modules, it is uncontroversial that many regions of the brain are able to communicate with each other, or, in technical terms, that they are *integrated* (Note that "reintegrated" is also the term used in the *Severance* world to describe someone like Petey whose severance procedure has been reversed). For example, as you are reading this chapter, your visual cortex is processing the shapes on the page, and your motor cortex handles your eye movements. Your Broca's area enables you to understand the structure of the sentence, and your Wernicke's area works out the meanings. Your angular gyrus associates the visual input with your linguistic knowledge, your corpus callosum facilitates communication between your right and left hemispheres, and your prefrontal cortex ties it all together into a unified whole. Reading, as with almost every cognitive ability, relies on the integration of different parts of your mind.

Episodic Memory

Is there evidence for modularity of mind in the *Severance* world? The premise behind the severance procedure is the existence of modularity, that it is possible to seal off parts of the outie from parts of the innie with no leakage between the two. Indeed, there is robust evidence in the series for the existence of some modularity in severed minds. This evidence comes primarily from examining the characters' *episodic* memories, that is, their explicit memories about their own lives, the stories they can (and cannot) tell about where they have been and what they have experienced. Indeed, innie Dylan does not know that outie Dylan plays hide and seek with his son. Outie Irving does not know that innie Burt offered a kiss to innie Irving, or that innie Irving declined the kiss despite his deep infatuation with innie Burt. Innie and outie Mark do not know about each other's experiences–vastly different but both deeply intimate–with outie Gemma (i.e., innie Ms. Casey). When Petey shows up at Pip's restaurant, outie Mark does not recognize him, nor does he understand Petey's reference to innie Irving's signature line: "Hi kids, what's for dinner?" The severance procedure has worked as planned, bifurcating the characters' episodic memories. I will argue, however, that other kinds of memory in a severed mind are shared between innie and outie, and that, in fact, these other types of memories are equally personal, equally constitutive of selfhood.

Memory Consolidation

Cognitive science has established that different types of memories are stored in different parts of the brain and that damage to one part of the brain can impair one type of memory while leaving other types intact. A classic example is the case of H.M., a patient who had a medial temporal lobectomy to treat severe epilepsy.[15] Following the surgery, H.M. could not remember any events from the years directly preceding his surgery but could remember events from earlier in his life. This is because of *Ribot's law*[16]: Over time, episodic memories are consolidated, meaning, they become less detailed and move from the medial temporal hippocampus where they are initially stored to the cortex for compact storage. This is why memories from long ago often feel more gist-like and less vibrant: they literally are more gist-like and less vibrant. When Petey says that his memories from Lumon feel as old as those from when he was five years old, he is describing the psychological effects of memory consolidation. In H.M's case, the older, consolidated memories in his cortex were unaffected by the surgery, whereas the newer, unconsolidated memories in his medial temporal hippocampus were destroyed.

H.M.'s ability to form new memories was also affected. He could form a specific type of new memory (called *implicit* memory, see below), but could not form other types of new memories, such as new episodic memories (the type that is encapsulated in severed minds) or semantic memories (see below). From studying H.M. and subsequent patients with similar neurological profiles, scientists now have a fine-grained understanding of different types of memories, both how they are experienced psychologically and how they are represented in the brain (Fun fact: The protagonist in the film *Memento* was inspired by H.M.'s condition![17]). Below, I contrast episodic memory, described above, with two other types of memory explored in *Severance*: *semantic* memory and *implicit* memory.

Semantic Memory

Semantic memory is memory for facts. If you know that *Severance* streams on Apple TV, you have that fact stored in semantic memory. If you remember sitting on the couch eating popcorn while watching the first episode of *Severance*, you have that experience stored in episodic memory. The series is clear that, unlike episodic memories, semantic memories are largely retained in severed minds. In the very first scene, Helly is questioned to ensure that the severance procedure was successful.[18] "Who are you?" she is asked. "What color were your mother's eyes?" The tragedy of that moment, the reason her heart sinks, and the viewer's heart sinks too, is the erasure of her episodic memories: the erasure of where she came from and who she is. But: "Name any U.S. state or territory," she is commanded. "Delaware," she whispers. Aha! Here is a major clue about the nature of memory in severed minds: Semantic memory stays integrated.

This integration is confirmed throughout the series. Helly immediately knows the English language, has general knowledge about things in an office, is aware of social tropes. The same is true for all of the characters, who are able to imagine that their outies live on a riverboat (Dylan), or that they have had affairs with older married women (also Dylan). Irving listens with glee, drawing on his semantic memory, as Ms. Casey tells him that his outie is adept at swimming and is an excellent lover. Innies do not wake up on the table as infants. They bring with them their outies' years of hard-earned knowledge.

With one exception: The fourth question in innie Helly's input survey is, "What is Mr. Eagan's favorite breakfast?" This is a semantic memory question, a question about a fact, and yet innie Helly does not remember the answer. Immediately prior to her severance procedure, Milchick had supplied outie Helly with the (nauseating) answer to this question: three raw eggs with milk.[19] Here again is Ribot's law. Outie Helly learned this fact too close to the procedure for it to be integrated, and innie Helly cannot access this memory.

Implicit Memory

Both episodic and semantic memory are types of *declarative* memory. Declarative memories are conscious, and therefore, can be put into words (declared). Outie Helly could have answered the questions about her mother's eye color and Mr. Eagan's favorite breakfast. In contrast to declarative memory, implicit memory is unconscious memory. If you are able to type on a keyboard without looking at the keys, but you cannot name the keys from left to right without looking, you have implicit but not declarative memory of keyboard layout. Implicit memories feel psychologically different from declarative memories, and they are stored in completely different areas of the brain. For this reason, H.M. was able to retain his implicit memories from before his surgery and was able to create new implicit memories as well.

There are many other studies demonstrating that loss of declarative memory does not entail loss of implicit memory. For example, Korsakoff syndrome[20] is an acute disorder caused by prolonged severe alcohol abuse and resulting in impaired declarative memory. In an experiment, Korsakoff patients are given a puzzle to complete. An hour later, they are shown the same puzzle. The patients, lacking the declarative memory, attest that they have never seen a puzzle like this before. However, when they are asked to complete the puzzle, they do so much more quickly than they had an hour before. In other words, they have an implicit memory of completing the puzzle. They just don't know that they have this memory. There are many similar studies in typical populations. For example, people tend to judge sentences they have previously heard as more credible than sentences they have not previously heard, even if they have no declarative memory of having heard the sentences.[21] (This partly explains the efficacy of propaganda.[22] Over time, people begin to believe what they hear, mistaking the sensation of familiarity for truth.) The distinction between implicit and declarative memory also explains infantile amnesia: Most people cannot access explicit memories from before the age of two or three, but experiences from infancy, recorded as implicit memories, have a profound, lifelong effect.[23]

Implicit memories seem to be immune to the severance procedure. Innie Helly can immediately sit up, stand, and walk. She knows how doorknobs work and knows how to assault Mark by throwing a speaker at him. She even understands nuance and tone. When Mark tells her she is a replacement (for Petey), she asks, "Why are you saying that you like you hate it?"[24] In other words, she has immediate access to outie Helly's implicit memories. Implicit memories are not only procedural (i.e., not only memories for how to perform actions). They can also hold emotional connections.

Memory and Emotion

Over a 14-year period, a small team of doctors made hundreds of visits to patient E.P., who lost the ability to create new declarative memories following viral encephalitis.[25] Although throughout the years, E.P. always claimed not to remember the doctors who came to his door, over time he treated them with greater warmth, demonstrated a more relaxed demeanor, and opened the door more quickly to let them in his home. E.P. came to trust the doctors, who always treated him with kindness and respect. He remembered them, even though he didn't remember that he remembered them.

Moreover, an experiment with amnesic patients directly demonstrates the persistence of emotional memory absent episodic memory.[26] Participants watched a series of sad videos and were asked questions about their emotional states immediately following the videos, and again a half hour later. On another day, they watched a series of funny videos and were asked the same questions about their emotional states. Although on both days, the participants had no declarative memory of having watched the videos a half hour after doing so, their reported emotional states at these times were consistent with the mood of the videos they had watched.

Is the same true in severed minds? Tracking Mark's emotional state throughout the series, especially during moments when his mood diverts from his usual sullen and restrained manner, may give us some insights on the possibility of this crossover. When Petey surprises outie Mark at Pip's restaurant, Mark does not have an episodic memory of him. But perhaps Mark does implicitly recognize him. Mark, the eternal conflict-avoider and risk-averter, the man so allergic to any challenging emotions that he voluntarily had his brain severed to avoid grief, does not treat Petey as a stranger. He listens calmly, intently to Petey, accepts Petey's letter, and trusts Petey when he flippantly says, "I'm your best friend. You're my very good friend."[27] Mark, the rule-follower, calls out from work the next day and hides Petey, because above all else, Mark is a loyal friend, and he knows, implicitly, that Petey is his friend.

After innie Mark is emotionally tortured in the break room in Episode Two, outie Mark goes on his date with Alexa and then gets in an argument with the Whole Mind Collective (i.e., the anti-severance activists). This is another scenario when Mark acts in a manner that is counter to the painfully polite approach he generally takes. It seems as if those experiences from earlier in the day are raging inside him, though he can't name their cause, and he uses the argument as a form of release. Similarly, when outie Mark explains to Petey that he values the opportunity to forgo his pain for eight hours a day, Petey gently corrects him: "You carry the hurt with you. You feel it down there too. You just don't know what it is."[28]

The fortitude of this kind of emotional implicit memory is put to the ultimate test in innie Mark's wellness sessions with Ms. Casey (i.e., outie Mark's wife, Gemma). In observing the sessions, Ms. Cobel seems confident that they do not remember each other, that the severance procedure blocked their emotional connection, but I think there is evidence that this implicit memory, a tiny glimmer of it, persists. In one wellness session, Ms. Casey lights Gemma's Christmas candle, which presumably releases a scent that outie Mark, but not innie Mark, would recognize. Lighting the candle seems to spark something in innie Mark, who absentmindedly sculpts a Christmas tree out of clay, suggesting that part of him does remember, and perhaps he not only remembers the scent and its association with Christmastime, but he also remembers how he felt spending Christmas with his beloved Gemma.

Mechanisms of Reintegration

It is probably not a coincidence that the trigger for Mark's momentary reintegration was scent. There is robust evidence for this connection, called the Proustian Effect, after the author who explored scent and emotional memory in his novel *In Search of Lost Time*.[29] There is a neuroscientific reason for the Proustian Effect: Unlike any other sensory system, the olfactory system, which processes scent, is directly linked to the limbic system, which processes emotional memory.[30] For this reason, a familiar smell can very rapidly trigger an emotional response tied to an implicit memory. This scene is a powerful example of how we can use visceral experiences and rituals to strengthen integration, uniting past and present, implicit and declarative memory.

We see the impact of this kind of symbolic action in another scene as well. After outie Mark rips up the photograph of Gemma, he carefully tapes the fragmented image back together. Through this symbolic action, Mark tunes into the locus of the emotional connection that both of his parts share with Gemma/Ms. Casey. Momentarily reintegrating himself, Mark assumes Ms. Casey's wellness session cadence and recites, "My wife was extraordinary. My wife was allergic to nutmeg. And when she sneezed, she always sneezed twice. My wife liked other people's dogs. My wife thought cardigans looked ridiculous. I loved all these things about her. Equally."[31]

Dreaming is a final mechanism of reintegration, where subconscious feelings and desires can be richly experienced. Sigmund Freud popularized dream interpretation at the turn of the twentieth century when he wrote about dreams as a vehicle for processing the day's experiences and realizing unfulfilled wishes.[32] Today, scholars investigate dreams from the perspectives of neuroscience,[33, 34] consciousness,[35] memory consolidation,[36] evolutionary biology,[37] and medicine,[38] among others. In *Severance*, innie Irving has a recurring dream in which black sludge pours thickly over his keyboard and onto his hands, enveloping his cubicle. We eventually see outie Irving drinking coffee into the night to force himself to stay awake so he can paint Lumon's long, dark hallway over and over again, slathering the black sludge on his canvas. Both within his dreams and while painting, Motörhead's hard rock anthem "Ace of Spades" [39] blares around him, contributing to the scene's frenetic energy, which stands in polar opposite to Irving's usual placid propriety. By the end of Season One, we don't yet know Irving's full story, but we see glimmers of Irving's reintegration through dreaming, art, and music.

Philosophies of the Self

This chapter began by exploring the great debate in cognitive science over modularity of mind. Are we a collection of parts, or are we a whole? Throughout the series, many of the characters weigh in on this debate. The most staunchly pro-modularity character is Irving. Irving is boundaried in all elements of his life, and this includes his views about his friends' minds and his own. For example, when innie Dylan, grief stricken, recounts meeting the son he did not know existed, Irving corrects him that the boy is his outie's son, not his. Irving maintains these boundaries because he desperately wants to believe that obeying them will give meaning to a life that is otherwise ostensibly devoid of meaning. As Irving explains, "It's an unnatural state for a person to have no history. History makes us someone. Gives us a context. A shape. But waking up on that table, I was shapeless."[40] He hopes that rigid rules will give him some shape. It is as reasonable a strategy as any in dystopia.

The seventeenth-century philosopher John Locke and twentieth-century philosopher Derek Parfit would perhaps agree with Irving. According to Locke, personal identity stems from linking memories of the past with awareness of the present.[41] Without this unified consciousness, there is no self. Though Parfit's work three centuries later diverts from Locke's in important ways, he argues for some of the same core properties of selfhood. In a famous thought experiment, Parfit asks his readers to imagine a teleportation device that can scan a body, record all of its memories and thoughts, destroy the original body, and then use the recorded information to recreate an identical body, with identical memories and thoughts, at a different location.[42] Parfit argues that the two bodies, though made of different physical matter, share a single personal identity, which is determined not by physical continuity but by shared memory. Parfit argues that, in contrast to the teleportation example, if a person takes a pill that causes them to lose their memories, the person loses their selfhood as well.

Outie Mark sees himself as a single self that travels between worlds, with the severance procedure a vehicle for this travel, equivalent to alcohol in his outie life. He is not a different person when he is drunk than when he is sober, or when he is at work than out of work, even though his experiences in each state are different. Outie Mark makes this perspective clear at the dinnerless dinner party. When Danise comments, "I'd always be wondering about the other one," outie Mark retorts, "There isn't another one. They're both me."[43] He expresses this same philosophy of the self in his altercation with the Whole Mind Collective, who protest the "forced labor" committed by outies on their innies. Mark counters, "Forced labor, really? So people can just like self-imprison. Are you captive right now? No, seriously, because your past self chose to walk you down here to be an infantilizing jerk to people." Rooted in a philosophy of the self as continuous, Mark's rebuttal provides a compelling counterpoint to the Whole Mind Collective's assertion that the severance procedure strips its victims of volition. Mark's philosophy here could be thought of as compatibilist, an idea first put forth by the Stoics in ancient Greece[44] and further developed in modern times by philosophers such as Harry Gordon Frankfurt.[45] The general idea of compatibilism is that the world is deterministic—the present follows directly from the past—but as long as a person's current actions follow from their current desires, they are still acting with free will.

Reghabi shares this view in describing innie Mark to his outie: "For all intents and purposes, he is you. Do you really think he's different down there? Combs his hair differently, laughs at different jokes?"[46] As Reghabi articulates, personalities appear consistent across personas. Helly is consistently brazen and indignant. Mark is consistently reserved and loyal. Despite a lack of shared explicit memories, the personas appear to share a self. The eighteenth-century philosopher Immanuel Kant would perhaps agree with outie Mark and Reghabi. Kant's philosophy distinguishes between the empirical self (the self as experienced in the world) and the transcendental self (the unifying consciousness that structures experience).[47] Amnesia disrupts the continuity of the empirical self but not the transcendental self, which endures even if the empirical self undergoes changes.

In contrast to outie Mark and Reghabi, outie Helly is scathingly direct about her view that her two personas are not both her. In a video to her innie, outie Helly asserts, "I am a person. You are not. I make the decisions. You do not."[48] Many people have a sense, as outie Helly does, that some parts of themselves are not their true self. A person with a hot temper might tell their anger, "I am in control. You do not get to overwhelm me." A person with an addiction might have a similar conversation with themselves. Someone who makes an error while sleep-deprived might say, "That wasn't me. That was my exhaustion." Scores of self-help materials claim they will help you find "your best self."

When innie Dylan accuses innie Irving of fraternizing with innie Burt and jeers that the ghost of Kier can officiate at their wedding, innie Irving rebukes, "This is inappropriate workplace commentary, and I am self-reporting you."[49] By "self-reporting," I surmise, he means that his true self is his good self, the senior-most Macrodata Refiner. This other Irving, the one who is all hot and bothered by Burt, is some unruly sidekick who relies on the real Irving to keep matters in check. This philosophy of the self is central in some (often very effective) approaches to psychotherapy, such as Internal Family Systems, that attest to the existence of a true self, which can only emerge if the auxiliary parts are properly (gently, compassionately) managed.[50]

Death and Immortality

Considerations on death and innie retirement also reflect the characters' views on selfhood. The Perpetuity Wing displays quotes proclaiming the existence of fundamental immortality: One quote by Kier reads, "The remembered man does not decay"[51]; another by Jame Eagan reads, "History lives in us, whether we learn it or not."[52] Similarly, innie Burt astonishes innie Irving in his recitation of a line by Kier recorded in an early version of the Lumon handbook: "And I shall whisper to ye dutiful through the ages. In your noblest thoughts and epiphanies shall be my voice. You are my mouth and through ye, I will whisper on when I am ten centuries demised."[53] Despite the dystopian context in which the quotes are showcased, they poignantly capture the doctrine that all of us live on through the ideas and actions we impart on the world, and all of us are born into a body and world imbued with the ideas and actions of our ancestors. This belief is akin to the nineteenth-century philosopher Georg Wilhelm Friedrich Hegel's notion of *Geist* (roughly, "mind" or "spirit"), which, he argues, evolves through history as ideas are transmitted and refined throughout the generations.[54]

On retirement, innie Mark has (or at least professes to have) a different perspective than his outie persona when he tells innie Helly that if she quits, she will effectively die, since she only exists at Lumon. The dubious expression on innie Helly's face, and her subsequent actions, suggest that she is more aligned with outie Mark's perspective. She is not concerned that quitting, even through extreme measures, will cause her to stop existing. The eighteenth-century philosopher David Hume might be aligned with innie Mark. Hume challenges the idea of a continuous and unchanging self. He argues that our sense of self is a bundle of perceptions and experiences, without any underlying, permanent substance.[55] Hume famously states that when he introspects, he cannot find a self—only a collection of changing thoughts and sensations. He rejects the notion of a substantial and enduring self and suggests that our belief in personal identity is based on the regular succession of our mental states rather than on the existence of a persistent self.

It is hard to know what to make of outie Burt's retirement video, at once absurdist and poignant, propagandistic and sincere: "Though today is my last day with you, I'm certain you will remain with me in spirit in some deep, yet completely inaccessible corner of my mind. The impression you've left on me is indelible, though I'm unaware of it on a conscious level, and I will never forget any of you, even though sitting here right now, I have no recollection of actually ever meeting you and no idea of your names or any of your physical characteristics or even how many of you there are."[56] More candidly than any other character, outie Burt describes his innie's experiences as explicitly forgettable but immortalized within his own implicit memory. Or, in innie Dylan's plain terms, "Maybe love transcends severance."[57]

Notes

1. Plato, *Phaedo*. Translated by G. M. A. Grube. Hackett Publishing Company, 1981.
2. *Severance*, "Half Loop."
3. Ibid.
4. *Severance*, "Defiant Jazz."
5. Jerry A. Fodor, *Modularity of Mind*. Cambridge, MA: MIT Press, 1983.
6. Nancy Kanwisher, "The Quest for the FFA and Where it Led." *Journal of Neuroscience* 37, no. 5 (2017): 1056–1061.
7. Mengjin Li, Hong Huang, Bingbing Guo, and Ming Meng. "Distinct Response Properties Between the FFA to Faces and the PPA to houses." *Brain and Behavior* 12, no. 8 (2022): e2706.
8. Sherryse L. Corrow, Kirsten A. Dalrymple, and Jason JS Barton, "Prosopagnosia: Current Perspectives." *Eye and Brain* (2016): 165–175.
9. Oliver Sacks, *The Man Who Mistook His Wife for a Hat*. New York: Harper & Row, 1985.
10. Raika Pancaroglu, Charlotte S. Hills, Alla Sekunova, Jayalakshmi Viswanathan, Brad Duchaine, and Jason JS Barton, "Seeing the Eyes in Acquired Prosopagnosia." *Cortex* 81 (2016): 251–265.
11. Nancy Kanwisher, "The Quest for the FFA and Where it Led." *Journal of Neuroscience* 37, no. 5 (2017): 1056–1061.
12. Michael Tarr and Isabel Gauthier, "FFA: A Flexible Fusiform Area for Subordinate-Level Visual Processing Automatized by Expertise." *Nature Neuroscience* 3 (2000): 764–769. https://doi.org/10.1038/77666.
13. Irene Sperandio and Philippe Chouinard, "The Mechanisms of Size Constancy." *Multisensory Research* 28 (April 30, 2015): 253–283. https://doi.org/10.1163/22134808-00002483.
14. Roger N. Shepard, *Mind Sights: Original Visual Illusions, Ambiguities, and Other Anomalies, with a Commentary on the Play of Mind in Perception and Art*. W.H. Freeman and Company, 1990.
15. Suzanne Corkin, "What's New with the Amnesic Patient H.M.?," *Nature Reviews Neuroscience* 3 (2002): 153–160. https://doi.org/10.1038/nrn726.
16. Morris Moscovitch, "11 Memory Consolidation and Transformation: The Hippocampus and Mental Time Travel." Scientists

Making a Difference: One Hundred Eminent Behavioral and Brain Scientists Talk about their Most Important Contributions (2016): 53.

17. "Frequently Asked Questions for *Memento*." *IMDb*. Accessed November 11, 2023. https://www.imdb.com/title/tt0209144/faq/.
18. *Severance*, "Good News about Hell."
19. *Severance*, "Defiant Jazz."
20. H. Beaunieux, B. Desgranges, C. Lalevée, V. de la Sayette, B, Lechevalier, and F. Eustache, "Preservation of Cognitive Procedural Memory in a Case of Korsakoff's Syndrome: Methodological and Theoretical Insights." *Percept Mot Skills* 86, no. 3 Pt 2 (June 1998): 1267–1287. https://doi.org/10.2466/pms.1998.86.3c.1267.
21. A. Hassan and S.J. Barber, "The Effects of Repetition Frequency on the Illusory Truth Effect." *Cognitive Research* 6 (2021): 38. https://doi.org/10.1186/s41235-021-00301-5.
22. Nora Isacoff, "The Psycholinguistics of Propaganda: Mechanisms of Subjugation and How to Challenge Them." *East European Journal of Psycholinguistics* 9 (December 26, 2022). https://doi.org/10.29038/eejpl.2022.9.2.isa.
23. Cristina M. Alberini and Alessio Travaglia, "Infantile Amnesia: A Critical Period of Learning to Learn and Remember." *Journal of Neuroscience* 37, no. 24 (2017): 5783–5795.
24. *Severance*, "Good News about Hell."
25. R. Insausti, J. Annese, D.G. Amaral, and L.R. Squire, "Human Amnesia and the Medial Temporal Lobe Illuminated by Neuropsychological and Neurohistological Findings for Patient E.P." *Proceedings of the National Academy of Sciences of the United States of America* 110, no. 21 (May 21, 2013): E1953–E1962. https://doi.org/10.1073/pnas.1306244110.
26. Justin S. Feinstein, Melissa C. Duff, and Daniel Tranel, "Sustained Experience of Emotion after Loss of Memory in Patients with Amnesia." *Proceedings of the National Academy of Sciences of the United States of America* 107, no. 17 (April 27, 2010): 7674–7679. https://doi.org/10.1073/pnas.0914054107.
27. *Severance*, "Good News about Hell."
28. *Severance*, "In Perpetuity."

29. Marcel Proust, *In Search of Lost Time*. Translated by C. K. Scott Moncrieff and Terence Kilmartin. New York: Vintage Books, 1982.
30. Cretien Van Campen and Julian Ross, “The Hippocampus of Proust: The Making of Sense Memories in the Brain.” In *The Proust Effect: The Senses as Doorways to Lost Memories.* Oxford: Oxford Academic, 2014. https://doi.org/10.1093/acprof:oso/9780199685875.003.0006.
31. *Severance*, “Defiant Jazz.”
32. Sigmund Freud, *The Interpretation of Dreams.* Translated by Abraham Arden Brill. 3rd ed. New York: The Macmillan Company, 1913.
33. Benjamin Baird, Sergio A. Mota-Rolim, and Martin Dresler, “The Cognitive Neuroscience of Lucid Dreaming.” *Neuroscience & Biobehavioral Reviews* 100 (2019): 305–323.
34. F. Siclari, B. Baird, L. Perogamvros, et al., “The Neural Correlates of Dreaming.” Nat Neurosci 20 (2017): 872–878. https://doi.org/10.1038/nn.4545.
35. Marco Pantani, Andrea Tagini, and Antonino Raffone, “Phenomenal Consciousness, Access Consciousness and Self across Waking and Dreaming: Bridging Phenomenology and Neuroscience.” *Phenomenology and the Cognitive Sciences* 17 (2018): 175–197. https://doi.org/10.1007/s11097-016-9491-x.
36. Matthew P. Walker, “The Role of Sleep in Cognition and Emotion.” *Annals of the New York Academy of Sciences* 1156, no. 1 (2009): 168–197.
37. Antti Revonsuo, “The Reinterpretation of Dreams: An Evolutionary Hypothesis of the Function of Dreaming.” *Behavioral and Brain Sciences* 23, no. 6 (2000): 877–901.
38. C.H. Schenck and I. Arnulf, “Parasomnias: Clinical Characteristics and Forensic Implications.” *Sleep Medicine Reviews* 44 (2019): 27–37.
39. Motörhead, “Ace of Spades.” Ace of Spades, 1980.
40. *Severance*, “In Perpetuity.”
41. John Locke, “Of Identity and Diversity.“ In *Essay Concerning Human Understanding,* reprinted in John Perry. Berkeley: University of California Press, 1975.
42. Derek Parfit, *Reasons and Persons.* Oxford University Press, 1984.
43. *Severance*, “Good News about Hell.”

44. Ricardo Salles, "Compatibilism: Stoic and Modern" Archiv für Geschichte der Philosophie 83, no. 1 (2001): 1–23. https://doi.org/10.1515/agph.83.1.1.
45. Harry Frankfurt, "Alternate Possibilities and Moral Responsibility." *Journal of Philosophy* 66 (1969): 829–839. Reprinted in Fischer (ed.) 1986 and Frankfurt 1987.
46. *Severance*, "Defiant Jazz."
47. Immanuel Kant, *Critique of Pure Reason*. Translated by Norman Kemp Smith. New York: Palgrave Macmillan, 2007.
48. *Severance,* "The You You are."
49. Severance, "Hide and Seek."
50. Richard C. Schwartz and Martha Sweezy, *Internal Family Systems Therapy*. Guilford Publications, 2019.
51. *Severance*, "In Perpetuity."
52. Ibid.
53. *Severance,* "The You You are."
54. Georg Wilhelm Friedrich Hegel, *Phenomenology of Spirit*. Translated by A. V. Miller. Oxford: Oxford University Press, 1977.
55. David Hume, *Treatise of Human Nature*. Edited by L. A. Selby-Bigge. 2nd ed. London: Oxford University Press, 1978.
56. *Severance*, "Defiant Jazz."
57. *Severance*, "Hide and Seek."

Bibliography

Alberini, Cristina M., and Alessio Travaglia. "Infantile Amnesia: A Critical Period of Learning to Learn and Remember." *Journal of Neuroscience* 37, no. 24 (2017): 5783–5795.

Baird, Benjamin, Sergio A. Mota-Rolim, and Martin Dresler. "The Cognitive Neuroscience of Lucid Dreaming." *Neuroscience & Biobehavioral Reviews* 100 (2019): 305–323.

Beaunieux, H., B. Desgranges, C. Lalevée, V. de la Sayette, B. Lechevalier, and F. Eustache. "Preservation of Cognitive Procedural Memory in a Case of Korsakoff's Syndrome: Methodological and Theoretical Insights." *Percept Mot Skills* 86, no. 3 Pt 2 (June 1998): 1267–1287. https://doi.org/10.2466/pms.1998.86.3c.1267.

Corrow, Sherryse L., Kirsten A. Dalrymple, and Jason JS Barton. "Prosopagnosia: Current Perspectives." *Eye and Brain* (2016): 165–175.

Corkin, Suzanne. "What's New with the Amnesic Patient H.M.?" *Nature Reviews Neuroscience* 3 (2002): 153–160. https://doi.org/10.1038/nrn726.

Fodor, Jerry A. *Modularity of Mind*. Cambridge, MA: MIT Press, 1983.

Freud, Sigmund. *The Interpretation of Dreams*. Translated by Abraham Arden Brill. 3rd ed. New York: The Macmillan Company, 1913.

Hassan, A., and S.J. Barber. "The Effects of Repetition Frequency on the Illusory Truth Effect." *Cognitive Research* 6 (2021): 38. https://doi.org/10.1186/s41235-021-00301-5.

Hegel, Georg Wilhelm Friedrich. *Phenomenology of Spirit*. Translated by A. V. Miller. Oxford: Oxford University Press, 1977.

Hume, David. *Treatise of Human Nature*. Edited by L. A. Selby-Bigge. 2nd ed. London: Oxford University Press, 1978.

Insausti, R., J. Annese, D.G. Amaral, and L.R. Squire, L.R. "Human Amnesia and the Medial Temporal Lobe Illuminated by Neuropsychological and Neurohistological Findings for Patient E.P." *Proceedings of the National Academy of Sciences of the United States of America* 110, no. 21 (May 21, 2013): E1953–E1962. https://doi.org/10.1073/pnas.1306244110.

Isacoff, Nora. "The Psycholinguistics of Propaganda: Mechanisms of Subjugation and How to Challenge Them." *East European Journal of Psycholinguistics* 9 (December 26, 2022). https://doi.org/10.29038/eejpl.2022.9.2.isa.

Kanwisher, Nancy. "The Quest for the FFA and Where It Led." *Journal of Neuroscience* 37, no. 5(2017): 1056–1061.

Kant, Immanuel. *Critique of Pure Reason*. Translated by Norman Kemp Smith. New York: Palgrave Macmillan, 2007.

Li, Mengjin, Hong Huang, Bingbing Guo, and Ming Meng. "Distinct Response Properties Between the FFA to Faces and the PPA to Houses." *Brain and Behavior* 12, no. 8 (2022): e2706

Locke, John. "Of Identity and Diversity." In *Essay Concerning Human Understanding,* reprinted in John Perry. Berkeley: University of California Press, 1975.

Moscovitch, Morris. "11 Memory Consolidation and Transformation: The Hippocampus and Mental Time Travel." *Scientists Making a Difference: One Hundred Eminent Behavioral and Brain Scientists Talk about their Most Important Contributions* (2016): 53.

Motörhead. "Ace of Spades." *Ace of Spades.* 1980.

Pancaroglu, Raika, Charlotte S. Hills, Alla Sekunova, Jayalakshmi Viswanathan, Brad Duchaine, and Jason JS Barton. "Seeing the eyes in acquired prosopagnosia." *Cortex* 81 (2016): 251–265.

Parfit, Derek Parfit, *Reasons and Persons*. Oxford University Press, 1984.

Proust, Marcel. *In Search of Lost Time*. Translated by C. K. Scott Moncrieff and Terence Kilmartin. New York: Vintage Books, 1982.

Revonsuo, Antti. "The Reinterpretation of Dreams: An Evolutionary Hypothesis of the Function of Dreaming." *Behavioral and Brain Sciences* 23, no. 6 (2000): 877–901.

Sacks, Oliver. *The Man Who Mistook His Wife for a Hat*. New York: Harper & Row, 1985.

Salles, Ricardo. "Compatibilism: Stoic and Modern." *Archiv für Geschichte der Philosophie* 83, no. 1 (2001): 1–23. https://doi.org/10.1515/agph.83.1.1.

Schenck, C.H., and I. Arnulf. "Parasomnias: Clinical Characteristics and Forensic Implications." *Sleep Medicine Reviews* 44 (2019): 27–37.

Schwartz, Richard C., and Martha Sweezy. *Internal Family Systems Therapy*. Guilford Publications, 2019.

Shepard, Roger N. *Mind Sights: Original Visual Illusions, Ambiguities, and Other Anomalies, with a Commentary on the Play of Mind in Perception and Art*. W.H. Freeman and Company, 1990.

Siclari, F., B. Baird, L. Perogamvros, et al. "The Neural Correlates of Dreaming." *Nat Neurosci*, 872–878 (2017). https://doi.org/10.1038/nn.4545.

Sperandio, Irene, and Philippe Chouinard. "The Mechanisms of Size Constancy." *Multisensory Research* 28 (April 30, 2015): 253–283. https://doi.org/10.1163/22134808-00002483.

Tarr, Michael, and Isabel Gauthier. "FFA: A Flexible Fusiform Area for Subordinate-Level Visual Processing Automatized by Expertise." *Nature Neuroscience* 3 (2000): 764–769. https://doi.org/10.1038/77666.

Index

A

Advanced-stage capitalism, 43
Aesthetics, 3, 20, 63, 67, 85
Agency, 4, 37, 43, 53, 106, 108, 121, 158, 159, 164, 173, 174, 176, 177
Aging, 4, 122, 245, 246, 248, 249, 251, 255–257
Alienation, 4, 38, 39, 44, 52, 63, 75, 76, 78, 105, 117, 118, 120–123, 129, 131, 154
Alter, 2, 27–39, 84, 144
American Civil War, 216, 218, 223, 226
Amnesia, 27, 175, 187, 268, 273
Anesthesia, 221, 223–225, 227–232, 235
Anesthesiology, 4
Architecture, 2–4, 83–93, 145, 174, 261
Art, 1–3, 20, 29, 32, 33, 35–37, 39, 63–68, 76–78, 88, 101, 118, 157, 195, 246, 253–255, 271
Authentic, 4, 53, 106, 107, 130, 131
Autonomy, 4, 99, 106, 172, 173, 180, 232, 249

B

Biopolitics, 146
Biotechnology, 2, 69, 215, 217, 230
Bodily autonomy, 171, 176, 182
Body, 15, 27, 52, 81, 144–146, 172, 173, 175–177, 179–181, 185, 186, 193–195, 200, 209, 219–221, 223, 231, 234, 262, 272, 274
Brain, 121, 130, 131, 135, 138–141, 148, 149, 173, 215, 229, 262–266, 268, 269
Break room, 23, 51, 86, 92, 105, 144, 146–148, 158, 162, 176, 205, 206, 233, 234, 269
Bureaucracy, 50, 51

C

Camus, Albert, 4, 118
Capacity, 28, 39, 64, 93, 173

N. M. Isacoff and J. Dawes (eds.), *Reintegrating Severance*,
https://doi.org/10.1007/978-3-031-57448-1

Capitalism, 3, 4, 24, 28, 38, 39, 43, 44, 46–51, 64, 84, 91, 93, 102, 117, 154, 157, 160, 245, 256
Change, 2, 17, 23, 33, 37, 39, 44, 48, 54, 55, 69, 74, 78, 98, 100, 101, 103, 104, 127, 145, 164, 176, 179, 184, 204, 221, 224, 248, 273
Character engagement, 197, 202
Childbirth, 4, 91, 176, 177, 183–185, 216, 225
Church, Frederic Edwin, 72
Cinematography, 82
Civic participation, 100
Civil rights, 173, 177
Class, 2, 31, 34, 38, 39, 48, 52, 87, 120, 123, 129, 222
Cognition, 68, 197, 263
Cognitive dissonance, 4
Commute, 4, 98
Consciousness, 16, 22, 34, 38, 39, 45, 69, 78, 105, 155, 167, 172, 215, 216, 224, 228, 229, 231, 250, 271–273
Consent, 64, 130, 171–173, 175–177, 181–186, 195, 196, 232
Conspicuous production, 99, 101
Consumption, 222
Control, 21, 23, 27, 28, 36–39, 49, 50, 53, 54, 75, 86, 87, 91, 100, 101, 103, 104, 106–108, 139, 140, 145, 146, 163, 165, 193, 200, 216, 256, 273
Corporate culture, 14, 24, 25, 160, 216, 223
Corporate mythology, 3, 13, 180
Corporation, 22, 28, 85, 118, 125, 127–129, 131, 138, 140–142, 144, 145, 148, 156, 158, 160, 171, 172, 174, 221, 255
COVID-19, 2, 99, 171
Critique, 25, 39, 44, 99, 117, 137, 154, 155, 161, 162, 166
Cultural history, 3

D

Data, 137, 138, 140, 141, 164, 181, 233, 234, 262, 263
Death, 13, 33–35, 93, 142, 173, 200, 256, 257, 273
Deleuze, Gilles, 3, 30, 139, 140, 148
Design, 1, 4, 7, 63, 65–67, 75, 77, 78, 82, 83, 85–88, 90, 91, 98, 107, 122, 123, 125, 126, 144, 147, 174, 182, 196, 201, 208, 226, 253, 254
Dichotomy, 15, 98–100, 103
Discipline, 1, 54, 216, 222
Discursive, 144
Disorientation, 82, 85, 93, 99, 249
Disruption, 34, 107, 148, 249, 256
Dissociative, 27, 176
Diversity, 5, 32, 100, 196
Domination, 22, 43, 49, 51, 54, 72, 78
Dreaming, 30, 271
Dubois, W.E.B., 3
Dystopia, 2, 28, 43, 103, 108, 127, 173, 245, 248, 257, 262, 271, 274

E

Eagan, Kier, 15, 21, 27, 30, 32, 51, 52, 72, 88, 126, 127, 135, 139, 141, 155, 156, 161, 164, 165, 178–180, 216, 217, 223, 253, 254
Efficiency, 4, 50, 104, 119, 120, 136, 165
Emotion, 4, 52–54, 66, 71, 78, 121, 123, 124, 138, 144, 160, 162, 177, 184, 194, 196–198, 201,

202, 205, 216, 220, 223, 227–229, 233, 235, 262, 268–270
Encapsulation, 264, 265
Episodic memory, 265–267, 269
Ether, 37, 73, 74, 216, 222–228, 232, 235
Ethics, 159, 177, 180, 184
Eugenics, 135, 148, 149
Exploitation, 38, 45, 99, 106, 154, 158, 160, 161, 167, 173, 174, 185, 186

F
Fascism, 3
Feminist, 4, 154, 182, 184
Fodor, Jerry, 263, 264
Foucault, Michel, 3, 83, 145
Founder Worship, 4, 158, 165
Frankfurt, Harry Gordon, 272
Friedrich, Casper David, 3, 63, 71, 76
Fusiform Face Area (FFA), 263, 264
Futuristic, 166

G
Government, 45, 49, 53, 119, 131, 226, 236
Guattari, Félix, 84, 88, 148

H
Hegel, Georg Wilhelm Friedrich, 118, 274
History, 3, 4, 13, 14, 17, 19–21, 29, 32, 33, 44, 54, 69, 88, 167, 171, 175, 178, 203, 216, 218, 223, 231, 246, 248, 251, 254, 271, 273, 274
H.M., 266, 268
Hopper, Edward, 3, 63, 75
Humanity, 50, 53, 137, 141, 149, 166
Human rights, 100, 176, 185
Hume, David, 274

I
Identity, 3, 14–17, 19, 23, 27, 33–36, 106, 107, 135, 136, 140, 146, 161, 171, 173, 176, 177, 184, 196, 197, 216, 218, 223, 235, 246–250, 252, 254, 261, 271, 272, 274
Immortality, 149, 273
Implicit memory, 266–268, 270, 274
Incentives, 4, 17, 19, 21, 87, 88, 105, 118, 126, 154, 158, 159, 161, 162, 164–166
Industrial revolution, 44, 47, 77, 117, 118, 122, 131
Infantilization, 105, 272
Innie, 2, 4, 16, 17, 19–21, 23–25, 43–46, 49, 53, 77, 81, 82, 88–91, 97, 98, 103, 105–108, 129, 136, 142, 149, 154, 155, 157–159, 161–163, 165, 166, 173–178, 180–185, 193–209, 215–218, 228–236, 247, 250, 253, 255–257, 262, 265, 267–274
Innovation, 154
Internal Family Systems, 273

K
Kafka, Franz, 4, 118
Kant, Immanuel, 64, 65, 68, 273

L
Labor, 17, 28, 36, 38, 47–50, 52, 84, 91, 101, 102, 108, 117–120, 127, 137, 138, 154, 155,

159–164, 166, 167, 171, 182–184, 218, 225, 228, 233
Labor camp, 43
Labor exploitation, 171–173, 176, 177
Labor theory, 4
Learning, 119, 202, 261, 263
Liberation, 44, 54, 55
Locke, John, 271, 272
Lumon, 2, 3, 7, 13–24, 27–39, 44–46, 49–53, 55, 64–70, 75–77, 81, 85, 87–95, 97, 98, 102–108, 111, 124–127, 129, 130, 135–149, 154–159, 161–167, 173–185, 194–200, 202–207, 209, 211, 215–217, 220, 221, 223, 225, 227–231, 234–236, 238–241, 247, 250–257, 266, 271, 274

M

Mapping, 14, 22–24, 91–94, 138
Marx, Karl, 3, 44, 47–51, 117–121, 129
Mechanisms of control, 143
Medicine, 216, 217, 219, 223, 227, 228, 238, 271
Memory, 19, 22, 28, 32, 64, 70, 109, 119, 135, 136, 138, 140, 142, 143, 146, 149, 163, 175, 176, 193, 198, 209, 215, 256, 261, 263, 265–272
Memory consolidation, 266, 271
Mind, 2, 17, 28, 33, 37, 54, 64, 65, 67, 68, 81, 93, 98, 119, 129, 144–146, 155, 180, 198, 199, 203, 223, 224, 237, 256, 261–267, 269, 271, 274
Minimalism, 67
Modern period, 3
Modularity, 263–265, 271
Moral, 128, 141, 145, 160, 180, 193–202, 205, 207–211, 221, 222
Morality, 197, 198, 208–210
Multiplicity, 4, 142

N

Narrative, 28, 63, 69, 73, 74, 82, 98, 99, 104, 106–108, 138, 141, 143, 147, 166, 194, 196, 208, 210, 212, 216, 217, 223, 246, 248, 249, 254
Neoliberalism, 91, 196
Neuroscience, 4, 261, 271
Nineteenth-century, 22, 52, 216–223, 227–229, 232, 236, 274
Non-discursive, 144
Nostalgia, 3, 14, 17, 19, 22
Numbing, 4, 223, 228, 231

O

Office, 2, 4, 15, 29, 30, 37, 43, 64, 66, 69, 75, 77, 83, 86–89, 91, 92, 103, 117, 123–126, 135, 140, 145–149, 154, 156, 158, 163, 165, 171–174, 178–180, 193, 196, 197, 200, 201, 205, 217, 221, 235, 253, 267
Ontology, 29
Oppression, 4, 37, 38, 68, 154, 155, 157–159, 161, 164–167
Outie, 2, 4, 14, 16, 17, 19, 21, 23, 24, 45, 52, 53, 69, 77, 81, 89–91, 97, 98, 103, 105, 107, 108, 129, 135, 140, 142, 143, 148, 153, 157, 159, 161, 165, 166, 173, 175–178, 181–183, 185, 186, 193–198, 200–206, 208, 209, 212, 215, 228–235, 241, 249, 250, 252, 253, 256, 257, 262, 265, 267–274

P
Pain, 4, 45, 121, 130, 176, 183, 184, 216, 220, 221, 223–225, 227–229, 231–236, 239, 270
Palimpsest, 63
Panopticon, 30
Parfit, Derek, 271, 272
Perception, 23, 53, 69, 98, 142, 155, 198, 255
Perpetuity Wing, 13, 16, 18–21, 24, 31, 88, 92, 124, 141, 147, 155, 158, 160, 165, 166, 178, 180, 217, 218, 231, 254, 273
Philosophy, 4, 67, 78, 84, 139, 156, 179, 202, 219, 272, 273
Philosophy of mind, 261
Philosophy of work, 118
Plantation, 154, 157, 158, 160, 165–167
Political, 3, 4, 34, 39, 93, 139, 161, 250
Ponzo Illusion, 264
Postmodern period, 3, 63
Power, 4, 28–31, 34, 36, 38, 39, 47, 49, 64, 70, 71, 75, 83, 85–88, 91, 92, 94, 100, 102, 108, 122, 130, 139, 145, 154, 155, 157, 164, 171, 173, 182, 216, 220, 221, 224, 230, 232, 234, 246, 255
Pregnancy, 173, 176, 177, 180–182, 184, 185, 262
Process, 30, 73, 88, 100, 132, 138, 141, 161, 166, 167, 185, 210, 270
Product, 17, 36, 39, 49, 85, 92, 117, 128, 217–219, 221, 227, 238
Production, 36, 39, 47–49, 64, 83, 86, 94, 103, 107, 118, 119, 130, 137, 138, 144, 154, 247
Productivity, 3, 4, 47, 87, 104, 119, 120, 126–129, 133, 136–138, 154, 158, 161–163, 165, 249, 255
Propaganda, 75, 88, 268
Prosopagnosia, 263
Protest, 23, 272
Proustian Effect, 270
Psychology, 4, 66, 122, 261

Q
Queer, 4, 84, 245–247, 249–251, 254, 257
Quiet quitting, 3, 25, 118, 171

R
Racial injustice, 3
Rationality, 48, 50, 51
Realism, 39, 122, 127, 128
Recession, 2, 126
Reclamation, 4, 51
Reintegration, 91–93, 102, 156, 173, 198, 270, 271
Reproduction, 36, 154, 155, 157, 159, 165, 166, 186
Reproductive exploitation, 4, 182
Reproductive labor, 154, 173, 176, 177
Resistance, 4, 28, 29, 34, 38, 85, 91, 92, 99, 102, 107, 118, 156, 157, 164, 166, 167, 174, 204
Retirement, 17, 25, 34, 38, 126, 206, 209, 246, 255–257, 273, 274
Romantic period, 3

S
Sacks, Oliver, 263
Satire, 185
Scripture, 27, 28, 253
Security, 3, 27, 46, 86, 105, 121, 144, 146, 178–180, 205, 252

Self, 3, 4, 13–17, 25, 28, 30, 31, 33, 38, 39, 44, 49, 50, 53, 54, 81, 84, 88, 91, 94, 97, 98, 103, 106, 118, 132, 139, 148, 153, 154, 156–158, 184, 186, 193–195, 198, 202, 210, 216, 218, 220–222, 232, 233, 248, 261, 262, 272–274
Self-communication, 261
Self-help, 107, 158, 203, 273
Selfhood, 263, 266, 272, 273
Semantic memory, 266, 267
Semiotics, 4
Severance procedure, 14, 19, 23, 24, 29, 32, 44–46, 49, 53, 54, 82, 83, 89, 91, 97, 98, 105, 130, 135–140, 143–145, 148, 153, 156, 157, 175, 217, 221, 223, 227–229, 231, 249, 265, 267, 268, 270, 272
Severed floor, 7, 14–17, 21–25, 28, 29, 31–33, 35, 38, 81–84, 86–94, 99, 136–138, 140, 142–149, 164, 211, 247, 252
Sex, 165, 173, 180, 181, 185, 186, 221
Sexual exploitation, 173, 177
Sexuality, 1, 4, 165, 180, 186, 246, 247, 249, 253, 257
Slavery, 4, 47, 153, 154, 157, 159–163, 165–167, 186
Sociological imagination, 3, 44, 53–55
Solitary, 63, 71, 101
Space, 4, 14, 15, 22–24, 31, 50, 52, 63–66, 69, 73, 76, 77, 81–91, 93, 94, 98–104, 106–108, 121–125, 128, 136, 139, 140, 143, 146, 147, 158, 174, 193, 196, 217, 222, 233
Spaces of transition, 4, 98–103, 106–108
Spectatorial allegiance, 4, 194, 197, 199, 200
Stoics, 272
Subjectification, 139, 140, 142, 145, 147
Subjective experience, 4
Subjectivity, 36, 82–85, 88, 89
Surgery, 154, 155, 161, 164, 166, 223, 225, 228–230, 235, 266, 268
Surveillance, 21, 86, 129, 132, 133, 137, 145, 157
Symmetry, 4, 15, 81, 90, 129, 178

T

Textual analysis, 209
The Great Resignation, 3, 7, 174
The sublime, 63–65, 68, 69, 71, 72, 76, 77
Twenty-first century, 154, 160, 216, 221, 223, 227, 228

V

Video animation, 72
Viewer cognition, 194
Virtue, 35, 194, 205, 210
Visual, 3, 15, 20, 21, 28–30, 32, 34–39, 64, 66, 67, 75–78, 83, 88, 90, 138, 141, 146, 147, 196, 203, 216, 230, 265
Visual images, 81, 144

W

Waffle party, 88, 105, 162–166, 178–181, 220, 221
Wages, 2, 48, 118–120, 132, 137, 162
Waxworks, 20
Weber, Max, 3, 44, 50–52

Work, 2–4, 7, 15, 16, 24, 25, 27, 30, 32–34, 36–39, 43, 45, 47, 49–54, 64, 66, 69, 73, 78, 82, 84–87, 91, 92, 94, 97–104, 106–108, 119, 121–124, 126–128, 130, 131, 135–146, 148, 153–155, 159, 160, 162–166, 173–175, 177, 178, 180, 182, 184, 186, 193–196, 198, 206, 215, 218, 221, 222, 225, 228, 229, 231, 233, 234, 249, 250, 254, 255, 268, 269, 272

Work as play, 126

Worker, 2–4, 15–17, 21–25, 28, 34, 35, 38, 39, 43–54, 73, 84–88, 91, 92, 94, 99, 102, 104, 106, 107, 117–124, 126–130, 132, 133, 136–140, 142–147, 155, 171, 193, 198, 206, 220, 223, 225

Work/life balance, 2, 44, 45, 49, 78, 103, 107, 135, 143, 154, 161, 172, 173, 175, 183, 193, 201, 215

Work persona, 123, 215

Workplace incentives, 154, 164

GPSR Compliance
The European Union's (EU) General Product Safety Regulation (GPSR) is a set of rules that requires consumer products to be safe and our obligations to ensure this.

If you have any concerns about our products, you can contact us on

ProductSafety@springernature.com

In case Publisher is established outside the EU, the EU authorized representative is:

Springer Nature Customer Service Center GmbH
Europaplatz 3
69115 Heidelberg, Germany

www.ingramcontent.com/pod-product-compliance
Ingram Content Group UK Ltd.
Pitfield, Milton Keynes, MK11 3LW, UK
UKHW021949281225
466455UK00007B/269
* 9 7 8 3 0 3 1 5 7 4 4 7 4 *